ALSO BY DAN SAVAGE

The Kid
Savage Love

skipping towards gomorrah

THE SEVEN DEADLY SINS

AND THE PURSUIT OF HAPPINESS IN AMERICA

DAN SAVAGE

A PLUME BOOK

PLUME
Published by the Penguin Group
Penguin Group (USA) Inc., 375 Hudson Street, New York, New York 10014, U.S.A.
Penguin Books Ltd, 80 Strand, London WC2R 0RL, England
Penguin Books Australia Ltd, 250 Camberwell Road, Camberwell, Victoria 3124, Australia
Penguin Books Canada Ltd, 10 Alcorn Avenue, Toronto, Ontario, Canada M4V 3B2
Penguin Books India (P) Ltd, 11 Community Centre, Panchsheel Park,
New Delhi – 110 017, India
Penguin Books (N.Z.) Ltd, Cnr Rosedale and Airborne Roads,
Albany, Auckland 1310, New Zealand
Penguin Books (South Africa) (Pty) Ltd, 24 Sturdee Avenue, Rosebank,
Johannesburg 2196, South Africa

Penguin Books Ltd, Registered Offices: 80 Strand, London WC2R 0RL, England

Published by Plume, a member of Penguin Group (USA) Inc.
Previously published in a Dutton edition.

First Plume Printing, October 2003
10 9 8 7

Ⓟ REGISTERED TRADEMARK—MARCA REGISTRADA

The Library of Congress has catalogued the Dutton edition as follows:

Savage, Dan.
Skipping towards Gomorrah : the seven deadly sins and the pursuit of happiness in
America / Dan Savage.
p.   cm.
ISBN 0-525-94675-6 (hc.)
ISBN 0-452-28416-3 (pbk.)
1. United States—Moral conditions.   2. Deadly sins.   I. Title
HN90.M6 S28 2002
306'.0973—dc21   2002021252

Printed in the United States of America

for my brother, Bill . . .

CONTENTS

skipping towards gomorrah

We hold these truths to be self-evident, that all men are created equal, that they are endowed by their Creator with certain unalienable Rights, that among these are Life, Liberty and the pursuit of Happiness.

—The Declaration of Independence

*The best lack all conviction, while the worst/
Are full of passionate intensity.*

—W.B. Yeats

No virtuous man has ever painted a picture worth looking at, or written a symphony worth hearing, or a book worth reading.

—H.L. Mencken

Well Endowed

The truly revolutionary promise of our nation's founding document is the freedom to pursue happiness-with-a-capital-H. Unfortunately, this promise is considered problematic by some Americans. The very pursuits that make some Americans happy (some very happy indeed) are considered downright sinful by social conservatives. By itself, this attitude wouldn't be a problem if these other Americans were content to avoid activities they regard as sinful, live their lives according to their convictions, and recognize the right of their fellow Americans to do the same. While some Americans might choose to lead a less than virtuous existence, at least in William J. Bennett's estimation, what skin is it off Bennett's ass? If we aren't free to pursue our own version of happiness, then the first two items on Jefferson's wish list are without meaning. Life and liberty do us no good if we can't employ them—or waste them—in the pursuit of those things that make us happy.

Sadly, America's professional virtuecrats aren't content to mind their own business, to let their virtues be their own reward on earth, and to content themselves with thoughts of whatever reward they having coming to them in their heaven. Instead, Dr. Laura Schlessinger lectures us on the radio daily, Bill O'Reilly gripes at us on cable nightly, and William J. Bennett seems to produce a book a month. Fine, they have a right to their opinions, and they have a right to express themselves. However, the virtuous in America aren't satisfied with merely lecturing us. They want to give us orders, and to that end they've banded together in what appears to be a never-ending effort to shove their own virtues down all of our throats. They've convinced themselves that the pursuit of happiness by less virtuous Americans is both a personal and a political attack. Not content to persuade their fellow Americans to be virtuous—which, again, is their right—they want to amend constitutions and pass laws.

While the efforts of the virtuous to make their virtues compulsory haven't been successful—have you given up any of your vices?—the virtuecrats go largely unchallenged in the public arena. The virtuecrats haven't succeeded in halting the sale of rap CDs, the giving of blow jobs, or the getting of high; they have succeeded in convincing us that no one has a right to challenge them. They're virtuous, after all. They're good people trying to do good. Who can argue with good? By successfully framing the debate as virtue versus sin, and not the laws versus your freedoms, the virtuecrats have succeeded in silencing their political foes and the sinners who enjoy the happy pursuits virtuecrats seek to ban. So while tens of millions of Americans have listened (or have been forced to listen) to the Borks, Bennetts, Buchanans, Pat Robertsons, Dr. Lauras, and Bill O'Reillys go off about the dangers and immorality of, say, smoking pot, unbiased researchers have long since documented that marijuana is safe, harmless, less addictive than caffeine, and less harmful than alcohol. Despite this research, nothing remotely positive is ever written or broadcast by American news media about the recreational use of marijuana. Sure, medical marijuana gets some good press, but only because it plays to the media's obsession with victim stories; medical marijuana activists have an endless supply of sympathetic cancer patients, glaucoma sufferers, and AIDS patients at their disposal. But no one at a daily paper or a mainstream news program will risk saying anything truthful (and consequently positive) about recreational marijuana use for fear that William J. Bennett and Dr. Laura will swoop down and accuse them of sending the "wrong message" to kids. (Since when is the truth the wrong message?)

Some social conservatives, like Robert Bork, the author of the bible of social conservatives, *Slouching Towards Gomorrah*, go so far as to argue that our founding fathers were just kidding around about the pursuit of happiness. It was, at best, a rhetorical flourish on Thomas Jefferson's part, not anything we should take seriously, much less act on. Bork, ironically, is a leading proponent of the "original intent" movement in legal theory, which argues that judges should base their rulings solely on the intent of our founding fathers, which can be divined through a close reading of our nation's founding documents. Except, of course, for the first lines of our nation's first document. That "pursuit of happiness" stuff? That's just poetry. Americans shouldn't be free "to choose which virtues to practice or not practice," Bork argues, as that would entail, "the privatization of morality, or, if you will, the 'pursuit of happiness,' as each of us defines happiness." (Morality is apparently the only thing social conservatives don't want to privatize.) The pursuit of happiness is so rank and unpleasant a concept for Bork that he sticks it between quotes as if he were holding it with a pair of tongs.

Bork isn't the only social conservative who wants to rewrite our nation's founding document. In his best-seller *The Death of the West*, Patrick J. Buchanan simply deletes the pursuit of happiness from the Declaration of Independence: "Jefferson meant that we are all endowed by our creator with the same right to life, liberty, and property," Buchanan writes. If our founding fathers were as thoughtful and wise as original intenters and social conservatives are always telling us, we can only assume that our founding fathers selected "pursuit of happiness" over "property" for a good reason. Out of respect for our founding fathers' original intent, shouldn't we assume that they knew what they were doing? Shouldn't we assume that they meant it?

Apparently not. "Pleasure is an event; happiness is a process," Dr. Laura writes in her book *How Could You Do That?!* "Pleasure is an end point; happiness is the journey. Pleasure is material; happiness is spiritual. Pleasure is self-involved; happiness is outer- and other-involved." Happiness may be a spiritual process for Dr. Laura, but all Americans should be free to define happiness for themselves, and some of us find happiness in pursuits that Dr. Laura wants to see banned.

But Dr. Laura is hardly the most extreme of the virtuecrats. "According to the Declaration of Independence, our freedom comes from a transcendent authority," writes Alan Keyes in his book *Our Character, Our Future*. Keyes is an African-American conservative who ran for president in 1996 and 2000, and is the host of a talk show launched on MSNBC in early 2002. (Gosh darn that liberal media elite!) Keyes is obsessed with abortion and homosexuality, and he believes America wouldn't be in such "a dismal state" if only Americans would recognize that the Christian Bible trumps the United States Constitution in matters of law and public policy. Why is that? "The Declaration tells us clearly where rights come from: 'We hold these truths to be self-evident that all men are *created* equal, that they are endowed,' not by the Constitution, or the Bill of Rights, or the Supreme Court, or anybody else, they are endowed by their *Creator*." Since our rights flow from the Creator, we don't have the right to engage in anything specifically forbidden by Keyes's Creator. It's a willfully perverse reading of the Declaration of Independence. By invoking the Creator, Keyes argues, the authors of the Declaration of Independence meant to negate every other word they wrote.

Our founding fathers had ample chance to distance themselves from or completely disavow the pursuit of happiness when they gathered in Philadelphia in 1787 to draft the United States Constitution. They didn't seem to slouch into Philadelphia heavy with regret about the happiness line in the Declaration of Independence. In fact, they seemed pretty pleased with themselves, gathering in Philadelphia, as they wrote, "in order to form a more perfect union." (*More* perfect?) I'm no Constitutional scholar, I admit, nor have I had the honor of being nominated to the Supreme Court; I didn't serve my country as the first in a long line of wildly ineffective drug czars; and I've also never hosted a do-as-I-say call-in radio advice program that obsessed about sexual morality while at the same time nude pictures of me taken by a premarital sex partner were circulated on the Web. And I haven't, like Bennett, "served two presidents." (I did, however, serve Prince Edward and Joan Collins when I was living in London and supporting myself by waiting tables.) Nevertheless, it seems to me that if "Life, Liberty and the pursuit of Happiness" were such a big, fat, fucking mistake, then our wise founding fathers would have realized it in the eleven years that passed between the signing of the Declaration of Independence and the first meeting of the Constitutional Congress. If they felt "the pursuit of Happiness" was a mistake, they surely would have done something to correct it when they gathered to make our union just a little more perfect. (Our founding fathers failed, of course. It was their "original intent" to allow slavery to flourish and to deny women the right to vote. Talk about your imperfect unions.)

Many of my fellow Americans are deeply annoyed at the self-appointed virtuecrats and preening moralists who clog our airwaves and best-seller lists, and have warped our political conversation to the point that simple honesty and truth-telling about sex or drugs disqualifies someone from public office. (Dr. Joycelyn Elders, RIP.) I, for one, am sick of being told that I live in an immoral wasteland. Robert Bork is a best-selling author, former federal judge, and failed Supreme Court nominee who looks at the United States and sees Gomorrah, the biblical city-state destroyed by God (along with Sodom, a neighboring bedroom community). William J. Bennett is the Jesse Jackson of the right, the omnipresent former education secretary and federal drug "czar," who, like Jackson on the left, is the ass his party feels obliged to kiss. The author of *The Book of Virtues,* Bennett pops up on television whenever a Democrat ejaculates on an intern. (Bennett was somewhat less prominent when Newt Gingrich divorced his second wife and married a congressional aide.) Pat Buchanan is the conservative television pundit, Hitler-admiring two-time candidate for the Republican presidential nomination, and the Reform Party's candidate in 2000.

Bork's *Slouching Towards Gomorrah* was published in 1996, and in it Bork made the case for censorship (of rap albums, video games, and violent films), the rollback of reproductive rights, and the enforcement of sodomy laws, among other things. It's a thrilling read, and it set a new standard for conservative commentary. In books, magazines, speeches, and on television, Bork and other right-wing "scolds," as Andrew Sullivan has dubbed them, argue that the United States of America is in a state of moral collapse— Bennett says as much in the title of his latest book, *The Broken Hearth: Reversing the Moral Collapse of the American Family.* Buchanan paints a picture of the United States in *The Death of the West* that reads like a translation of an Osama bin Laden video. The United States is "a moral sewer and a cultural wasteland that is not worth living in and not worth fighting for," according to Buchanan. (Buchanan seems anxious to be president of this moral sewer, however.) "To look at America today," writes Ralph Reed, former director of the Christian Coalition, in his book *Active Faith*, "is to witness a nation struggling against forces as dangerous as any military foe it has ever faced. The threats, however, come not from without but from within." Those threats? Abortion, drugs, and single moms. "Bill O'Reilly is even madder today than when he wrote his last book, *The O'Reilly Factor*," reads the dust jacket to Fox

News personality Bill O'Reilly's latest book, *The No Spin Zone*. "He's mad because things have gone from bad to worse, in politics, in Hollywood, in every social stratum of the nation."

In this seemingly endless flow of America-the-moral-sewer books and op-eds, scolds argue that our nation is shot through with moral rot, weakened by the demands of the ACLU, feminists, immigrants, secular humanists, and gays and lesbians. The moral-rotters, according to conservatives, are aided and abetted at every step by the liberal media elite. (The same media elite that can't turn over a rock without offering a book deal and a show on Fox News to whatever is found crawling underneath.) As we learned on September 11, 2001, our moral rot can have deadly consequences with supernatural causes. According to Rev. Jerry Falwell, it was the presence of feminists, ACLU members, homos, and federal judges that prompted God to "lift the curtain" of protection from the United States, "and allow the enemies of America to give us probably what we deserve [on September 11]."

In the wake of the September 11 attacks, some people predicted that social conservatives would have to shut the fuck up. Writing in *The New Republic* after the attacks, Andrew Sullivan pointed out that the reaction of the American people to the attacks on our country by Islamo-fascists proved that the scolds—the Borks, Buchanans, Bennetts, Falwells, Robertsons, et alia—had been wrong about America all along:

> Not long ago, leading paleoconservatives were denouncing America as a country, in Robert Bork's words, "slouching towards Gomorrah." Moral decline was almost irreparable; civil responsibility was a distant memory; pop culture was sapping any social fiber we had; and the evils of feminism, homosexuality, and Hollywood were corroding the country's ability to believe in itself or defend its shores. None of this was ever true. . . . The response of the American people to the events of September 11 surely disproved these scolds once and for all.

Shortly after Sullivan wrote those words, Pat Buchanan's *Death of the West*—". . . [the United States is] a moral sewer and a cultural wasteland that is not worth living in and not worth fighting for. . . ."—shot up the *New York Times* best-selling list.

Curiously, after spending three hundred pages making the United States sound like Calcutta, Buchanan wraps up his book with a one-sentence paragraph about what a beautiful country this is. Speakers at the Republican National Convention do the same thing: Once they've finished telling us that the United States is a shithole, they wrap up their speeches with claims that the United States of America is unique in the world, a shining example to other nations, and the greatest country on earth. Oh, and God bless America.

It's difficult to square this circle: America speeds towards hell in a handbasket, year in, year out, through both Democratic and Republican administrations; things get progressively worse, never better; and yet the United States remains the greatest country on earth, year in, year out. How is this possible? How can we be the stinking moral sewer and the shining city on the hill at the same time? Gomorrah and God's country? Are all the other countries on earth so irredeemably awful, so squalid, so beyond hope that no matter how fast America falls we can't pass a single one on the way down? This explanation might cut it if the rest of the world were Syria, Sudan, and Serbia. But how do the Buchanans, Bennetts, and O'Reillys account for perfectly pleasant little countries like Sweden? Or the Netherlands? Or Canada? (By the way, someone needs to alert Pat Buchanan that Canada is not in Europe. On page 200 of *The Death of the West*, he writes, "Europe has begun to resemble the United States. Between 1960 and 2000, out-of-wedlock births soared in Canada from 4 percent to 31 percent, in the U.K. from 5 percent to 38 percent, in France from . . .")

The carping goes on year after year, book deal after book deal, with the Republican National Convention serving as a sort of quadrennial national checkup, during which we're invariably told that we're headed downhill fast. Watching the Republican National Convention is like going to the doctor every four years and being told your body is riddled with some horrible, disfiguring, fast-spreading, terminal cancer. We've been getting that same diagnosis from the same doctors every four years for—what? Twenty years? Longer? Am I the only one who sits through our national chemotherapy sessions with former drug czars and radio talk-show hosts and is not convinced we're so ill that we require such an annoying and toxic course of treatment?

Can't we get a second opinion?

Sometimes we do, but it's not all that helpful either. Americans are sinning, wimpy liberals meekly respond, but we're not sinning quite so much as Bill Bennett would lead us to believe. Americans may cheat on their spouses and smoke a lot of pot, but we don't cheat or smoke pot at the rate one might expect. If only a few more Americans would have Just Said No, liberals and conservatives agree, we could reverse our moral collapse and avoid the ignominious prospect of being a slightly less glorious nation than Canada, the sick man of Europe.

For anyone interested in genuine political arguments, the second opinion offered by liberals is deeply frustrating: it buys into the same values espoused by the people who gave us that faulty first opinion—namely, that "sin" is always bad. Terrified of being the pro-pot party or the pro-adultery party or the pro-sodomy party, the Democrats opt for virtue-lite politics and send junior varsity scolds like Sen. Joe Lieberman out to lecture Hollywood. Where is the politician who will look Bennett in the eye on television and say, "Some of the nicest, most virtuous, morally *uncollapsed* people I know smoke pot and commit adultery (with their spouses' permission)—it's how they pursue happiness, and so long as they're not hurting anyone else, why should they be made to feel guilty? Or any less virtuous than you, Bill Bennett?"

Bennett, like every moral scold who has ever compiled a big book on virtue, goes on and on about the deep sense of happiness and fulfillment he has derived from marriage and traditional family life. There's something deeply problematic about praising Bill Bennett—an activity that eats up an awful lot of Bill Bennett's time—for pursuing those things that make Bill Bennett happy (heterosexuality, sobriety, monogamy) while condemning someone else for pursuing the things that make him happy (say, homosexuality, pot, and the occasional three-way). Refraining from having sex with men and with women who aren't his wife makes Bill Bennett *happy*. And I'm all for Bill Bennett being just as happy a Bill Bennett as Bill Bennett can possibly be. But everyone should have the same right to happiness. Should the law coerce all of us into pursuing Bill Bennett's brand of happiness? Bill Bennett thinks so, and so do Bork and Buchanan. These men, so far as we know, derive happiness from things that have been labeled virtues, and hence they are praised for their pursuit of happiness. For others, the things that make us happy have been labeled sinful, and we're condemned for our pursuit of happiness. But if I'm not hurting anyone, my pursuit of happiness is no less virtuous than Bennett's.

To be fair, for some of the high-profile virtuous, living an upright life may not make them all that happy. In fact, it may make some of them miserable. There may be conservative pundits out there who desire to smoke dope or sleep around but deny themselves these pleasures, and their public calls for virtue are simply an externalization of their own inner struggle to be good. "Our virtues are most frequently but vices disguised," wrote La Rochefoucauld in his Maxims (1665), a point driven home by former television evangelist Rev. Jimmy Swaggart. Swaggart, you'll recall, condemned pornography and prostitution for years, and then was caught visiting prostitutes and "consuming" pornography. Swaggart had deeply conflicted feelings about pornography and prostitution, and he called for the more restrictive laws against both in hopes that the state might help keep him right with God. But those of us who enjoy pornography and prostitutes without conflict shouldn't have to go without to protect Swaggart from himself.

Whether virtue comes easy or the virtuecrat has to do battle with his desires, the virtuous all conspire to force their virtues on us sinners, which is not something sinners do. The existence of the virtuous is not regarded by sinners as a personal threat, nor do sinners attempt to stamp out virtue wherever we find it. No urban music lover has ever, to give one example, placed a gun to Robert Bork's head and forced him to buy a rap CD. Nevertheless, in *Slouching Towards Gomorrah*, Bork argues that no one should be *allowed* to buy rap CDs. "Is censorship really as unthinkable as we all seem to assume?" Bork asks in a chapter titled "The Case for Censorship." "I [suggest] that censorship be considered for the most violent and sexually explicit material now on offer [including] the more degenerate lyrics of rap music."

Personally, I never wanted to buy a rap CD until I read Bork's book, which is the strange—and strangely predictable—thing about censorship: It creates a demand for the very things the censors want to stamp out. Even if it were possible to scuttle the First Amendment—so much for original intent!—and ban rap music, the effort would fail. The Soviet Union, a police state with unlimited powers and spies in every workplace and apartment building, attempted to ban rock and roll music. It failed. It's hard to imagine how our government could enforce a ban on rap music in a country whose citizens own almost as many CD burners as they do guns. Not that I would put it past John Ashcroft. Social conservatives will sometimes argue that rap music or violent movies or drugs need to be banned to protect the weak and vulnerable from taking up a life of sinful indulgence. It would be easier to take these arguments more seriously if the same social conservatives weren't opposed to laws that protect the weak and vulnerable from unsafe workplaces, flammable children's pajamas, and arsenic in our drinking water.

Rap versus show tunes; monogamy versus variety; pot versus Bud Light—different things make different people happy. It's such a simple concept, so—what's the phrase? Oh, yeah. It's so *self-*

evident. Why, then, do so many conservatives have such a hard time wrapping their heads around it?

Like a room full of Victorian spinsters with the vapors, virtue-crats would have us believe that the mere knowledge that sinners are out there having fun keeps them up nights; indeed, knowing that someone, somewhere, might be pursuing happiness in ways they disapprove of is a profound psychological torment to them. Therefore, they argue, it's in the best interest of society—and by *society* they mean, "me and everyone who agrees with me"—for the law to come between sinners and their vices. Not only will it save the sinners from themselves, but it will also make it easier for the virtuous to get their nine hours every night. Need it be said? Bork doesn't have to listen to rap music if he doesn't care for it; Dr. Laura doesn't have to engage in premarital sex (anymore) if she's opposed to it (now); Jerry Falwell doesn't have to join the ACLU; Bill Bennett doesn't have to have a same-sex marriage if he disapproves. Law-abiding Americans who listen to rap music, indulge in pre-marital sex, feminism, and agitate for gay marriage do no harm to those who don't enjoy these activities or share these goals. Bennett's marriage, for instance, doesn't appear to have been harmed by legal gay marriages in the Netherlands. (If straight marriage in the United States is such a delicate institution that even a national con-versation about gay marriage can destroy it, as Bennett argues in *The Broken Hearth*, then the institution of straight marriage isn't long for this world. The next light breeze should blow the thing away.)

What the moaners and groaners at the Republican National Convention, Fox News, and on the op-ed pages of the *Wall Street Journal* refuse to accept is that freedom isn't a one-way street. It's not even a two-way street. Freedom is space, weightlessness, room to maneuver, to go your own way. It's people blasting off in all di-rections. We should agree to disagree about certain things like, say, drug use or premarital sex, and, when necessary, establish reason-able rules to prevent people from slamming into each other—such as laws against assault, rape, and murder, laws that set an age of consent for sexual activity, laws against drinking and driving. Beyond these simple rules, however, the freedom to pursue happiness must be regarded just as Thomas Jefferson described it—an inalienable right, God-given—or all our rhetoric about freedom is meaningless.

Do some people get harmed in the pursuit of happiness? Aren't people—and neighborhoods and whole cities—harmed by, say, the drug trade? Aren't prostitutes frequently harmed by violent clients? Doesn't adultery destroy homes? Yes, yes, and yes. But much of the harm done by drugs, prostitution, and adultery should be laid at the feet of the virtuous. It's their meddling that often creates the harm, not the sins in and of themselves. There would be no money, and therefore no gangs or violence, in the drug trade if drugs were legalized and their sale taxed and regulated. When was the last time beer distributors killed each other? Oh, yeah: prohibition. If prostitution were legalized, an American prostitute with a violent client or abusive pimp could turn to the police for protection, just as prostitutes do in the Netherlands. If every couple were encouraged to have a realistic, rational conversation about the near-inevitability of infidelity in long-term relationships, fewer homes would be destroyed by adultery. But the political right wing doesn't allow for realistic, rational conversation about anything—tune into Fox News anytime to see irrational, unrealistic nonconversation twenty-four hours a day. Furthermore, the law shouldn't be concerned with preventing people from harming themselves. Our bodies and minds and souls are our own, and we should be free to use and abuse and dispose of them as we see fit.

Not all sinners lack virtue, and not everyone who's technically virtuous is ethical. A woman who commits adultery with her husband's permission—or in her husband's presence—has to be viewed as more virtuous than a faithful man who's married to a woman he emotionally abuses. Yet adulterers are universally condemned by the virtuecrats, without any regard for their particular circumstances. Similarly, all users of illegal drugs are condemned. Yet a man who smokes a small amount of pot every day in his own home is doing himself and society less harm than a man who drinks himself drunk every night in public. The man who goes to a prostitute doesn't seek to harm the man who doesn't go to a prostitute; the man who goes to a gay pride parade in a lime-green thong doesn't seek to harm the man who goes to church fully clothed.

Indeed, it has long been my belief that the "bad" are frequently *more* virtuous in their private pursuit of vice than the good are in the public pursuit of compulsory virtue. Sinners, unlike the virtuous, do not attempt to impose their definition of happiness on others. I've never met an adult dope smoker who wanted to force a non-dope-smoking adult to smoke dope against his will. Yet our nation crawls with non-dope-smoking adults who want to force dope-smoking adults to stop smoking dope. Likewise, I've never met a homosexual who wanted to make a straight person into a gay person, but straight church groups take out full-page ads in newspapers trying to convince gay people to become straight people. Prostitutes don't force anyone to patronize them; the virtuous, however, seek to throw prostitutes in jail for tending to the needs of their clients.

There are millions of ethical, fully moral sinners in America, and I've grown sick of listening to the right wing bitch and moan about them while the left wing refuses to defend them. No one sticks up for the sinners—not even the sinners themselves. Some of the best Americans I know are sinners, but they lack the necessary conviction to defend themselves, their sins, and their right to be sinners. Meanwhile, the worst—the Bennetts, Borks, and Buchanans—are filled with a passionate intensity. Some sinners are no doubt scared. They worry that speaking up for themselves will prompt Bill Bennett to call them names in the op-ed pages of the *Wall Street Journal*. Sinners are bullied and coerced into remaining silent, and as a result, only the self-proclaimed "virtuous" are heard from in public. How much longer can American sinners sit by and say nothing while the vices we enjoy and know to be perfectly harmless are maligned?

To explore the lives of virtuous sinners, I decided to leave home and walk up and down in the United States, committing in turn all the seven deadly sins, except one, which, try as I might, I simply couldn't do. I wanted to meet and sin with other virtuous sinners. I write in praise and defense of the American sinner—those wonderful, freedom-loving, fun-seeking adulterers, gamblers, and gluttons I met during my travels through the moral sewers of the United States of America: through the Gomorrahs of Los Angeles; New York; San Francisco; Seattle; Dubuque, Iowa; Plano, Texas; and Buffalo Grove, Illinois. Part travelogue, part memoir, part Bork-and-Bennett bitch slap, this book is a love letter to Thomas Jefferson, American freedom, and American sinners.

A Quick Note on the Seven Deadly Sins

Why the seven deadly sins?

Well, why not the seven deadlies? The sins themselves—greed, lust, sloth, gluttony, anger, pride, and envy—are conveniently vague, which afforded me a wide variety of representative sins from which to choose. I might have focused on the Ten Commandments, I suppose, but, Christ, who hasn't taken the Lord's name in vain? Or dishonored their stupid parents? (Dr. Laura doesn't even speak to her mother!) And there are ten of them, which would've meant more work for me, and I'm a slothful kind of guy. What's more, I wanted to commit the sins I was writing about, and while bearing false witness is something I'd happily do ("Yes, your honor, I saw Robert Bork smoke dope with a male prostitute in a casino before he ate a dozen Krispy Kreme doughnuts. . . ."), I couldn't see killing someone to sell a few books, as I don't wish physical harm on anyone. I'd even brake for Bill O'Reilly.

Interestingly, the seven deadly sins aren't mentioned anywhere in the Bible, which may come as a surprise to some readers—it certainly came as a surprise to me. While I'd never run across the seven deadly sins while reading the Bible, I nevertheless assumed that the seven deadlies were in the Bible somewhere, perhaps in a psalm I'd somehow missed or the directors' cut of the Sermon on the Mount. But the collective idea of the seven deadly sins, as it turns out, has its roots in the pre-Judeo-Christian era, and the sources for the tradition are not at all clear-cut. Most scholars believe the roots of the seven deadly sins lie in a conflation of Babylonian astronomy, which argued that the cosmos was a series of seven spheres with earth at the center, and the Greek belief that the soul descends from heaven, acquiring sin as it takes on a mortal body.

The earliest list of seven sins appears in the *Greek Testament of the Twelve Patriarchs: Testament of Reuben,* supposedly written by

Reuben, one of the twelve patriarchs of the tribes of Israel, around 106 B.C. Another list of deadly sins was drawn up by Horace, the Roman poet (65–8 B.C.), who ticked off eight mortal crimes or passions: avarice, desire, vanity, envy, wrath, sloth, drunkenness, and sensuality. It wasn't until Evagrius of Pontus (d. ca. 400), an early Christian monk who lived in Egypt, made his list of eight cardinal sins that a list of non-biblical sins entered the Christian tradition. Evagrius served for a time as archdeacon of Constantinople before traveling to Jerusalem and then into the Nitrian Desert to become a hermit. It was a more gregarious monk, John Cassian (d. ca. 435), who brought Evagrius's list from Egypt to Europe. In his De Institutos Coenobiorum (ca. 420), Cassian listed Evagrius's eight sins: gluttony, lust, avarice, wrath, sadness, sloth, vainglory, and pride. (Fun fact: Cassian considered the first two sins, lust and gluttony, "natural," since the existence of humanity depends, to some extent, on eating and fucking.)

It was Saint Gregory the Great (Pope Gregory I, d. 604) who cut Evagrius's eight cardinal sins down to seven, as he added envy to the list, eliminated vainglory, and merged sadness with sloth. But Gregory's list of seven deadly sins—pride, anger, greed, envy, sloth, gluttony, and lust—was unknown outside of monastic circles until the Catholic Church made confession mandatory in the early part of the thirteenth century. Parish priests in England were instructed to teach their parishioners about the seven deadly sins after 1231, in the hopes that their parishioners would have less to confess if they knew what to avoid. That was what transformed the seven deadly sins from a Dark Ages obscurity to pop culture phenomenon, insofar as pop culture existed in the thirteenth century.

Got all that? Good. Now let's do some sinnin'.

GREED

The Thrill of Losing Money

Affluence brings with it boredom. Of itself, it offers little but the ability to consume, and a life centered on consumption will appear, and be, devoid of meaning. Persons so afflicted will seek sensation as a palliative, and that today's culture offers in abundance. —Robert Bork

Consumption, sensation, meaninglessness—Robert Bork wasn't writing about Las Vegas when he wrote those words, but he sure nailed the place.

Before I ever set foot in Las Vegas—before I sipped my first foot-long margarita—I despised the place as much as or more than I assume Bork does. To me, Las Vegas was a place where cocktail waitresses went to die, where swag lamps swung, and where gangsters were gunned down midmassage. Elvis and Frank and Liberace may have left the building, but Vegas was still their cheesy town, not mine. Las Vegas was strip clubs and slot machines, Zsa Zsa Gabor and Robert Urich. Las Vegas was for people who lead lives centered on consumption, devoid of meaning. It was a place where topless showgirls in smoky showrooms paraded before fat businessmen, their unhappy wives stewing at their sides. Glued together by greed, tarted up with acres of tinted mirrors, Las Vegas was a throbbing neonscape powered by the Hoover Dam, its acres of grass watered by what's left of the Colorado River.

I thought life was seriously out of balance in Las Vegas.

My impression of Las Vegas wasn't shaped by personal experience—not even the briefest of visits—but by two films I saw in my formative years: *The Godfather: Part II* and *Koyaanisqatsi*. After seeing both movies during my freshman year of college, I made up my mind never to set foot in Las Vegas, certain that both the city and anyone who enjoyed it were beneath me. So sure was I in my judgment, so smug in my superiority, that I dismissed the opinions of people that I knew and respected who had been to Las Vegas and claimed to have enjoyed themselves.

If the insufferable, clenched-butt snob I was in college could see me now, he'd never stop throwing up. I have to confess that I've fallen in love with Las Vegas. In my defense, it wasn't love at first sight; Las Vegas's charms where entirely lost on me the first time I visited. In fact, each and every prejudice I held about the city was confirmed on that first trip—even before my Vegas-bound plane could get off the ground.

I was thirty years old when I first visited Vegas in the flesh, and I went under duress. It was a business trip of sorts, and not one I had been looking forward to. My worst *Godfather–Koyaanisqatsi* fears about Las Vegas were realized before my plane could push away from the gate. The man who plopped down next to me was so fat he couldn't put his tray table down, and so pushy that he set his meal—four cherry Danish (!) and a rum and Coke (!!)—*on my tray table without asking permission*. I had long suspected Las Vegas to be a city larded with pushy, greedy gluttons, and the man sitting next to me was solid—massive!—proof that I was right. I dreaded the idea of spending three days in a hotel filled with people like him: greedy gamblers, fat-assed gluttons, and hopeless drunks.

But no one had warned me about the clowns.

All done up in shades of pink and white, Circus Circus Hotel Resort and Casino has—can you guess?—a circus theme. "Circus Circus is what the whole hep world would be doing on Saturday night if the Nazis had won the war," Hunter S. Thompson wrote in *Fear and Loathing in Las Vegas*. "This is the Sixth Reich." I'm not sure what Hunter means exactly, but Circus Circus is as creepy as any other place filled with clowns; in fact, there isn't a corner of the hotel's gigantic lobby or casino that escaped the wrath of Circus Circus's clown-mad decorators. A twelve-story-high neon clown greeted me out front, bas-relief clowns assaulted me at reception, clowns on slot machines dinged and whistled. Like all sensible adults, I loathe clowns, and being trapped in a clown-themed hotel for three days was not my idea of fun. It wasn't my idea *at all,* actually, and I made up my mind to order a horse head put in my travel agent's bed when I got home. When I found myself alone in my clown-themed hotel room, which I rode to in a clown-themed elevator, I wanted to hide under the clown-themed bedspread and cry.

Needless to say, my feelings about Las Vegas didn't change as a result of that first, traumatic visit. Besides eating (at the clown-themed buffet) and gambling (in a clown-themed casino), there was little to do at Circus Circus, and I wasn't allowed to stray far from the hotel. As I'm not a gambler and only an occasional, guilt-ridden glutton, when I checked out of Circus Circus after three miserable days, I vowed never to return to Las Vegas. But return I did, and it was on my second trip that a love affair that has yet to end was sparked. And, irony of ironies, I returned to Las Vegas to prove to a friend that it was just as bad as I'd told him. After listening to me complain, my best friend wanted to see this American Gomorrah for himself, and so I tagged along on his first trip to Vegas. I wanted to make sure he had just as bad a time in Las Vegas as I did. This time, I wasn't going for work—and I wasn't going for three days, either, just overnight. This time I was slumming in Las Vegas, and I planned to spend the day making snide remarks at the expense (and the expanse) of all the other visitors to the city.

But a funny thing happened on the way to making sure my best friend hated Las Vegas just as much as I did. Maybe it was staying in a hotel that was clown-free (MGM Grand), or maybe it was my best friend's infectious enthusiasm, or the fact that we stayed one night instead of three. But by the time we wound up strapped to the Big Shot ride atop the Stratosphere Hotel and Tower—imagine sitting in a chair on top of the Empire State Building and being shot a hundred feet into the air, and then free-falling back down to the roof—I had to admit that I was having a . . . good time. I was having a great time, actually, in Las Vegas. *And it wasn't a coincidence.*

When Las Vegas was just a gleam in the eye of America's organized crime families, the lure of legalized gambling was enough to attract hordes of none-too-demanding gamblers and tourists. As there weren't any places to gamble legally outside of Nevada, Las Vegas's first wave of hotels didn't have to offer much beyond slots and cheap drinks and the occasional sleazy floor shows to lure the suckers into the building. Today, of course, things are very different. First of all, Americans no longer have to travel far to gamble. The first legal casino in the United States may have opened in Lake Tahoe, Nevada, in 1931, but by the end of the 1990s, there were lotteries in thirty-seven states and some kind of legalized gambling in forty-seven states. Today only the residents of Hawaii, Tennessee, and Utah are unable to gamble in their home states. Even people who live in these holdout states, except Hawaii, don't have to roam far afield to gamble; chances are, wherever an American lives, a riverboat or a Native American casino is only a short drive away. Cities that used to be punch lines to jokes about towns with nothing going on—Biloxi, Mississippi; Dubuque, Iowa; Gary, Indiana—have become regional gambling meccas, petite Las Vegas knockoffs. And with the advent of on-line gambling, there's really no such thing as a gambling-free state anymore. We can place bets on our computers in our bedrooms, dens, and offices. Even in Hawaii.

Around the same time gambling was being transformed from a sinful and largely illegal activity to America's pastime—which was around the same time gambling got a new name: gaming—resort owners in Las Vegas realized that they had to offer something more than just slots and craps and cards to keep people coming to a strip of hotels in the middle of a friggin' desert. Most Americans live within a forty-minute drive of legal craps tables, card games, and slot machines. To keep pulling in gamblers, Las Vegas had to offer us things smaller casinos could not. In the early 1990s, Las Vegas transformed itself into a "family friendly" destination spot, with amusement parks for the kids, floor shows suitable for children, and, of course, casino gambling for the parents. Family-friendly Las Vegas is lately giving way to adults-only Las Vegas, with bare-breasted showgirls making a comeback at otherwise "respectable" hotels. But family-friendly or bare-breasted, Las Vegas knows it has to wow us to keep us coming back. Gambling isn't enough anymore.

My first trip to Vegas, as it turns out, was poorly timed. Most of the big, new resorts were still under construction, and all I saw on that first trip were clowns; construction cranes; boarded-up, soon-to-be-imploded old hotels; and dingy, depressing casinos with few attractions for the nongambler.

On my second trip, I wandered over to the Bellagio and its art gallery and fountains; then over to New York, New York, where I rode the roller coaster; and finally to the Stratosphere Hotel and Casino and its mind-blowing Big Shot ride. Paris was going up, along with its one-third scale Eiffel Tower, the Aladdin was being rebuilt, and the canals were being dug for the Venetian. All of a sudden, what was going on outside the buildings was as interesting as the gambling going on inside. Old Las Vegas was a collection of big boxy hotels built over big, smoky casinos. To make money, all a resort owner had to do was build a stack-the-suckers tower over a soak-the-suckers box. Fill the tower with hotel rooms, fill the box with slot machines, open the doors, and watch the money roll in.

By the mid-1990s, full-size warships were sinking outside of Treasure Island, Cirque du Soleil had taken up residence at the Bellagio, the Blue Man Group was imported from the actual New York

City, and a real show, the Broadway revival of the musical *Chicago,* was running at MGM Grand. No longer did you have to be a gambler to appreciate the spectacle of Las Vegas. The casinos, while still the moneymaking machine that fed Las Vegas, were no longer the focus. They were a given, and everything else—four-star restaurants, legit theater, the decorative arts—had taken center stage. And each of the huge, new casino-resorts had huge, new shopping malls (the Forum Shops at Caesar's Palace, Desert Passage at the Aladdin), which were filled with the same stores that can be found in every other mall in North America. Setting aside the bizarre notion that shopping is a recreational activity—and never mind why someone who lived in a city with malls of its own would get on an airplane and go to Las Vegas only to spend all of his time shopping in stores he could drive to or walk to at home—this was still something new.

And I fell for it. Many of the new hotels and resorts were beautiful, and I'm just a sucker for the decorative arts, I guess, so even the fake Paris charmed me. Still loud and crass, yes, and outsized, but beautiful. I didn't feel like a loser walking into the Venetian or the Bellagio. I felt like a guest, not a mark.

Oh, don't get me wrong: there's still a lot of crap in Las Vegas. Even the big new hotels are crap, really. It's just bigger, bolder crap, more contemporary crap. Some people still spend all their time at appallingly ugly old hotels, of course, like the somebody-implode-me-please Tropicana. You can still catch David Cassidy in a bloated show at the Rio, or Tommy Tune in a bloated show at the MGM Grand, and rumor has it that the reanimated corpses of Siegfried & Roy are still playing the Mirage. At the Tropicana one day, I saw an animal act that Chuck Barris would've gonged thirty years ago. But you don't have to spend your time at the Las Vegas of Bugsy Siegel, not if you don't want to. What Las Vegas has now that it once lacked—what it didn't have when *The Godfather* and *Koyaanisqatsi* were filmed—is some balance. You can take in the naked boobies of the showgirls at the Tropicana or the subversive artistry of the

Blue Man Group across the street at the Luxor. You can spend all your time in all-you-can-overeat buffets or dine in expensive restaurants run by big-name chefs who serve tiny portions.

And Americans are flocking to Las Vegas. Wandering around the casinos of Las Vegas you don't see a lot of urban types. The people conservatives believe are leading to the moral collapse of the country—feminists, immigrants, gays and lesbians, African Americans—are underrepresented in the most sinful city in the United States. Las Vegas's casinos are filled with little old ladies, respectable-looking soccer moms, and conservative-looking dads. In the lobby of the Venetian on my last trip to Las Vegas, I started asking people who they voted for in 2000: Bush or Gore? Among the sinners in Las Vegas, among the gamblers, drunks, and sleazily dressed women, Bush—President Abstinence, President Born Again, President Doesn't Drink—won by a landslide. Of the forty-six people I asked before a security guard told me to knock it off, thirty-two had voted for Bush.

The list of sins I haven't committed isn't very long. You name it and, with the exception of cunnilingus, I've done it. I've burned with lust, eaten myself sick, envied people who were smarter or better looking than I am, and lain around the house watching television when I was supposed to be studying or writing. Gambling, however, was a seedy, sinful pursuit that I could resist with very little effort. I've never made friendly wagers, I don't own stock, I've purchased lottery tickets three times in my adult life—and felt like an idiot every time. So while everything else in Las Vegas attracted me, the casinos in themselves held all the appeal to me that I imagine a thorough prostate exam has for Tom DeLay.

Even after I got over my anti-Vegas animus, I still felt dirty walking into casinos. Being in a casino said something about a person that I didn't want to say about myself. It said, "I am greedy and gullible." The losers far outnumber the winners—everyone knows this, right? That there are and always will be, by design, many, many losers in Las Vegas isn't a secret. Casinos aren't run like tobacco companies; they don't make much of an effort to hide the bad news.

The reason that I always had fun in Las Vegas—going to restaurants, shows, stores, and getting the occasional overpriced massage at the spa—was because I avoided the casinos. I never looked around Caesar's Palace or the Bellagio and thought, "Hey, I'm gonna take this place for all it's worth." Ironically, by not gambling I *was* taking the house. Resort owners lose money on hotel rooms; they make money when their guests *gamble,* not when guests check out. So while I never left Las Vegas with more money than I came with, I never left Las Vegas out more than the cost of my room, food, and entertainment. Las Vegas lost money on me—and, being Catholic, I felt guilty about it. In a city built on sin, the nonsinner is the transgressor.

So after seven trips to Las Vegas, I succumbed. Guilt got the best of me. If I wanted to keep going to Las Vegas—and I did—I would have to learn to gamble, if only to give the hotels a chance to start breaking even on me. And here was this sinful pleasure—gambling—that was so attractive that a multibillion-dollar industry had been created to indulge people who longed to commit it. It didn't look like fun to me, true, but neither does cunnilingus, and lots of people seem to enjoy the hell out of *that.* And if gambling was all about greed, as I suspected it was, hey, I'm greedy. I could be flattering myself, I suppose, and claim that I don't care about money. But I love money just as much as the next guy. And someone had to be making money somehow—I mean, if everyone lost, and lost big, every time they came to Las Vegas, well, people would stop coming, right? I'm a pretty smart guy—at least I like to think I am—maybe I could, with some practice and a little help, beat the house at the gaming tables instead of just at checkout.

First, slots.

There's not much strategy to slots. Find a slot machine in a maze of slot machines, one that hopefully isn't too close to a smoker or a granny hooked up to an oxygen tank (most of whom are also smokers), park your ass on an upholstered chair that's bolted to the floor, and start pumping in quarters. The slot machine tootles and bleeps; it may even speak; every casino has at least one bank of slot machines that scream "Wheel! Of! Fortune!" day and night. You put in a coin and push a button. (No one pulls the "arms" of one-armed bandits anymore; most slot machines still have arms, but they seem to be vestigial.) The computer program spins some apples or cherries or sevens or stars around, the machine tootles and bleeps or wheel-of-fortunes some more, and then one at a time, from left to right, the apples or cherries or sevens or stars stop spinning. And you're out a quarter. So you put in another quarter in hopes of winning your last quarter back. Repeat.

I lost about a hundred dollars in one hour the first time I played slots, which for sentimental reasons I did at Circus Circus. The whole time I was feeding quarters into a slot machine, I somehow couldn't shake the feeling that maybe this slots stuff was for suckers. Or clowns. People do win money playing slots, of course—there are pictures of them on the walls in some of the casinos. Still, more people lose money than win, as any fool knows. You can't tell this by listening to slot machines, however. The noise when someone wins is loud—slot machines don't actually drop coins into the stainless steel trays underneath them. They *spit* the coins into their steel trays. The coins hit the trays with a loud clang that can be heard all over the maze, bolstering the hopes of losers like me. ("People are winning! I might be next . . . must . . . keep . . . gambling . . .") Your perception is warped, of course, because none of the slot machines makes any special sound when someone loses a quarter or a silver dollar or, over in the high-stakes slots area, a five-, ten-, or twenty-five-dollar slug.

So what's the appeal of slot machines? Familiarity would be my guess. At every casino, the slot machines are laid out in a confusing maze of dead-end streets, spirals, and cul-de-sacs—a lot like the suburbs most gamblers live in. Like the suburbs, slot machines are isolating; you don't have to interact with other gamblers or a dealer to play the slots. The only person you have to interact with is a cocktail waitress. Someone may be playing the machine right next to you, but you're supposed to mind your own business, just like you would in the 'burbs. Craps and card tables, on the other hand, are intimidating urban areas, at the very center of the casino, laid out in a grid. You're jammed elbow to elbow with strangers at card tables, and while you avoid making eye contact, as you would in a subway or crosswalk, at the same time you keep close tabs on what the people around you are doing. Craps and card tables, consequently, can seem intimidating to new gamblers—especially suburban gamblers—while the maze of slot machines seems familiar and homey. What's more, today's slot machines are almost all computers—and what could possibly be more reassuringly familiar to American workers than sitting in front of a computer all day? At work, we're paid to sit in front of a computer. In Las Vegas, we pay to sit in front of a computer. And at home or in Vegas, we rely on alcohol to get us through.

But there's a price to pay for the comfort and familiarity of slot machines. The odds are stacked against the gambler at the slot machines. Of course, the odds are still stacked against the gambler at the gaming tables, too, they're just not stacked so high. Since my odds of winning at slots were less than they would be at any other game, I would have to learn some of the other games in the casino. Or try to.

I thought about playing craps, which according to the gambling books I was reading presents the knowledgeable player with his best odds of winning. Unfortunately, becoming a knowledgeable craps player takes twenty or thirty years. Trying to learn the game at Caesar's Palace, I stood with a group of people around a craps table while a charismatic old dealer taught us how to play. He was tall, bald, and gaunt, and he smiled like a cop: the corners of his mouth turned up, but his eyes were hard. The odds of beating the house, the dealer said, were indeed better at craps than at any other game in the casino. A tipsy frat boy nodded and smirked. Both the long-and short-term consequences of too many beers were quickly catching up with him (i.e., he wouldn't be needing that r much longer). Soon-to-be fat boy turned to his friends and boasted that he would "soak this place." They all high-fived each other. The dealer smiled wolfishly. Then he raised his arms and made a grand, sweeping gesture, taking in the whole room.

"Look around, son," the old dealer said, chuckling at the frat boy joylessly. We all took in the gaudy, over-the-top, brass-and-smoked-glass, football-field-size casino floor. It was Angie Dickinson vintage, but it was still very, very impressive. "Does it look like we get taken very often? I said your odds were *better* at craps. But they're not better than the casino's odds. They never are."

Craps is the most complicated game ever devised by the mind of man. The table is a rectangular oval with foot-high sides that looks like a strange sort of shallow bathtub lined with green felt. The felt surface is covered with numbers and boxes, and the table itself is surrounded by four or five dealers and sometimes twenty or more players. One of the dealers wields an intimidating-looking stick. The game is played with dice, and everyone who steps up to the table has to take a turn throwing the dice. There are about ten million different kinds of bets you can make, and one bad throw of the dice can cost everyone at the table a whole lot of money.

"Dice tables bring out the emotions more than any other game," writes the author of a book on craps. "There's a certain camaraderie among players that for some reason doesn't occur at any other tables. Players feel free to yell, shout, scream, applaud, and cheer. . . ."

Which means, of course, that craps tables invariably attract big, loud, drunk assholes. Frat boys, angry suburban dads, Wall Street types, good ol' boys with their mouths full of chewing tobacco: these are the guys who play craps. Cigar smokers play craps. Mobsters play craps. Bullies play craps. They all scream and yell at the

person who has the dice, which is why I just couldn't bring myself
to play the goddamned game. Being an unathletic, uncoordinated
fag in high school left me with many unhappy memories of being
the person who had the kickball or the soccer ball or the bat. While
other players yelled and shouted, I would invariably disappoint.
Knowing how angry a group of junior-varsity boys can get with
only the honor of defeating another group of junior-varsity boys, I
couldn't face a table full of angry adult male gamblers with actual
money at stake. If I was going to gamble, I would have to learn to
play cards. I played cards with my mother as a kid, but I couldn't
find any gin or hearts tables in the casinos I was in. And just when
I thought I might have to learn to play poker or blackjack I discovered . . .

$\mathbf{C}$asino War! Remember war? It's a kids' game, played with two
fifty-two-card decks. Two players simultaneously turn over one
card. The higher card takes the lower. If the players turn over cards
of identical value, you go to war: You both put two cards facedown,
then one more card faceup. The winner takes all the cards. Winning "wars" is the only way to win the game—and wars are rare.
Consequently, a single game of war can take hours, which is why
my parents taught it to their four children. It kept us occupied
while they sinned. Well, war only recently arrived in Las Vegas,
where it's played primarily by nongamblers. I stumbled over the
game in the casino of the Venetian, one of the big new hotels, and
I knew that this was a card game I could play. The rules were a little different, though. The players didn't get their own decks; instead, the dealer gave you one card, then dealt himself one card. If
your card was higher, you won. It was so simple that I figured I
couldn't mess it up.

So I pulled up a chair. Pretty soon I had a complimentary cocktail in my hand, and I was chatting away with the other warriors at
the table. While we played, the dealer treated us to a long, humor-
ous monologue designed to discourage us from ever playing

Casino War again. He pointed out again and again that the best we could hope to do was leave his table with the money we sat down with. The fifty-fifty odds meant we were likely to break even, but unlikely to win.

While the dealer tried to talk us out of playing War, some frat boys gathered to watch as we played. Soon they were making fun of us.

"Oh, they're playing War," one said. "Watch out! High rollers! Give these whales some breathing room!"

"What a pussy game," said another.

"Bock, bock, bock," said a third, flapping his arms like a chicken.

No security guard came to shoo away the frat boys who were calling us names, and the dealer didn't seem to mind them. Why should he? He was trying to talk us out of playing this game himself.

When I got up from the table two hours later, I wasn't even, as the dealer predicted. I was ahead. I sat down with $100 in five-dollar chips, and got up with $150 in chips. But some of my fellow warriors weren't so lucky. A smiling Asian man made dozens of hundred-dollar bets and lost almost every time. A slightly tipsy, very chatty woman who was sitting next to me burst into tears when she lost her last chip. And a man who claimed to have won three thousand dollars the night before at the Bellagio left the Venetian after two hours with the same money he sat down with.

Sitting at the table with strangers, playing a pussy game, I felt as if I were watching the American tragedy restaged as farce. Losers come to Las Vegas in hopes of feeling like winners, if only for an evening, and winners come to Las Vegas because they can afford to lose once in a while. Out there in real-life America, the winners and losers live in separate worlds: winners in gated communities, losers in ever-harder-to-find "affordable housing." Only in hyperunreal Las Vegas do the winners and losers rub shoulders—some sitting right next to each other at the card tables—and enact a highly ritualized, booze-soaked version of the striving, winning, and losing at the heart of American life.

Historically, Christian moralists in America have opposed gambling. Dice, cards, slots—the sin of gambling was right up there with adultery. By placing their faith in chance, gamblers were refusing to submit themselves to the will of God, making a false idol of money, worshiping luck and not Christ. Gambling was long seen as a form of stealing, because for someone to win at a game of chance, someone else has to lose. Duh. The winner profits at the expense of the loser and gives nothing in return, which was seen as violating Christ's instruction to love thy neighbor. Christian moralists believed that gambling encouraged the sin of envy, and while gambling is not forbidden anywhere in the Bible, there are many passages that discourage the love of money or wealth:

"The lover of money will not be satisfied with money; nor the lover of wealth with gain" (Ecclesiastes 5.10). "No one can serve two masters . . . you cannot serve God and Mammon" (Matthew 6.24). "Be sure of this, that no fornicator or impure person, or one who is greedy, has any inheritance in the Kingdom of Christ and of God" (Ephesians 5.5).

And let's not forget those Roman soldiers who threw dice for Christ's robes.

Considering the long tradition of antigambling sentiments and agitation (see *Guys and Dolls*) among Christian conservatives, it's strange that gambling rarely comes in for criticism from the Bill Bennetts and Robert Borks. The gambling issue doesn't get a lot of play with reliably conservative members of the U.S. House or Senate either. How did something that was once viewed as a sin comparable to adultery become so widespread in a country filled-to-bursting with self-appointed virtuecrats, moral scolds, a Christian Coalition, and hundreds of conservative members of Congress? Do they all agree with the gaming industry when it argues that gambling isn't a moral issue at all, and certainly not a sin?

Or is it the money, honey?

House Speaker Dennis Hastert visited Las Vegas in August of 1999. "Hastert rarely missed an opportunity Wednesday during his visit to Las Vegas to rip vocal gaming industry opponent Rep. Frank Wolf, R-Va.," the *Las Vegas Journal-Review* reported.

> "They are (his) own personal views and certainly not the views of the party leadership," Hastert, R-Ill., told Las Vegas reporters. . . . Hastert repeated the line during a private meeting with Mirage Resorts Chairman Steve Wynn and a midday fundraiser with gaming industry executives, who donated an estimated $600,000 to the Republican Congressional Campaign Committee. . . . "The consensus in the Republican conference is anti-personal gaming but pro the right to choose," said one House observer. "A majority in the Republican conference do not personally like to gamble and do not gamble, but most of them don't want to restrict the rights of others to do so."

So let me see if I have this straight: Republicans are pro-choice, pro-personal-freedom, and anti-restricting-the-rights-of-others when it comes to *gambling,* but not when it comes to anything else. When it comes to gambling, conservative Republicans will ignore thousands of years of moral teaching, Scripture, and tradition to support "personal gaming" because adults have a right to choose. Hey, Dennis: How about the right of adults to choose to have an abortion? Or commit adultery? Or listen to rap music? Or visit a prostitute? Or smoke pot?

"Gambling has become accepted as part of America's mainstream culture, alongside leisure activities such as attending movies, athletic events, and the theater." So begins *Keeping It Fun: A Guide to Low-Risk Gambling,* a pamphlet produced by the American Gaming Association. "The vast majority of Americans who gamble do it recreationally without any adverse consequences. . . . Keep gambling what it should be—entertainment. Know how to set limits, and, most importantly, know when to stop." According to the American Gaming Association, no one should gamble alone, no one under age should gamble, and no one should gamble to compensate for feelings of depression or low self-esteem. It's good advice—in fact, it's the exact same advice I would give pot smokers, adulterers, and gluttons.

"**B**et with your head, not over it. 1-800-BETS-OFF."

That message was brought to me courtesy of a cash machine in Dubuque, Iowa. Gambling long ago left Las Vegas, and I figured it was about time I did, too. Las Vegas is an overwhelming place, and the longer you stay in the city the less it charms. Two days is the ideal length for a visit to Las Vegas, and I had been spending weeks at a time in the city. So I decided to leave Nevada and visit the first American city to welcome riverboat gambling. Only after making that decision did I learn that city was Dubuque.

Iowa and I have a rather unpleasant history. During the 2000 presidential primaries, I went undercover as a volunteer for Gary Bauer's campaign while I had the flu (where I may or may not have licked Bauer's doorknobs, staplers, and officer supplies in an attempt to give him the flu), but more problematically, I may or may not have broken the law when I participated in Iowa's presidential caucuses. People don't actually vote in Iowa's caucuses, they "express a preference" in an informal balloting. When I found out that you didn't need a state ID or proof of residency to "express a preference" in Iowa's caucuses, I thought that was pretty fucked up. What was to stop out-of-state campaign staffers and activists who flood the state during the caucuses from showing up at caucus sites and expressing their preferences? A wealthy candidate like, say, Steve Forbes could flood caucus sites with paid supporters. (Forbes, in fact, placed a rather mysterious second in the 2000 Iowa caucuses.)

I pointed all of this out in my story, imagining myself to be something like a reporter who goes downtown, buys drugs, and then writes about how easy it is to buy drugs downtown. No one arrests those reporters, do they? There was much yowling from conservatives about the doorknob licking, and the Drudge Report, the *New York Post,* and *Free Republic* came after me in a big way. A few weeks after the piece appeared on Salon.com, I was charged with felony vote fraud, and Iowa tried to put me away for six years. I signed a confidentiality agreement with the state of Iowa and Gary Bauer that prevents me from commenting any further. But please see these footnotes, which will hopefully explain everything on my behalf.[1,2]

The particular ATM with the antigambling message sat in the lobby of a three-story brick building that housed a restaurant, buffet, and the Iowa Welcome Center. The building also served as the entrance to the *Diamond Jo,* a riverboat casino moored in the muddy stretch of the Mississippi River that flows past Dubuque, Iowa. There was also a small rack on top of the ATM filled with information about gambling addiction. It was kind of like going to a crack house and finding a picture of Nancy Reagan and her JUST SAY NO slogan hanging on the door.

---

1. Dan's lawyer, Mark Weinhardt, has these comments: In January 2000, Dan came to Des Moines to write a piece for the Internet magazine Salon.com regarding Iowa's "first in the nation" presidential caucuses. Searching for an angle from which to write about one of the far-right Republican candidates, Dan decided to go undercover. He became a volunteer in the presidential campaign of former Reagan domestic policy advisor and rabid gay-basher Gary Bauer.

Dan wrote about his few days with the Bauer campaign, which he actually found disturbingly pleasant. He also wrote about his being deathly ill with the flu while at Bauer headquarters. Then the flu and politics in his article merged. Incensed over Bauer's intolerance of people like, well, Dan, he wrote that he decided to try to get candidate Bauer sick with his flu. This would sap the Bauer campaign of momentum, literally and figuratively, before the critical New Hampshire primary, next on the agenda. Dan wrote that he prowled through an empty Bauer headquarters one day licking doorknobs, staplers, and other objects, hoping to transmit the flu to the candidate.

Dan's aside about political biological warfare was not exactly the centerpiece of his article, but it became the centerpiece of the reaction. Conservatives in Iowa, and even some moderates were outraged, and they said so in the local media. In fact, Dan didn't lick, cough, or sneeze on anything. It was a joke. (No one in the Bauer camp claimed to have gotten sick.) In true gonzo journalistic fashion, Dan bent the truth a little bit to make a point about his outrage. But no one in Iowa was getting the joke.

This little tempest in the media teapot would have been forgotten in days, but, almost as an afterthought, Dan wrote in his article about attending the actual Republican caucus for the precinct in Des Moines that included his hotel. It's hard to go to a caucus in Iowa without finding

Dubuque had the first riverboat casino in the United States, but the *Dubuque Diamond Jo Casino*—this particular boat—was actually the second riverboat casino moored at Dubuque. The first, "the majestic Casino Belle," according to Dubuque's daily paper, the *Telegraph Herald,* was replaced by the "spartan Diamond Jo," after the owners of the *Casino Belle* moved their boat to Alabama. I didn't find that out until after my first visit to the *Diamond Jo,* but even so, I knew something wasn't right about the *Diamond Jo* the first time I laid eyes on it. The three-story brick building that serves as the casino's entrance literally towers over the *Diamond Jo.* The scale is all wrong. Sitting next to the building built to complement the larger and more "majestic" *Casino Belle,* the *Diamond Jo* looks like a Honda Civic parked in front of Tony Soprano's four-car garage.

Staying in downtown Dubuque can be a very lonely experience. The streets were empty, and the downtown retail core felt abandoned. When I checked into the Dubuque's "historic" Julien Inn in late October 2001, I was the only person in the lobby besides the clerk. Once a fine, old Victorian hotel, the Julien had been remod-

---

some national media ogling the event, but Dan took journalism a step further. When he got to the front desk of the caucus and was offered a voter registration form, he filled it out, putting down as his address the hotel where he was staying. When it was time for the nonbinding straw poll for presidential candidates, which fascinates the media, Dan grabbed one of the little squares of paper passed out in the meeting room, checked the name of a Republican candidate, and handed it in.

Though a number of people were upset by Dan's phony claim of "doorknob licking," there was no credible theory in the criminal law under which he could be prosecuted for making such claims. Sometimes, however, someone will commit an act that arouses public indignation, and then he will just happen to be prosecuted for something else, much more mundane, at about the same time. That happened to Dan.

The following April the Polk County Attorney's Office filed two criminal charges against Dan. One of them, a misdemeanor, charged him with voting in a "primary election" when he was not qualified to do so. The other charge alleged that he falsely claimed that he was a resident of Iowa on the voter registration form, a class D felony with a maximum five-year-sentence.

There was no real dispute about the facts of what Dan did at the caucus. The battleground instead was the legal meaning of what he did. The vote fraud statutes under which Dan was charged are incredibly ambiguous. No one could remember the last time anyone had been prosecuted under those statutes. With no reported cases to guide the court, the lawyers on both sides would be making scads of "How many angels can dance on the head of a pin?" legal arguments about what is meant by words like *vote, resident,* and *primary election.*

eled in 1965 to look like the lair of some minor-league villain, the kind of evil subgenius Sean Connery disposed of in the first reel, and it doesn't seem to attract many paying guests these days. In fact, the clerk seemed genuinely startled when I walked in and asked for a room. She quickly transitioned to vaguely suspicious when I made it clear that I was serious, and after I asked for one of the hotel's one-bedroom apartments (a steal at $225 a week), she idled on hostile for the rest of our time together. I rode the elevator up to my room on the eighth floor of the hotel all by myself; I ate dinner in the hotel's German-themed restaurant, the Alte Glocke, all by myself; I had a beer in the hotel's deserted bar all by myself. The only time I saw anyone else on the eighth floor was when an older man in a motorized wheelchair left his room for his weekly trip to the nearby pharmacy that stocked a small selection of groceries.

"Dubuque was founded in 1788 by French-Canadian fur trader Julien Dubuque," reads the historic marker in front of Dubuque's red-and-white county courthouse, an impressive wedding cake of

---

For months the prosecutor insisted that the only alternative to a trial was if Dan pleaded guilty to the felony. That was anathema to us, not only because we didn't think Dan committed the felony, but because the consequences of a felony conviction can be severe. So we appeared inexorably headed for a public spectacle of legal quibbling, probably on Court TV. Then in the fall, for reasons I have never figured out, the State's position softened. The State ultimately agreed to resolve the case for a guilty plea to a misdemeanor, a little bit of community service performed in Dan's hometown, and a $750 fine.

Neither Dan nor I were crazy about pleading guilty to anything, but it would end the whole thing. Dan pled guilty without a single media person noticing, finally resolving his case on November 7, 2000. Election Day.

2. Randy Cohen writes the weekly column "The Ethicist" for *The New York Times Magazine:* During the 2000 presidential campaign, Dan Savage did his darnedest to give Gary Bauer the flu; I don't think this is so terrible. (Full disclosure: I may be influenced by the piece Mr. Savage contributed to my own book, and by my admiration for his column, but I've never even met the guy, and so I feel it's not out of line to offer a defense of his tactics.)

Were we perfect, we'd all make a real effort not to give colds to one another and would, for instance, don surgical masks at the first cough to keep our viruses to ourselves, like many people do in Japan and China but few of us do here in America. If we are not harried from cough-drop counter to Kleenex shelf for our heedlessness, why assail Dan Savage? Savage was striving to pass on only a minor malady. (And as an ethical matter, it is essential that he was absolutely certain that

a building constructed in 1891. "[Dubuque] joined with the Mesquake [sic] Indians to exploit the rich lead mines of the area. In 1833, [the area] was opened for American settlement, and the resulting lead rush created a boomtown." I know enough about American history to be deeply mistrustful of historic markers, especially ones in lily white parts of the country that speak of whites "joining with" local Indian tribes. While Julien Dubuque may have been a nice guy who was soliticious of the Mesquake Indians in the extreme, I didn't see any Indians during the weeks I spent in Dubuque. I did see a lot of white people, though, and no one seemed to know what had happened to the Mesquakes. And who the hell ever heard of a lead rush?

Like many of the dying river cities along the Mississippi, Dubuque's civic boosters hope to lure visitors to the city with its many fine examples of Victorian architecture. ("Dubuque: Masterpiece on the Mississippi," is the city's official tourist slogan.) But an earlier generation of Dubuque's civic boosters went on an urban renewal binge in the late 1950s and 1960s, tearing down everything in sight—including block after block of Victorian buildings in downtown Dubuque. Nothing much besides parking lots was ever

---

it was a minor malady and not a more serious illness.) He had the flu, not malaria. Had he been an *Anopheles* mosquito, I'd have urged him not to bite Gary Bauer on the behind. Had he been a plague-infested flea riding around on the back of a rat, I'd have persuaded him with what eloquence I could muster (using single syllable words that his flea-brain could comprehend) not to nestle down in Gary Bauer's hair. But he was only a scribbler with a bad cold. True, his tactics did risk inflicting collateral damage on other doorknob or stapler users in Bauer's office. And his is not a form of political protest I'd want to encourage, but the thrashing he came in for seemed out of proportion to any harm he did or could have done.

The spectacle of someone licking not only a doorknob but an alarming array of office supplies is disgusting. However, I don't defend it as an aesthetic act but as a political one. Savage practiced—invented—bio-satire. His was the outrage of someone personally affronted by the hate speech of a political extremist, and he found a fitting—and in my view, very funny—way to express his indignation. It was as if Jonathan Swift hadn't merely written about eating the babies of the poor, but actually sprinkled one infant with salt—unattractive, perhaps, but hardly fatal.

What if everyone did it? Unfortunate, but unlikely. A better way to apply the test of the categorical imperative would be to ask, What if during every presidential campaign one irate journalist tried to give one fringe candidate a bad cold? The Republic might tremble (vomit, grow feverish and exhausted, and take to its bed), but if it rests and drinks plenty of fluids, it will endure.

built to replace these buildings lost to "urban renewal." In the right light, Dubuque looks like a tintype of a smiling Victorian woman who had half her teeth knocked out. Worse yet for Dubuque, other nearby cities didn't tear down any of their older buildings in the 1950s, leaving them with more charming—and hence more touristed—Victorian city centers. Even today Dubuque's architectural heritage can't seem to catch a break: a row of Victorian buildings in the downtown area was evacuated during my stay in Dubuque when a parking lot being constructed directly behind the buildings destabilized their foundations. The buildings will probably have to be torn down. Adding insult to injury, downtown Dubuque needs another parking lot like Jerry Falwell needs another chin.

There was another reason I decided to leave Las Vegas and head to Dubuque: I wanted to feel like a whale. In gamble-speak, a high-roller is someone willing to lose a hundred thousand dollars on a trip to Vegas; a whale is someone willing to lose up to a million dollars or more. The average bet for a whale is ten thousand; 70 percent of whales are Asian men. At the Bellagio in Las Vegas, the maximum bet is a closely guarded secret, falling somewhere between twenty and forty thousand dollars. Maximum bets can be higher in the exclusive and intimate gaming rooms Las Vegas casinos have been building to attract "superwhales" like *Hustler* magazine publisher Larry Flynt, who is famous for betting ten, twenty, or thirty thousand dollars on a single hand. I'd never made more than a five-dollar bet in Las Vegas—not only wasn't I a whale in Vegas, I wasn't even a sea monkey. I probably wasn't plankton.

I could be a whale in Iowa, though. The state legalized gambling on riverboat casinos in 1989, and at that time the maximum bet in Iowa was five dollars; the most money any one gambler was allowed to lose in a twenty-four-hour period was two hundred dollars. I remembered reading about Iowa's prim betting and loss limits at the time the riverboat casino opened in Dubuque. The same lawmakers in Iowa who wanted to haul in the tourists and create new tax revenues and hundreds of jobs didn't want to be accused of exploiting problem gamblers—or creating them.

So that was the plan: Fly to Iowa, bet five bucks, and, hey, look at me! I'm uh . . . Christ, I'm Larry Flynt. Blech.

The *Diamond Jo* was small, and compared with the casinos I'd been to in Las Vegas (my only reference point), it was spartan—but, hey, compared to some of the newer casinos in Las Vegas, Vatican City is pretty spartan. And unlike the casinos in Las Vegas, the *Diamond Jo* was kind of cozy and intimate, something like what I'd imagined the private rooms for whales in Las Vegas to be. Unfortunately, the *Diamond Jo* was doing well enough to commission and produce its own jingle, which it plays over and over and over again, for hours on end, all day and all night: "The *Diamond Jo Casino*! Where the river runs wild! The *Diamond Jo Casino*! Where the cards run wild! The *Diamond Jo Casino*! Where the river runs wild!"

After getting my bearings, I sat down at an empty blackjack table. The dealer—a middle-aged man with a hangdog face and the skin of a lifelong smoker—seemed friendly and approachable, unlike some of the other dealers, who looked miserable. (Or were they just wearing their poker faces? Or perhaps that jingle was getting on their nerves?) Most important to me, there was no one at his table. Part of what makes card games so intimidating for the inexperienced gambler is the fear of making a fool of yourself in front of card players who know what they're doing. I was happy to be alone at his table—not that I was winning. I wasn't; I was losing, but I was losing in peace and quiet. I was losing five dollars at a time, one little red chip per hand, but that wasn't the maximum bet anymore. The sign on the table said, MINIMUM BET: $5/MAXIMUM BET $500. Five hundred dollars! My dreams of being a whale in Iowa were dashed.

Curious about what had happened to the five-dollar minimum bet, I contacted the business reporter of Dubuque's daily newspaper, the *Telegraph Herald*.

"This is a state and a community that has overwhelmingly supported gaming," said Matt Kittle, who covers the casinos for his paper. "Every eight years the voters in any county with gambling get to vote on whether or not gambling will continue to be allowed in their county. The last time we voted, about 70 percent of the voters were in favor of gambling continuing."

Gambling came to Iowa in 1984, when the state legalized "paramutual" gambling, that is, betting on dog and horse races. Any company that wanted to open a dog track would have to win a referendum in the county it wanted to build in. A referendum was quickly organized in Dubuque County, it passed, and the state's first dog track—The Dubuque Greyhound Park—opened in 1985. "You have to bear in mind that, while this is a conservative town, it's also overwhelmingly Catholic. Bingo primed the pump in Dubuque." (Eighty percent of Catholics gamble compared with 43 percent of Baptists.)

But a state allowing just a little bit of gambling is like a woman claiming she's just a little bit pregnant—it's a pretense that's difficult to keep up. So with dog tracks up and running, the Iowa state legislature soon passed a similar riverboat casino bill, and Iowa is now home to three dog tracks and ten riverboat casinos.

"Some of our 'riverboats' aren't even *in* rivers," said Kittle. "They're floating in ponds that were dug just for the casinos. It complies with the letter of the law, but the *Lakeside Casino Resort* in Osceola isn't near a river. It's a boat in a moat."

Kittle is sometimes surprised by just how thoroughly gambling has been woven into the fabric of corn-growin', pig-farmin', God-fearin' Iowa.

"First we had betting on dog races on dry land," said Kittle. "Then we had dog races on dry land, with slots, craps, and black-jack on boats so long as they were in the middle of the river." Iowa's riverboats were packed with tourists—busloads would come in every day from surrounding states. Then the state of Illinois introduced riverboat casinos on its side of the Mississippi, and other states legalized casino gambling, and Native American tribes opened their own casinos. Other states didn't require gamblers to float around the Mississippi while they gambled, and there were no limits on bets or losses. Pretty soon Iowa's boats were empty.

"Hearing the sounds of slot machines while you're stuck in the middle of the river is a circle in hell," said Kittle. "People would come to Iowa, lose their two hundred dollars in a half an hour, and they had nowhere to go and nothing to do for four more hours, while the boat cruised around. They had to sit there listening to the dings and chirps of the slot machines for hours and hours. It was a nightmare.

"So the state legislature passed a law doing away with the five-dollar maximum bet and the two-hundred-dollar loss limit, and changed the law so that the boats only had to 'cruise' one hundred days a year," said Kittle, "and our boats filled back up. Now we've got slots at the dog tracks and boats that are more or less permanently moored to their docks." And the law that requires riverboats to "cruise" the Mississippi at least one hundred times a year? The *Diamond Jo* meets this requirement by cruising on weekdays only during the summer between the hours of 5 and 7 A.M. The boat is usually empty when it goes out.

"Now Illinois is debating whether or not to allow video gambling in bars," said Kittle. "If they do that, we'll probably have to do that, too, to stay 'competitive,' just like we had to do away with the five-dollar maximum bet and the two-hundred-dollar daily loss limit."

You can't be a little bit pregnant.

"No, you can't." Kittle nodded. "You would think farm people would've known that all along."

Blackjack for beginners: You place a chip on the small circle on the felt in front of you. The dealer deals one card faceup to everyone at the table and then gives himself a card facedown. Then he deals a second card faceup to everyone at the table, before giving himself one card faceup. If the dealer has an ace up, he checks to see if he has blackjack; if he does, he wins. If he doesn't, the players can ask for more cards, to get as close as they can to twenty-one. Hopefully you won't take too many cards and bust your hand. When all the players have either busted or decided to hold, the dealer turns over his facedown card. The dealer draws more cards until he has seventeen or higher, and then he holds. If your hand is better than the dealer's hand—closer to twenty-one without going over—you win. If you bet five dollars, you win five dollars. If you bet five hundred dollars, you win five hundred dollars. If the dealer's hand is better than your hand, you lose five dollars. Or five hundred dollars.

A few hands after I sat down, another man joined me at the table. I didn't think my inexperience was obvious—it was blackjack, so all you have to do is count to twenty-one; how hard is that?—the experienced gambler could tell I was a novice and started offering me pointers. As it turned out, counting to twenty-one is a lot harder than it looks—the experienced gambler, who bore a passing resemblance to the actor Christopher Walken, was playing twenty-five-dollar chips. He walked me through different bets—double down, splitting my hand, playing two hands at once—while the dealer looked on, turning over cards and taking my chips from me one at a time.

"Blackjack is easy," the experienced gambler said, lighting a cigarette. "Gambling is easy—if you take the time to learn to play the game. And if you do that, son, you'll make money. But the only way to make *real* money is to do something stupid every once in a while."

The dealer didn't try to stop the experienced gambler from coaching me. He just kept on turning over cards, a little service-industry smile on his face.

"It's stupid time," the experienced gambler said.

The dealer caught my eye. I couldn't read his expression; his face was a blank.

The experienced gambler started making hundred-dollar bets—

hundred-dollar bets!—one right after another. He wasn't on a winning streak, though, and his stack of chips quickly disappeared. After about two dozen hands, the experienced gambler lost his last hundred-dollar chip.

"Well, that's it for me," the experienced gambler said. He got up, wished me better luck than he'd been having, and left for the craps tables.

The dealer looked down at me and held his palms out, asking me with a gesture if I was in or out. I moved a five-dollar chip out onto the green felt.

"Don't listen to him," the dealer said softly, leaning towards me. "Gambling isn't easy. If it was easy, they would call it *winning.*"

He turned over a few more cards and took my last chip from me.

"And just between you and me, stupid is just stupid."

For three nights in a row, I had returned to the *Diamond Jo,* sat at the same dealer's table, and lost seventy dollars. I always arrived intending to gamble larger sums of money, but I couldn't bring myself to put more than one five-dollar chip on the table at a time. I wasn't a whale in Dubuque—just an inept five-dollar-a-hand blackjack player. The dealer was always there, and he smiled when he saw me coming. He smiled exactly like the craps dealer in Las Vegas, like a cop. The fourth night I went to the *Diamond Jo,* the dealer didn't smile—he gave me a look. He even lifted his eyebrows.

"Welcome back," he said, gesturing to an empty chair. "Still haven't learned your lesson?"

He began taking my seventy dollars from me, as was our custom. I looked up at him, and he smiled—a real smile, the corners of his eyes crinkling up, his eyebrows rising on his forehead. He shook his head and asked me why I was doing this to myself.

"I've come to Dubuque to learn to play blackjack," I said. "How do you think I'm doing?"

"As far as the casino is concerned, you're doing beautifully."

I asked him if the experienced gambler, the man I played with the night before, came around often. I needed some more lessons.

"First of all, that 'experienced gambler' sat right next to you and lost a couple of grand in twenty minutes," said the dealer. "So I wouldn't recommend you model your game off of his. And all he taught you was how to place different kinds of bets. Which, if you don't know what you're doing with the cards, is as good as teaching how to lose money more quickly. He didn't do you any favors."

"But how complicated is blackjack, anyway?" I asked. "You give me two cards and I ask for more until I get close to twenty-one. That's pretty simple."

"You can play a simple game if you want to give the casino all your money," the dealer said. "But if you ever want to leave this boat with money in your pocket, you're going to have to learn how to play a more complicated game."

The dealer owned a used bookstore in downtown Dubuque, and he suggested I drop in sometime. He didn't think it would be right for him to give me advice, but he would happily sell me one of the paperbacks on gambling strategy that he had in stock.

I handed him my last five-dollar chip and said I'd see him in the morning.

Catherine's Used Books is one of the few nonpawn, nontavern, nonbarber retail operations in downtown Dubuque. A clean, white storefront with shelves that go up to the ceiling, Catherine's Used Books had, "Over 80,000 used books in stock—come in and count them!" and had that wonderful paper-ink-rot-dust smell that only a room packed with used paperbacks ever does. In addition to used books, the dealer who urged me to learn something about blackjack before running through my money at his table—his name was Bob—also sold Native American prints, dream catchers, and knickknacks in his shop. He opened the store a few years ago with his wife, herself a retired card dealer. His daughter, a dealer, also lives in an apartment above the store.

The store was empty when I dropped in to pick up a book on casino gambling. Bob was in the back shelving, heard the bell, and came to the front of the shop. He laughed when he saw me.

"So you've come for the book, eh?" he asked. "You might have saved yourself some money if you'd come for the book as soon as you got to town."

Then Bob asks me what I'm doing in Dubuque. I tell him the truth. I'm here to write about gambling. And sin. Bob stiffens and folds his arms across his chest.

"Don't write the same stuff that everybody writes," he said. "Don't you go on and on about, 'Oh, it's so awful, all these people losing their farms, their houses, all these people getting addicted.' "

But surely some gamblers lose their houses and farms and get addicted?

"Sure. I've seen it happen. But people who don't go to casinos lose their farms, too. It happens all the time. There are farmers who drink themselves bankrupt, too, but you don't hear a lot of calls for making alcohol illegal again."

He had a point—even if he was wasting it on me. I wasn't in Iowa to write about how awful gambling is or to call for its prohibition. Quite the contrary. I was here to celebrate the sin a bit, and to get to the bottom of gambling—what's the attraction? What's the appeal? Since the odds always favor the house, why bother? What brings people back—time and again—especially as their loses mount?

"Good jobs, jobs that pay good money."

Bob was still talking me into casinos. He set a stool down in front of the cash register and gestured for me to sit. Then he sat at a chair behind his register, leaned back, and continued.

"No one ever writes about that—the good jobs," said Bob. "The casino was the best thing that ever happened to me. I went from ten-dollar-an-hour district manager for a retail company to fifteen dollars an hour with the tips as a card dealer. Dealers in Chicago make more than that. Some make a lot more. You can have a life on a dealer's income."

But surely there were other good jobs in Dubuque before the casinos came to town?

"The only two good jobs in town were at the John Deere plant and the meatpacking company," said Bob. "John Deere hasn't hired anyone in twenty years, and the meatpacking company went out of business two years ago. Some people say it's not dignified work, that Iowans who used to make a living building things or farming have been 'reduced' to dealing cards. That's a city person's perspective. It's *hard* to make a living farming. And dealing is all that helps some people hold on to their farms."

But surely some people don't like dealing?

"They don't last, the ones who don't like it. They don't last! And what they don't understand is that they've got the best job in the world. *You get paid to play cards!* You're not working in a factory floor; you're not gutting pigs. You're out there on the floor, interacting with people, playing a *game*. And all people gamble—all human cultures have their gambling games. You want to talk about a sin? Talk about the lottery. Do you know what your odds are when it comes to a state lottery? Three hundred million to one. A casino owner would go to jail for offering odds like that. And the commercials on TV for the lottery make it look like it's only a matter of time before you win the lottery, if you just keep playing. That's a sin."

Bob and I are getting on like a house on fire—until I ask him to give me some pointers on improving my game.

"Oh, no, no, no." Bob shook his hands and held them out in front of himself, the way dealers do at the end of a session, to show that they have nothing in them. "No can do, no way, no how. I'd lose my job in a flash. Like that—" He snapped his fingers. "If the casino managers found out I was coaching gamblers in my free time, I'd be out a good-paying job. I'll sell you a book, that I can do. They sell that book in the gift shop at the *Diamond Jo,* so they can't be mad at me for selling you a used copy here. But I can't coach you, sorry."

Bob was nice guy, a wonderful guy, and I didn't want to get him in trouble with his boss. So I thanked him for the book and stepped out onto the street.

"You know what?" Bob called to me, leaning out of the door to the store. "The establishments around here are full of dealers. Dealers, retired dealers, fired dealers. That's just a fact I'm telling you."

"Man goes into a casino, loses four thousand dollars playing blackjack. Walks over to a slot machine, puts a dollar in, wins four thousand dollars. Is he even?"

Yes.

"No!" The old dealer slapped his hand down on the bar for emphasis. "Casinos have to report the names of people who win more than a certain amount. So that guy is going to get a note from the IRS telling him he owes them almost half of that money. So he's still two thousand dollars in the hole!"

Three old-time dealers—one hired, one fired, one retired—were trying to teach me a few things. I was sitting at a long, nicotine-stained bar, drinking Hamm's and talking cards while a sports show blared from one television and Fox News blared from the other. When I first walked in, I felt slightly suspect. It was a bright sunny day in late fall, but it was pitch-black inside the bar, and it took a few moments for my eyes to adjust. There were only two other men in the bar besides the bartender, and they were sitting together at one end. The rest of the bar was deserted. I sat on a stool at the other end of the bar, and the bartender ignored me for a few minutes, as if he hoped I might go away. When he finally walked over, he asked if he could help me—not if I wanted a beer, but if he could help me, as if I were lost and needed directions out of his bar. I asked for a beer, which I sipped at after the bartender returned to his other two customers.

Ten minutes later, the bartender looked over at me, and I raised my eyebrows, the international sign for "I need something." He acknowledged my raised eyebrows with a quick nod and then turned back to his other customers. I was confused. Was he ignoring me? Would he be right over? What should my next move be? When the bartender looked over at me again, I raised my eyebrows again. "I need something," my eyebrows said. The bartender sighed, told his other customers he'd be right back, and then walked over to my end of the bar.

"Something you need?" he said.

I asked him if he knew any card dealers who might be interested in giving a novice blackjack player a few pointers. He stared at me for a long, long time.

"Anyone want to teach this guy blackjack?" the bartender announced to the men at the other end of the bar. Two minutes later, the two other men in the bar—both dealers, as it turned out—were sitting beside me. The bartender stood and listened to our conversation, leaning against the back bar, his arms folded across his chest, one foot up on the beer cooler under the bar.

I had been playing blackjack at the *Diamond Jo* every night for almost a week, I explained, and I'd lost all my money every night for a week. I came to town to learn to play blackjack, and I had only two nights left, and I wasn't getting any better. I had to be doing something wrong, but I didn't know exactly what.

"The first mistake is showing up," said the bartender. "If you want to keep your money, don't show up."

"What are you doing?" asked the older of the two old dealers, fingering a cigarette. "What's your strategy?"

"You try to get to twenty-one, right? Isn't that everyone's strategy?" I said.

The two old dealers laughed; the bartender smirked.

"Blackjack is about busting the dealer," said the older of the two dealers, a man who looked like he could be Wallace Shawn's great-grandfather. He had the unmistakable pallor of the lifelong smoker: gray skin, deep lines on his face, yellow eyes. He didn't seem sickly; indeed, he was the very picture of health—relatively speaking, of course, and I only ever saw him in a dimly lighted bar. I felt like I

was in the presence of the proverbial old smoker, the lifelong nicotine addict constantly invoked by young smokers who refuse to
quit. ("I know a guy who's ninety-two years old, and has been
smoking two packs a day for seventy years, and he's never been
sick a day in his life!")

"If you're thinking about getting yourself to twenty-one," the
old smoker said, "you're playing your own hand, and you're not
going to get anywhere playing your own hand."

Whose hand am I supposed to play?

"The dealer's hand," the old smoker said.

"Always assume that the dealer has a ten in the hole," he said.
"His down card, it's a ten card, tell yourself that, it's always a ten
card. Now the dealer has to hit until he has seventeen or better, but
he has to hold as soon as he gets to seventeen—always remember
that. If he has a seven, eight, nine, or ten up, then you assume he's
got seventeen, eighteen, nineteen, or twenty. If the dealer has sixteen, seventeen, eighteen, nineteen, or twenty and you have between twelve and sixteen, you take a card. Always hit.

"But if the dealer has a two, three, four, five, or six card up, assume he's got a ten down and don't take a card. What you want is
the dealer to go bust instead. If he's got sixteen, he has to hit until
he gets to seventeen. So he'll bust most likely. If you're at thirteen,
and he's got fifteen or sixteen, just stay put. Let him take the card."

This was news to me. I didn't know you could hold at thirteen
when the dealer had fourteen, fifteen, or sixteen, and not automatically lose. I didn't know the dealer had to keep drawing if his hand
was below seventeen but higher than your hand.

"But what if the dealer's down card isn't a ten?" I asked. "What
if you held at twelve and the dealer has a five card down and a five
card up and then he draws, say, an ace?"

"It's the luck of the draw. This is strategy, just strategy. Remember, it's called gambling, son, and—"

"And not winning," I said.

"Right. Not winning."

The other dealer spoke, and I was startled by his voice. Also a smoker, this dealer didn't have as much luck as the old smoker. He appeared to be only about fifty, but his voice box had been removed, and he spoke with the help of a small, handheld amplifier that he held up to his throat. Cancer forced him to retire from dealing. He lived on disability and Social Security payments, but he was dressed like he had someplace to go. The old smoker, who was still dealing, was wearing a sweatshirt; the retired dealer was in a business suit.

"Be consistent," he said. "Play consistently, decide what your strategy is, and stick to it. People get sixteen and don't hit, and the dealer wins the hand, the next time they get sixteen, they think, 'I didn't hit the last time I had sixteen, and the dealer won. So I'll take a card this time.' And the dealer wins that hand, too. Now if you'd been playing consistently—always sticking on sixteen, or always staying on sixteen—you would've broken even on those two hands. But if you're always changing the way you play, if you're always playing the last hand you lost, you're going to lose and lose."

Anything else I need to know?

The bartender took his foot off the beer cooler and leaned on the bar.

"Okay, eighteen-point-six is the average winning hand," he said. "If you've got sixteen, on average, you're going to lose. And one third of the cards in the deck are ones, twos, threes, fours, and fives. That means, with sixteen, taking a hit gives you a thirty-three percent chance of getting a hand that's close to eighteen-point-six or better. That's a good chance. If you've got nineteen, don't take a hit—ever. Even if the dealer has a ten card up. Statistically speaking, nineteen is a winning hand."

The bartender had been a dealer once, and the other men deferred to him, even though he was at least twenty years younger. It was something of an honor to get pointers from the bartender, apparently, as the old smoker pointed at my notebook and made a little scribbling motion with his cigarette, letting me know that I needed to get this down. The bartender was once a dealer and a gambler; he would work an eight-hour shift in a riverboat casino in Davenport, Iowa, and then cross the Mississippi River to the Illinois side and play for twelve hours. He made piles of money, lost piles of money, and wound up getting fired when his gambling problem spun out of control. He made up his mind to stop gambling one day, got in his car, and drove to Dubuque where his uncle owned a bar. The bartender works days and does inventory, his uncle works nights. In a few years, the old smoker told me, the bartender's uncle is going to give him the bar.

"You need a strategy for your money as much as you need one for the game," the bartender said. "More. A lot of people come in, and they've thought about their strategy for the game, but not for their money. And the money is what you're there for, right? So think about the money. Say you put a five-dollar chip on the table. You win that hand. Now you've got ten dollars on the table, two five-dollar chips. Leave the ten on the table. You win another hand. Now you've got twenty dollars, four chips. Take five dollars off the table, and leave the fifteen dollars. How much have you got invested in that fifteen dollar bet? Nothing. Now you're playing with the casino's money. If you win another hand, you'll have thirty dollars, six chips. Leave twenty dollars on the table, take the rest, and you've got fifteen dollars in your hand. You've made ten dollars. You've tripled your money. You're not risking anything on the next hand. You're playing the casino's money. Even if you lose the next hand, you didn't lose twenty dollars, you made ten dollars. And then start over again, with a new five-dollar bet—and you're still playing with the casino's money."

"That's right," said the man with the voice synthesizer, "take risks with the casino's money."

So you can do something stupid, so long as it's the casino's money.

"Yeah, you can do something stupid," said the ancient smoker. "But when you're playing your own money, you want to be smart, you want to be conservative."

"But what you've got to remember is this," said the bartender. "If the cards aren't falling your way, the best strategy is to get up and go. If they're not falling your way, tip the dealer and get the hell out of the casino."

"This is the hard part," said the old smoker.

"You'll see a guy go in, and pretty soon he's down a hundred," the bartender continued. "So he says, 'I'll just keep gambling until I'm even.' The casino loves it when people think that way. So he gambles and gambles, and keeps losing, and pretty soon he's down fifteen hundred dollars. To make back a hundred bucks, he lost fifteen hundred dollars. That's not smart. If the cards aren't coming, leave. Come back another night. It cost me one career and two marriages to learn that little lesson."

The bartender wasn't the only one who developed a problem with gambling after Iowa legalized riverboat casinos. Between 1989 and 1995, "problem gambling increased in Iowa from 1.7 percent of the population to 5.4 percent," according to the Iowa Department of Human Services.

"Gambling is all about greed," said the bartender. "Everyone wants something for nothing. And some people are foolish enough to think they can actually get something for nothing."

I might have deferred to the bartender's experience and insight, I suppose, and taken his word for why people gamble; they're greedy, so they gamble. But I couldn't understand why someone who was greedy would do something so foolish as to gamble. The house always wins, the gamblers always lose, and that's why casinos are a business and not a charity. If someone loves money, why would he take the almost certain risk of losing it by playing slots or craps or blackjack?

"People aren't that smart," said the old smoker.

"People don't think that far ahead," said the man with the voice synthesizer.

"No," said the bartender, "that's not it at all. People who gamble think they're special. They think Jesus or fate or luck or the odds or some supernatural something or other is going to smile on them and frown on the poor bastards sitting on either side of them. To be a gambler, you have to be greedy—"

"But not all greedy people are gamblers," I said.

"Are you going to let me finish?" the bartender asked.

I nodded. The bartender paused, and he looked at me for a long time. I covered my mouth with my left hand.

"People gamble because they're greedy, first and foremost, but not all greedy people are gamblers. You're right. But all gamblers are greedy people who think they're special. They're full of themselves. Winning or losing, gamblers are deluded."

"That's right, he's right," said the old smoker, laughing. "When you're winning, you're special. Luck is smiling on you. And when you're losing, luck is picking on you, singling you out." He slapped the bar. "Win or lose, you're still special!"

I was about to get a deck of cards I'd been carrying around in my pocket when the bartender pulled one from a drawer under the cash register. He tossed the deck onto the bar, and the retired dealer picked it up, pulled the rubber band off it, and started shuffling the cards. Above the back bar was a wire rack with clips that held twenty or thirty small bags of pretzels, and the bartender yanked down three bags, tore them open, and dumped them on the bar.

"On you," he said, indicating the pile of pretzels, which he divided into four smaller piles, one pile for the old smoker, one pile for the man with the voice synthesizer, one for me, and one for himself. Then we played blackjack, all cards faceup, and slowly but surely something miraculous happened. The pile of pretzels in front of me on the bar grew. I was winning. It wasn't money, but it was something.

I thanked the old dealers and the bartender, and offered to pay for their beers, which they refused to let me do. I settled up— $6.75 for four beers and three bags of pretzels—and walked out the door a little unsteady on my feet, thanks to the four beers I downed in the two hours I'd spent with my coaches. No one else came into the bar during my coaching session in deserted, downtown Dubuque. Later on, back at my hotel room, I realized that I hadn't introduced myself by name to my coaches, nor had I thought to ask their names.

"One more thing," said the old smoker when he was standing in the door of the bar, saying good-bye. "You know the only thing worse than losing big the first time you go into a casino?"

"No," I said. "What?"

"Winning big."

Later that night I headed to the *Diamond Jo,* after I slept off a rare midday hangover at the Julien Inn. I got three hundred dollars out of the cash machine, checked my coat, and found an empty table. It was my regular dealer's night off, so I got a fresh start with a brand-new dealer, a younger guy, a dealer who didn't look at me, didn't smile, and didn't think of me as a total, hopeless, helpless loser. I did my best to play basic strategy, I was conservative with my money and stupid with the casino's money. I double-downed, and I always held on sixteen, and I played the dealer's hand, always assuming the dealer's down card was a ten. When he had five up and I had twelve in my hand, I held, hoping he would bust trying to get to seventeen, which he often did. When he had ten up and I had fifteen in my hand, I took a card, hoping I would get closer to 18.6.

I doubled my money—I more than doubled my money.

Two hours after I walked into the *Diamond Jo,* a week after I got to Dubuque, years after my first trip to Las Vegas, for the first time in my life, I walked out of a casino with more money than I walked in with—a lot more money. I sat down with $300, and I got up with $710. At one point, I had to remind myself to stop gambling. One of the dealers in the bar had warned me about people who gamble, get up a few hundred dollars, and then figure they're either geniuses or that their luck can't change. They'll keep gambling, fall back down to the money they came with, and they'll feel like they're in the hole, when they're actually breaking even. So they'll keep on gambling, trying to get back up to where they were, to their new "break-even" point, and they'll wind up losing all they came in the door with.

"I see people who could get up with three months' worth of rent in their pocket," the dealer-turned-bartender warned me, "or a half a year's worth of car payments. They get greedy, and then they blow it. You should decide before you go into the casino at what point you're going to be satisfied with your winnings. If it's double your money, then make yourself get up and get out when you've doubled your money."

I could hear his voice in my head after I doubled my money, but I played a few more hands. I went up some more, but I knew I was pressing my luck, and I didn't want to get greedy. I gathered up my chips. The other players at the table—three men had joined me, since I was winning, and gamblers like to sit next to winners—couldn't believe I would just get up and leave in the middle of a winning streak. But I had more than doubled my money—I won more than enough money to pay my bill at the Julien—so I cashed out and left the casino.

I wanted to rush back to the bar and buy a round of Hamm's for my coaching staff, but it was almost midnight when I got out of the _Diamond Jo_. Walking across the parking lot and over the bridge that connects the casino to downtown Dubuque was difficult; I was paying attention, I was playing basic strategy, and I was winning— and it was difficult not to attribute my little winning streak to an innate, freshly tapped skill, a heretofore undiscovered knack for playing blackjack. After spending one afternoon being coached by three card dealers, I was suddenly a card shark, if not a whale. That couldn't just be luck, right? I mean, with the tools they gave me, I was able to build a small fortune, right? I did that—I won $410! Me! And if it was an innate skill, some sort of gift, that turned my $300 into $710, why shouldn't I keep playing? And winning?

Walking into the lobby of the Julien, I thought, Shit, they're just giving money away on that boat. Why shouldn't I go back and take some more from them?

When I walked into my room, I flopped down on the couch to watch Angie Harmon work over a girl gangbanger on *Law & Order,* fully intending to head back to the casino when the culprit was safely behind bars. By the time the show was over, though, my moment of hubris seemed to have passed. In the hour I had to calm down, I remembered what my coaching staff tried to impress on me: The cards were just falling my way; I wasn't skilled, just lucky; and getting up from the table when I was up by $410 was the smart thing to do. I was ahead.

The bartender, the world's oldest living smoker, and the man without a voice box were all in the tavern when I dropped by the next day. I had tipped the dealers last night at the *Diamond Jo,* so why shouldn't I tip the dealers who really made my last gambling experience so profitable? I almost typed *enjoyable,* but even when I was winning, gambling didn't strike me as much fun. It was stressful. Oh, sure, there was a moment of elation when you won a hand, but that moment was brief, and a second after it was over, it was time to make another bet, time to slide another chip out onto the green felt, and then you were back in Stressville. Would I get a good hand? Would I bust? What's the dealer really got? Winning was better than losing, of course, but the actual minute-to-minute experience of it wasn't that much different.

I said hello, sat down next to the dealers, and the bartender came over and set a Hamm's in front of me before he returned to his regular leaning spot, his butt on the back bar, and one foot on the cooler under the front bar. It was only my second visit to his bar, and I was already a regular; he didn't wait for me to order a beer (at 12:20 on a weekday afternoon), he just brought me what I had the last time I was in. I told my three-man coaching staff that I won, that it went well, that I took their advice and it paid off. They were delighted—not at my skill, but at their own. I tried to give them each fifty dollars, but all three refused to take my money.

"You won it," said the bartender, "it's your money."

"Wouldn't feel right," said the ancient smoker.

"Spend it on your girlfriend," said the man with the voice synthesizer.

I asked them if I could at least buy them a round of drinks. That was acceptable, and I picked up their tab—which gave me an idea. Later that night, on my way back to the *Diamond Jo*, I returned to the bar. The dealer-turned-bartender was off, but his uncle, the bar's owner, was in. I asked if his bar ran prepaid tabs. Indeed they did. I opened a two-hundred-dollar tab for the ancient smoker and the man with the voice synthesizer.

The last time I walked into the *Diamond Jo*, I was on a streak. I went in with a strategy—my winning strategy. I played the exact same game I played the night before, the night I more than doubled my money. Before I arrived at the *Diamond Jo*, I made myself promise to rise graciously from the table and exit the casino just as soon as I doubled my money—I wouldn't be taking the stupid risks I took the night before, when I kept on gambling after I doubled my money. I wasn't going to get greedy.

My last night in Dubuque was my last chance to be a whale. I wouldn't be able to bet the maximum—$500 per hand—but I decided to up the ante. I added a zero to the amount of money I was prepared to gamble. Instead of $300 and $5 bets, I gambled $3,000 and made $50 bets. I went to a bank that morning and cashed a money order for three thousand dollars, and I was given a short stack of hundred-dollar bills. I expected three thousand dollars to make an impressive roll, not realizing that three grand is only thirty hundred-dollar bills. It's thick, but it doesn't look like something a gangster carries around with him. Still I was nervous on the walk from the hotel to the casino, which was deserted as usual. In the week I spent in Dubuque, I was the only person I ever saw walk from downtown to the riverfront. Everyone else drove.

It was on the walk to the casino that I made a fatal blunder: I began spending the money in my head. If I played as well as I played the night before—and why wouldn't I?—I would leave the casino with about seven grand, four of it profit. The three grand I brought to gamble with would go back in the bank, of course, but I would return to the tavern and establish a thousand-dollar tab for my coaching staff before I left Dubuque. Every morning for breakfast, I went to a small café around the corner from my hotel, a place called Dottie's, and every day the same waitress took my order. If I won big, I would leave her a hundred-dollar tip. Shit, I'd give her a grand, too. The rest of my winnings, the other two grand, well, I would donate it to some charity or other, or to a group trying to legalize nonmedical marijuana. I would put my ill-gotten gains to good use, I swore, as I walked into the *Diamond Jo* and found an empty table. Two old men wouldn't have to worry about their bar tabs for a long, long time, and I would use the rest of the money to make the world I live in a slightly better place. I wasn't greedy; I was good.

Do I even need to mention that I walked out of the *Diamond Jo*—four hours later—without a cent in my pocket?

Leaving the *Diamond Jo* after losing three thousand dollars was one of the hardest things I've ever done. You would think a person who just lost three grand playing cards would be anxious to get the hell out of the casino. That wasn't the case. I had to force myself to keep walking—off the boat, past the cash machine, out the doors, over the bridge, up the street to the Julien Inn, across the deserted lobby, onto the elevator, down the hall, into my room, over to the couch. Every step was a battle. I didn't want to leave the casino: I wanted to run back to the ATM, withdraw another five or six hundred dollars, sit back down at a table, and try to win back all the money I'd lost. The urge was overwhelming—it was what the bartender at the tavern had warned me about. The cards weren't falling my way, and I didn't get up and go. I kept playing, and now that I was in the hole, all I wanted to do was go back to the casino and keep playing until I made it right, until I won the money back.

I couldn't quite understand how it had happened. What about all the good things I planned to do with my winnings? Didn't that count for anything? What about the tab I established for my coaches? Didn't that count? I played the exact same game, the same game I played the night before, when I turned $300 into $710. Playing that same game twenty-four hours later, I turned $3,000 into zero dollars. How was this possible? It wasn't as bad as my first attempts at blackjack, when I would sit down, lose fourteen straight hands, then get up and go. Shit, I was up much of the night. But the times I was up I wasn't up by much, and those times started coming further and further apart as the night wore on. In between the short times I was up, I fell into the hole, and as the night wore on, the holes kept getting deeper and deeper. I was up $200; then I was down $500. Then I was up $100; then I was down $1,000. Then I crawled back up to around $2,700; then I started falling, falling, falling. When I got down to $1,000, I thought maybe I should quit. Then the money was all gone.

I walked back over the bridge to downtown Dubuque. I had to force myself to keep walking, remembering not to turn around. Turning around and looking back at the *Diamond Jo* wouldn't turn me into a pillar of salt, like Lot's wife. It would, however, pull me back in. I knew that if I turned my head to look, my body would turn with it, and then my feet would carry me back to the casino. I felt as if I were turning inside out, like I was walking through thin sheets of acid, as if each step that took me closer to the empty Julien Inn peeled off a layer of my skin. My heart was pounding. I was raw and I felt exposed and violated and . . . and . . . completely . . . desperately . . . alive.

Back at the Julien Inn, skinned alive but safe in my room, I sat next to the window and looked at the *Diamond Jo*. Every once in a while, a car went over the bridge, carrying some other sucker down to the boat. I suddenly remembered that woman playing War in Las Vegas, the woman who burst into tears when she lost her last chip. She took a risk, she lost, she cried. She felt something specific and painful—and something personal, since it was her pain. She wasn't living vicariously through Nicole Brown-Simpson or Princess Di or New York City firefighters or an unhappy couple hashing things out on *Oprah* with Dr. Phil. Something happened to her. She had a sensation, something sharp and specific and personal. We live in a culture that celebrates and elevates the victim, so perhaps that woman secretly enjoyed her safe, packaged, consensual victimization at the hands of that casino. She sat in a plush room, on a padded chair, had a complimentary cocktail, and wagered her way to victimhood. And when it was all over, she got to have a good cry—for herself, not for Diana or Nicole or New York City.

I'd been victimized, too—by my own greed and my own inability to get up and leave the casino when it was clear the cards weren't falling my way. Three thousand dollars is a lot of money, but sitting in my room, the lights and TV off, looking out over the *Diamond Jo* and the Mississippi River, I had to admit that I didn't regret the gambling, even after losing so much money. The feelings I had walking back over that bridge the night I won $410 and the night I lost $3,000 were intense and, I had to admit, worth it.

We know the house always wins—the house even tells us so. Shit, the house rubs our noses in it. They give us free cocktails, as if to say, "We make so much money off you suckers that we can afford to give booze away." They build billion-dollar hotels and resorts and rent us rooms at less than it costs to have our room cleaned every day, as if to say, "We make so much money off you suckers that we can run the hotel part of this business at a total loss and still make millions." They fill their casinos with brass and glass and marble and gold and carpets and chandeliers, as if to say, "We make so much money off you suckers that we have to sit up nights thinking of new shit to blow it on." The casinos make money because once we're in Las Vegas or on the boat or at the Indian casino in the middle of nowhere, they know we're going to gamble, and when we gamble, we lose. We know we're going to lose, because they told us so, and yet we gamble anyway. So I don't think greed is the reason people gamble—greedy people own casinos; they don't visit them. People gamble because they want to feel what I felt the night I lost three grand, or that woman felt the night she busted playing War.

"Affluence brings with it boredom," according to Robert Bork, and I think on this one occasion he's right. "Of itself, it offers little but the ability to consume, and a life centered on consumption will appear, and be, devoid of meaning." When Robert Bork worries about bored, affluent Americans seeking out ever more degraded sensations, he's slamming the entertainment industry—gangsta rap, teen sex comedies, and TV sitcoms in which small, smart, fictional children disrespect their elders. But entertainment doesn't really provide us with true sensations, only vicarious ones. Films and television rub our noses in the exciting lives of people who almost never seem to be watching films or television. Americans sit in theaters or our living rooms and watch Brad Pitt or Julia Roberts or Denzel Washington take risks, live their lives on the edge, and court disaster. Movies and television feeds us an almost constant diet of cliffhangers, with protagonists making a half a dozen life-and-death choices in under two hours.

In real life, though, how often do we experience a cliffhanger? Our entertainment is aggressively overstimulating because our real lives are oppressively predictable. Bork's right, we're bored—even after September 11, we're bored. Compared to our entertainments and our collective, subconscious fantasies, our lives are too safe, and we're constantly working to make them safer and more boring and predictable. In film and television, however, in our collective fantasy lives, the world is a dangerous place filled with excitement and cliffhangers and life-and-death choices. We learn how to kiss watching movies, we learn how to lie, how to fight, we learn how to break up—all the things we used to learn by observing each other, we now learn by observing a few highly paid stars. We can't help but compare the lives we lead to the fictional lives we consume. We're encouraged to live vicariously through the impossibly exciting lives of fictional characters. In a hotel room recently, I was half-listening to the previews on the in-room movie channel while I sat in the tub; for a small fee, I could watch *Spy Game, Behind Enemy Lines,* and *Lord of the Rings* in the safety and comfort of my own room. Suddenly a smarmy voice-over started asking me questions: "So who do you want to be? A CIA operative? A downed fighter pilot? A sorcerer's apprentice? With On Command, you can be whoever you want, whenever you want. So who is it you want to be?" The exciting lives we're encouraged to fantasize about, the lives we dream about, the lives that are implanted in our subconscious by film and television, are enormously out of step with the lives we actually lead. The comparison between the lives we lead and the lives we watch can be pernicious and suffocating. There is very little suspense in real life, very little drama, risk, or danger.

Except in a casino.

Observing the action at one of the newer hotels on the Vegas strip one night, I was reminded of Mecca, Islam's holiest city. There is a mosque in Mecca built around a rock that Muslims believe the prophet Mohammed was standing atop before he ascended into heaven. That rock now sits in the middle of the mosque's enormous courtyard, and during the hajj, Muslims crowd into the mosque's courtyard, swirling around Mohammed's last known whereabouts, trying to get themselves a little closer to heaven. I thought to myself, Las Vegas is the American Mecca, a holy city, site of the American hajj, a place in the desert where we gather to worship our American God, money. Like the courtyard of that mosque in Mecca, Las Vegas's casinos swarm with people, circling the casino, but instead of circling the last known whereabouts of a long-gone prophet, we circle slot machines and card tables and craps games. It's all about money, I thought, greed, worshiping money.

I was wrong. It's not about money, it's about risk and danger and purchasing a little of the action we see on the screen. In a casino, you can sit down at a table with a drink in your hand and treat yourself to a night filled with cliffhangers. You're taking risks, and the bigger your bets, the more you have at stake, the closer you get to feeling like you're making life-and-death decisions. I felt burning alive—or cinematically alive—when I walked into that casino with three thousand dollars in my pocket, ready to risk it all. And I felt flayed alive, but alive, walking out three hours later with nothing left. And it was worth it.

Americans don't gamble because we're greedy for money, but because we're greedy for reality, for a sensation that isn't a palliative, for the real deal, a real risk, a risk that's our own and not Brad Pitt's. We gamble because we want a cliffhanger of our own. I don't think it's a coincidence that gambling exploded in the United States at the end of the Cold War, when our daily lives were no longer lived in the shadow of nuclear war. Nor do I think it's a coincidence that America's casinos were empty in the days and weeks after September 11, 2001, when we felt like our lives were filled with risk. And I don't think it's a coincidence that Americans returned to casinos just as soon as the war on terrorism became another television show, another thing we watched on TV that was so much more exciting than the lives we actually live.

LUST

The Erotic Rites of David and Bridget

At one time, wearing a wedding band meant you were off limits. Today that is less and less the case. —William J. Bennett

The public scandal is what constitutes the offence. Sins sinned in secret are no sins at all. —Molière

There were a lot of wedding bands on a lot of left hands at the Tropicana Hotel one recent weekend in August. Thousands of married couples from dozens of states were strolling in and out of the hotel's casino and convention center. Couples were saying hello to friends they hadn't seen since last year's convention, comparing tans, and gathering in even-number clumps to gossip and catch up. Most of the couples in the hotel were holding hands or engaged in some form of PDA. Couples strolling through the casino would suddenly stop and kiss—and, really, why shouldn't they? This weekend was a long-planned, much-anticipated romantic getaway, a time when the normal pressures and expectations of daily life were supposed to fall away. Over the next three days, the couples planned to dress up, drink, gamble, and dance.

Oh, and commit adultery. For while the couples at the Lifestyles 2001 convention at the Tropicana Hotel in Las Vegas were most decidedly married, none were off-limits. (I know, Las Vegas again. But, come on, it's a book about sin. More than one trip to Las Vegas was inevitable.) Married heterosexual swingers, aka "playcouples," had descended on Las Vegas and taken over the hotel.

Lust was in the air.

As you might recall from the first chapter, lust is one of two "natural" sins (gluttony is the other), and to explore the dynamics of lust, I decided to hang out with adulterers, people who give in to this natural sin. Selecting adultery, of course, had one big perk: I would have to commit adultery myself, and my boyfriend couldn't really complain, since it was, you know, my job.

"We're not technically married," my boyfriend pointed out when I explained to him that the terms of my book contract obligated me to cheat on him. "Can unmarried couples even commit adultery?"

Faced with a relationship crisis grounded in a theological debate, I decided to call on a member of the clergy to settle this dispute. My boyfriend and I are not regular churchgoers and we don't know any priests or ministers, so I called a prayer line I saw advertised on a Christian cable network. A very nice Baptist minister working from his home in North Dakota explained to me that it was impossible for me or any gay man to commit the sin of adultery.

"You aren't married and you never will be married and that means you can't come together in a holy sexual union that pleases God," my prayer partner explained. "Only man and wife can do that. What you do is fornicate, and fornication is a sin. God hates all fornication, and all fornicators are sinners. Fornicating with another homosexual does not make you an adulterer. It's only makes you a fornicator."

Which I already am?

"Which you already are."

I asked my prayer partner if God would prefer that I be monogamous, even if I was being faithful to a man.

"I'm trying to be clear here. On Judgment Day, God isn't going to say, 'Oh, I see here that you fornicated with only one man.' God doesn't care if it was one man or one thousand men. All fornicators go to hell."

And a little extra fornicating isn't going to make the lake of fire any hotter?

"Fire is fire," my prayer partner warned me.

Much to my boyfriend's delight, adultery was a sin I could only observe, not indulge in. Crap.

*W*ife-swapping was first mentioned in the media in the mid-1950s after a small group of military officers in Southern California gave birth to the modern swinging movement. In swinging circles, legend has it that a tight group of Cold War–era military men shared their wives to cement their bond. (Organized wife-swapping among military officers in the 1950s and 1960s, particularly in the air force, is well-documented and routinely denied.) Nonmilitary swing clubs started popping up in the early 1960s, first in arch-conservative Orange County, then in San Francisco, Hollywood, and Los Angeles. Clubs started out as gatherings in members' homes; then certain bars began catering to swingers. In 1971, social scientist Gilbert Bartell claimed in *Group Sex: A Scientist's Eyewitness Report on the American Way of Swinging* that 1 million people—half a million couples—were involved in organized swinging.

The host of the world's Lifestyles 2001 convention in Las Vegas, the Lifestyles Organization (LSO), grew out of a California swingers club called WideWorld, founded by Robert and Geri McGinley in 1969. Their club, according to LSO's Web site, was founded "to provide recreational opportunities to couples who yearned to lead lives free from archaic religious and political restrictions." The group held its first convention in 1973, which was attended by 125 couples. The convention I attended in 2001 attracted more than three thousand couples—six thousand men and women wearing color-coded plastic wristbands that identified them as swingers. Most of the men dressed in conservative sportswear—chinos, polos, bolos—while most of the women were dressed more revealingly. There was an awful lot of cleavage on display. Some of the couples were young, some were old, but it was always the woman who was on display.

LSO's founder Robert McGinley is widely regarded as the father of the modern swinging movement. In his brief history of swinging, he cites an unnamed (and unpublished) report by "two well-known sociologists" that predicts 15 percent to 25 percent of all American married couples—some 22 million people—will become swingers at some point in their marriage, a statistic that should be taken with about a hundred thousand grains of salt. But it's impossible to dispute McGinley's claim that organized swinging is going on all over the United States. The Internet has emerged as a powerful tool to facilitate swinging, and a quick Internet search turns up swingers' clubs in every corner of the country—including clubs in "red" states like North Carolina, Mississippi, Indiana, Idaho, and Utah.

LSO is the granddaddy of swingers' organizations, and remains the largest swingers' organization in the country, with twelve full-time employees, an in-house travel agency (Lifestyles Tours & Travel), and a clubhouse in California. A large chunk of LSO's Web site is dedicated to answering questions and demystifying the *lifestyle,* a term the group embraces as passionately as they reject the term *wife-swapping.* According to its Web site, LSO speaks out "in public and private forums" to advance the "playcouple" philosophy: "Sex between consenting couples is natural, wholesome behavior and to pretend it is not is to encourage physical and mental disorder." A large chunk of the site is dedicated to Q&A-style fact sheets that seek to reassure couples who might be curious about attending a swing club or a Lifestyles Convention:

"But we've never been to anything like this before. . . ."

"You won't be alone. . . . What you'll find are a lot of people—everyday people just like you—who are only interested in an open and friendly atmosphere where people are not afraid to talk about

fantasies. . . . No one gets attacked. No one is pressured to do anything they don't want to. There's no rituals, no initiations. There
are, however, a lot of people having fun."

"**F**or me the question was, could I be a good Jew and a
swinger?" David paused, looked across the table, and opened his
hands, palms up, as if he had nothing to hide.

"There are a lot of 'shall nots' in the Torah," he says. "But it
seemed to us that if we were honest with each other, then we
weren't committing adultery."

"If you're lying to your partner, that's adultery," says Bridget,
David's wife, nodding.

We're eating hot, salty pretzels with yellow mustard in the Tropicana's coffee shop, a dingy hole in the wall that wouldn't be out of
place in a Trailways bus depot. Tall and muscular, David is an impressive example of Jewish manhood—picture a slightly younger
version of former Israeli prime minister Benjamin Netanyahu with
a head full of dark hair. David has muscular arms and shoulders
and was wearing a tank top and a pair of running shorts when we
met. Bridget was a red-haired, green-eyed woman of Irish descent
wearing blue-jean overalls and a small star of David on a chain
around her neck. Bridget's mother was Jewish and her father was
Irish-Catholic; her mom got to pick the faith her children were
raised in, while her dad got to pick their names. Bridget has two
older brothers, Sean and Patrick, both practicing Jews.

David and Bridget are in their early forties, but neither looks a
day over thirty-five. They've been married for ten years but "in the
lifestyle," as they call it, for four. They attend at least two parties a
month and sometimes more at one of the nine swingers clubs in
the suburbs of Chicago. They have three children, all boys under
the age of ten. They keep kosher, attend services at least once a
week, and are giddy with anticipation about their boys' impending
bar mitzvahs. Before meeting me in the Tropicana's lobby, David
and Bridget spent an hour in their hotel room reading the Torah.

"The Torah talks about deception being part of the offense when someone commits adultery," says David, when I ask how they reconcile their conservative religious beliefs and their liberal attitudes towards sex. "So is adultery having sex with someone who isn't your spouse? Or is it hiding that sex from your spouse?"

"We realize we're doing something that would be frowned upon in our moral community," says Bridget, "and that it may be a contradiction. But people are complex." Bridget feels the Torah is on their side. "This is something we feel helps our bond as husband and wife. Torah says a man should leave his parents and cleave to his wife," and David and Bridget feel that swinging brought them closer together, that is, it helps them cleave.

God forbids adultery in the Sixth Commandment. In the Jewish tradition, sin requires an action. "Judaism doesn't legislate thought," says Bridget. "Even coveting requires an act in furtherance of the desire." In the Christian tradition, however, adultery isn't just a sin in deed alone but also in thought. Wanting to commit adultery, according to the Christian God, is every bit as bad as actually committing adultery. It may seem harsh that God would condemn millions of straight American men to eternal torment for, say, wanting to fuck Jennifer Aniston, the actress married to Brad Pitt, but, hey, who are we to question God? (As God points out to Job, we weren't around when he was hanging the stars, so who the fuck are we and what do we know about anything?)

Early Christians believed that the act of lusting after someone was not only a sin on the part of the luster but also potentially the *lustee.* "Someone who consciously seeks to induce lustful thoughts (or actions) in another is guilty of sinning," according to Míceál Vaughan, a professor of English at the University of Washington and an expert on the liturgy of the Catholic Church. "Sin in Catholic tradition is only the result of one's personal thoughts, actions, and consent to them, so a person who is the object of lust is not thereby guilty of sin. It's on other grounds entirely that the object of lust becomes guilty of sin," such as behaving or dressing in ways that they know make others lust after them. Which means, of course, that Brad Pitt, Heath Ledger, and Tom Cruise—all three appeared shirtless on the cover of *Vanity Fair*—have sinned grievously, as their actions inspired lust in my heart and the hearts of millions of other straight women and gay men. When someone's dress (or lack thereof), actions, or words tempt others to sinful thoughts or deeds (or both), "[that is] what is called making one's self an 'occasion of sin,' and there is potentially some guilt incurred by that," added Vaughan.

Since Jennifer Aniston and Brad Pitt make themselves the "occasion of sin" about as often as I make myself toast, Jennifer can expect to roast in hell for prancing around on *Friends* in her underwear, and Brad will burn right beside her for splashing his abs all over the cover of *Vanity Fair*.

And here's some more bad news for Brad and Jennifer: Man and wife, according to early church fathers, were asked to love each other like brother and sister. Lust even within marriage was considered a form of adultery, believe it or not, *which means it's not okay for Brad and Jennifer to lust after each other*. The remedy for lust, marital or casual, was chastity—with some kinds of chastity considered better than others. Virginity was the best kind of chastity, according to church fathers, which led some early Christians to castrate themselves. If you couldn't be a virgin, the second-best chastity was widowhood. If you weren't disciplined enough to be chaste or lucky enough to be widowed and too horny to go without sex, "it's better to marry than to burn," Saint Paul said. Hardly a ringing endorsement of the institution of marriage.

But despite all the compliments the "ancient" and "sacred" institution of marriage gets from American clerics and candidates (who ignore the many ways in which the "unchanging institution of marriage" has evolved and changed over the centuries), early Christians regarded marriage as vastly inferior to celibacy. Which is still the Catholic Church's position. Unlike the Jews—an embattled tribe trying to make as many babies as possible—early Christians believed the world was coming to an end. Jesus said as much: "And he said unto them, 'Truly I tell you, there are some standing here who will not taste death until they see that the Kingdom of God has come with power (Mark 9.1, Matthew 16.28).' " With the world coming to an end, the early Church discouraged its members from bringing more children into the world. With the Kingdom of God at hand, Jesus H. Christ, who had time to arrange for child care?

Judaism isn't so insanely antisex, according to David and Bridget.

"In the Jewish tradition, sin is 'missing the mark,' " Bridget explained to me in Las Vegas. "Being damned isn't a Jewish concept. King David was very promiscuous, but he is still seen as the greatest king and a Jewish hero, so maybe missing the mark sexually isn't so serious a sin."

David and Bridget got into swinging the same way most swinging couples get into the lifestyle; David asked his wife is she might want to attend a party. He'd gone to a few with his previous long-term girlfriend, enjoyed them, and thought Bridget would like them just as much as he did. Bridget was afraid the parties would be sleazy.

"I told her we could leave at any point," says David, "and that we didn't have to do anything. She would be in charge. I told her that going to a club is like going to the most fun bar you've ever been to."

It only took one visit to convince Bridget that David was right.

"People let loose and were really free," says Bridget. "And unlike most bars, it's completely safe for women. Nothing is going to happen that you don't want to have happen. None of the men are obnoxious or drunk, since they know they'll be asked to leave if they make any of the women feel uncomfortable."

Women can do just about anything they like at a swingers' dance or in a swingers' club—they can be aggressive, demanding, passive, and casually bisexual. The same isn't true for men. Men who touch women without permission are shown the door, as are drunk or obnoxious men, and there's a taboo against casual same-sex play among men. "I doubt that all the men in this hotel or at parties are straight," admitted David, tearing apart another pretzel, "that just doesn't seem likely, not with so many of the women being bisexual. Male bisexuality is seen as a threat by a lot of straight men, and male bisexuality is seen as a threat to women, since bisexual husbands are likelier to have HIV than husbands who only want to watch their wives and other men's wives."

The swinging movement would collapse if women felt unsafe or threatened, David explained, so clubs have to create an environment where women feel safe and free to lose themselves in the moment. "Men, on the other hand, can't cut loose," said David. "We have to be on our best behavior at all times." Single men are not allowed at swing clubs, so that men don't outnumber women, and clubs refuse admittance to men suspected of hiring prostitutes to accompany them to parties. "We're constantly monitoring how our actions are being perceived by the women, to make sure we're not doing anything that might make any woman uncomfortable."

In his book *The Lifestyle: A Look at the Erotic Rites of Swingers,* investigative journalist Terry Gould describes the swinging scene as a matriarchy. David agreed with that description.

"Women have all the power. If a woman says, 'He touched me when I asked him not to,' then you're warned. Do it again, and you're out. So you're careful and respectful because you don't want to be asked to leave. It's too much fun in there; it's a man's fantasy come true. All the women, all that sexual energy, all that fun and possibility—and I get to share all of it with the woman I love. It's paradise, and any sane man would do whatever he had to in order to stay in paradise. It's wonderful."

It's also illegal.

Illinois, where David and Bridget keep kosher and attend swingers' parties, is one of the twenty-seven states that still have adultery laws on the books. While no one has been prosecuted by the state of Illinois for "open and notorious" adultery in the last forty years, adultery laws in other states are still enforced—and more recently than you might think. In October of 2001, Jerry Ward of Taylersville, North Carolina, was found guilty of having sex with his live-in girlfriend, who was estranged from her husband. (Ward was fined ninety dollars plus court costs.) In New York State, there have been twenty-five arrests and convictions for adultery in the ten years *before* Bill Clinton moved to the state. Ironically, the U.S. military, where modern swinging got its start, is the most aggressive prosecutor of known adulterers. In 1997, the year the U.S. Air Force famously charged Lt. Kelly Flinn, the first female B-52 bomber pilot, with adultery, sixty men and seven other women were also prosecuted by military courts for adultery. One of the women, Lt. Col. Karen Dwyer (U.S. Air Force) committed suicide five days after she was convicted.

"In extramarital affairs, there *are* victims," William Bennett writes in *The Death of Outrage,* the book in which he scolded the American public for not falling in line behind Republican efforts to hound Bill Clinton from office over a few lousy blow jobs. "Adultery is a betrayal of a very high order, the betrayal of a person one has promised to honor," according to Bennett. "It violates a solemn vow. When it is discovered, acute emotional damage almost always follows, often including the damage of divorce."

Not to mention the occasional despairing suicide or ridiculous impeachment.

There don't appear to be any victims at the Tropicana Hotel, though, just a lot of married men and women having a good time. Over the course of the weekend, swingers from all over the United States and the world attended the fellatio workshop, the pool parties, the Sexy Safari Jungle Party, and the Sexy Sci-Fi Party. Christian activists are famous for crashing gay events, from pride parades to private parties, and videotaping gay men being overtly sexual in public. Copies of these tapes are sent to elected officials in an effort to convince them that gay men are a threat to the American family.

Walking through the Erotic Arts Exhibition at the Lifestyles 2001 Convention, an art show that features dozens of images of bondage and bestiality, I wondered where the Christian activists were. Surely an art show by and for heterosexuals that promoted bondage and bestiality—sometimes both at once!—had to be a bigger threat to American families than whatever gay men do when there aren't any straight people around.

The Lifestyles Organization forbids "public play," that is, sex at the workshops, pool parties, and dances. There is, however, a lot of flirting, groping, and dirty dancing. When couples decide its time to carry the flirting and groping into actual acts of adultery, they take it up to their rooms and suites, away from the eyes of nonswinging couples who happen to be at the hotel, hotel employees, and scribblers with notebooks. While there's no public sex at the Lifestyles Convention, there is plenty of skin on display, most of it belonging to females. The only event that showed a lot of male skin was the Best Buns contest, the male beauty pageant that compliments the Miss Lifestyles contest. At both events the announcers told the crowd where each contestant was from, and most seemed to be from "red states," places like Arkansas, South Carolina, and Georgia, all conservative states that George Bush carried in 2000. When the crowd was informed that a woman in the Miss Lifestyles contest was from Texas, a big cheer went up.

"There are lots of Texans here tonight!" the announcer shouted, and the whooping continued.

Three thousand couples attended the Lifestyles 2001 Convention, and if each of those couples managed to find one other couple to play with, that means twelve thousand separate acts of adultery were committed in one hotel on the Las Vegas strip in one weekend. That has to be some sort of record—even for Las Vegas.

In *The Broken Hearth: Reversing the Moral Collapse of the American Family*, Bill Bennett identifies numerous threats to the American ever-imperiled family, which he describes as being "under siege." He frets about the rise in illegitimate births (which dropped in 1999 to 1990 levels), divorce rates (also falling), cohabitation, and single parenthood (which has leveled off). But the gravest threat to the American family, according to Bennett, is gay marriage. There are just six chapters in what is, for Bennett, a relatively slim book (189 pages). By far the largest chapter is devoted to the grave threat gay marriage poses to the American family. And why would homosexual marriages present such a threat to heterosexual ones? Bennett's chief argument against gay marriage is the fact that so few gay men are or want to be monogamous:

> Advocates would have us believe that homosexuals do not want any change in the obligations that marriage entails, namely, fidelity and monogamy. . . . [But] some who claim to be more "traditional" in their views find the strictures of family life to be too much. Andrew Sullivan, in a candid admission at the end of his book *Virtually Normal: An Argument about Homosexuality*, writes that homosexual marriage contracts will have to entail a greater understanding of the need for "extramarital outlets (pp. 115–116)."

Marriage, Bennett argues, is not and cannot be an "open" contract. "Its essential idea is fidelity. Obviously that essential idea is not always honored in practice. But it is that to which we commit ourselves."

Bennett believes the existence of nonmonogamous, legally married gay couples would undermine heterosexual marriages. (Or that's what he would like us to believe he believes.) And how would gay marriages undermine straight marriages? Married gay male couples—with our trendy haircuts, Phillipe Stark sofas, and extramarital outlets—would present an irresistible example to impressionable straight couples. Married straight couples might find out that their married gay neighbors weren't monogamous and conclude that they could be legally married and nonmonogamous, too, just like the gays. And while Bennett concedes that lesbian couples are likelier to be monogamous than either gay *or* straight couples, he doesn't support marriage rights for lesbians despite the good example lesbian marriages would set for everyone else.

Now I'm not going to waste anyone's time arguing that most or even many gay male couples are monogamous. The notion that gay couples are likelier to come to an understanding about extramarital outlets is not a right-wing plot or an anti-gay stereotype. It's a fact. Researchers who've studied male couples found that the vast majority did make allowances for some outside sexual contact. But even if every gay couple on earth were strictly monogamous—if gay men were as faithful as lesbians—Bennett overstates the impact gay marriage would have on impressionable straights. While some heterosexuals may turn to homosexuals for fashion tips and sex advice—more should, God knows—very few straight couples take gay couples as their role models.

And it's not as if America's married heterosexuals are hanging back waiting for gay marriage to be legalized before they cheat. To take one famous example, gay marriage was illegal in the United States when Bill Clinton ejaculated on Monica Lewinsky—gay marriage is illegal in the United States *thanks* to Clinton, who signed the Defense of Marriage Act in 1996. Clinton isn't the only married man in America who has ejaculated on someone to whom he isn't married. Peggy Vaughan, author of *The Monogamy Myth,* estimates that 60 percent of married men and 40 percent of married women will have an extramarital affair at some point in their marriage. Since these people are not always married to each other, Vaughan believes that 80 percent of heterosexual marriages are "touched" by adultery.

If Bennett is truly worried about the bad example of non-monogamous married couples—if that's not just his excuse for denying gay couples the right to wed—one would expect that Bennett is more concerned about the gatherings like the Lifestyles 2001 convention at the Tropicana Hotel than the "outlets" gay men in couples permit each other.

Let's crunch some numbers:

There are 60.7 million American men between the ages of eighteen and fifty. The best estimate of the percentage of American men who identify as gay is 3.7 percent, which means there are only 2.2 million gay men between the ages of eighteen and fifty, the years men are likeliest to marry or remarry. If gay marriage were legalized, the maximum number of gay married couples in the United States would be 1.1 million—provided, of course, that every one of those 2.2 million American gay men could find a husband in one day. (And even if gay marriage were legalized there would still be gay men who didn't want to marry, gay men no other gay men would want to marry, and gay men who didn't want to leave the priesthood in order to marry.) So keep in mind that the 1.1-million-gay-marriages estimate is probably high.

Now consider that there are currently 1.1 million straight couples involved in the swinging movement, according to researcher Richard Jenks, a professor of sociology at Indiana University Southeast who researches alternative sexualities. These aren't *potential* nonmonogamous married couples Jenks is talking about, but *actual* nonmonogamous *heterosexual* married couples who are, if we agree with Bennett, *setting a very bad example for other heterosexual couples.* That 1.1 million figure represents 2 percent of the 54.4 million married couples in the United States, which means the number of swinger couples in the United States has doubled since the 1970s. There are currently as many actively swinging, nonmonogamous straight couples as there are potential gay married couples.

The average heterosexual couple is likelier to socialize with other heterosexual couples; they're likelier to look to other heterosexual couples as role models and for advice; and they're likelier to look to other heterosexual marriages for an idea of what's possible in their own marriage. Considering these facts, it seems clear that if anyone is setting a bad example for monogamous heterosexual couples, it's the growing number of married, nonmonogamous, heterosexual "playcouples" who crowded into the Tropicana Hotel and Resort for Lifestyles 2001.

What's more, unlike homosexuality, swinging is a *learned* behavior. Homosexuality is not a choice—I don't care how many "ex-gay" Christian conservatives can trot out for the cameras. My proof that homosexuality is not a choice? A question for my straight male readers: Is there anything I could do or say or write that would convince you to willingly, happily, eagerly, anxiously, deliriously, lustfully put my dick in your mouth and leave it there until I had an orgasm? I rest my case.

Monogamous straight couples, however, can be talked into swinging. During the Lifestyles 2001 convention, the Tropicana was crawling with formerly monogamous married straight couples who either read about the lifestyle on the Web or met someone involved in the lifestyle and decided to check out a party for themselves. Swingers define fidelity differently, they pursue "extramarital outlets," they call it a lifestyle—and they recruit. A straight couple I know were invited to dinner by their new next-door neighbors, who wined them, dined them, and hit on them. Their new neighbors were swingers, they announced, and they invited my friends to join them at the next party they attended. My friends went, and now they're swingers. A lawyer I know was approached by a senior partner in his law firm about attending a swingers' party at the senior partner's home. The offer put my friend in an awkward spot: Could he refuse the invitation without jeopardizing his position with the firm? (He declined the invitation, and the feared retaliation never materialized—my friend is a partner in his firm now.) Swingers organizations advertise themselves and their conventions, local clubs put up Web sites, individual couples have home pages and take out personal ads—all in an effort to attract new, previously monogamous couples into the lifestyle.

Every evil action that conservatives accuse gays of—recruiting, cheating, living a "lifestyle"—these married heterosexual couples are actually guilty of.

Bennett should be appalled. He should be frightened. Anyone who believes that the American family is threatened by non-monogamous gay male couples should be apoplectic about the growth of the swinging movement. Make no mistake, Mr. Bennett, these radical swingers are on the march. Terry Gould writes, ". . . swinging has grown substantially. The annual Lifestyles convention is a megaevent. Miniconventions are taking place every Saturday night in the smallest towns, and new clubs are opening all the time . . . [and] we are entering an era in which the playcouple lifestyle is going to take a big jump in popularity." Swingers clubs, like the ones David and Bridget attend in the suburbs of Chicago, send out newsletters and maintain Web sites. "It is inevitable that more and more straight people will run across these ads," Gould writes. "[Thanks to the Internet], thousands will certainly find their way to clubs no one suspected of being up and running within a fifteen-minute drive from home."

For someone who regards fidelity as the "essential" to marriage, Bennett seems strangely incurious about organized, nonmonoga-mous heterosexual couples committing adultery en masse. Modern swinger conventions, playcouple parties, and contact magazines and Web sites are nowhere to be found in Bennett's book. But Ben-nett has time to round up all the usual gay suspects: Anne Heche, Ellen DeGeneres, Julie Cypher, Melissa Etheridge, Bruce Bower, Andrew Sullivan, Jonathan Rauch, Elizabeth Birch, John Boswell, Rosie O'Donnell, Robert Mapplethorpe. Gays come up seventy-one times in *The Broken Hearth*'s index, but there's just one mention—one!—of heterosexual swinging. It's on page 22, *and it's in the past tense*. Bennett ridicules a book on "open marriages" published in 1972, and then blandly states that, "wife-swapping and 'open mar-riage' did not become the rage in American life."

Surely Bennett is aware that swinging wasn't canceled in 1974 along with *Love, American Style*. Roger Stone, an adviser to Bob Dole's 1996 presidential campaign, was forced to resign after re-porters discovered that he and his wife were regulars at various swing clubs and conventions. Mr. and Mrs. Stone also advertised in swingers' magazines looking for younger men, preferably military types, to have sex with Mrs. Stone while Mr. Stone watched. Bennett was an adviser to the Dole campaign, so he must have known Roger Stone—Stone was active in Republican politics for years—and Bennett had to have been aware of the scandal. But Bennett would have us believe swinging is something a few loopy straight people experimented with in the early seventies—did Bennett's research assistant rent Ang Lee's *The Ice Storm* and call it a day?—and Stone doesn't rate a single mention in a book about the "moral collapse" of the American family.

In August of 2002, the Lifestyles convention was held in Reno, Nevada. For three days in August of 2003, Lifestyles Organization will transform yet another big American metropolis into the swingers' Vatican City, playcouples' temporal and spiritual capital. Lifestyle conventions aren't held in secret; they're heavily advertised on the Web, hotels and resorts compete to host them, and with each passing year, the conventions earn increasingly favorable coverage in local and national media. If Bennett doesn't believe that heterosexual couples are passionate about nonmonogamy—some are eager to proselytize about it—I'll buy Bennett a ticket to the Lifestyles 2003 Convention and introduce him to thousands and thousands of straight couples for whom wife-swapping and open marriage are indeed the rage.

Bennett doesn't have to trek to Reno or Las Vegas to find married, nonmonogamous heterosexuals committing adultery. Bennett lives with his wife in Chevy Chase, Maryland. Two miles up the road in Silver Springs, Maryland, the Hartford County Swing Club hosts regular parties and social events for heterosexual couples. According to their Web site, "HCSC is a group of couples . . . who come together to have fun and make new friends." Hosted by Cookie and Ron, the Hartford County Swing Club sponsors gatherings year-round, including winter holiday parties with "gift exchange supervised by 'The Nekkid Elf.' "

The Hartford County Swing Club has been helping Bill Bennett's married, heterosexual neighbors commit adultery since 1999. But while Bennett's married, heterosexual neighbors seek extramarital outlets right under his nose, Bennett is more concerned with how gay men *might* behave *if* we could get married. (If Bennett is interested in meeting some of his swinging neighbors, he can e-mail The Hartford County Swing Club at swingclub@aol.com for directions to its next party. But you'll have to bring the wife, Bill, as single men are not allowed.)

Cultural conservatives like Bennett are always complaining about people who profit from violent movies and music, accusing this music label or that movie studio of making money by promoting immoral behavior. At the Lifestyles Convention, I picked up brochures for more than a dozen resorts that cater to playcouples or described themselves as "lifestyle-friendly" places with names like Blue Bay Resorts, Hedonism, Caribbean Reef Club, Solare Resorts, and Plato's Repeat. They're all making money off organized mass adultery, and yet Bennett has no comment. Swinging is even making inroads into popular culture. In *How the Grinch Stole Christmas*—one of the worst movies I've ever seen—the adult Whos down in Whoville are shown at a drunken party tossing keys into a bowl by a window, echoing the infamous "key party" scene in *The Ice Storm*. Director Ron Howard portrayed the Whos in Whoville as swingers—*and this is a movie marketed to our children*!

Excuse me, but where the fuck is Bill Bennett's outrage? Why hasn't Bennett called for Opie's head?

Buffalo Grove, Illinois, isn't anyone's idea of Gomorrah (or Whoville, for that matter). A conservative, largely Jewish bedroom community in the northern suburbs of Chicago, Buffalo Grove is a few square miles of ranch and old farm houses. Most of the homes in Buffalo Grove are a short walk from at least one synagogue. During the week, Buffalo Grove's lawyers and office workers make their way to downtown Chicago on commuter trains and express buses, in minivans and SUVs.

Buffalo Grove is one of those places that isn't. There's no downtown, no town square. To quote a famous Jewish dyke, "when you're there, there's no there there." (Gertrude Stein was speaking of Oakland, California.) With the exception of a few depressing malls filled with the same three dozen stores you'll find in every other mall in North America, there's nothing much in Buffalo Grove. But the place is, as the saying goes, a fine place to raise a family; there are good schools, quiet neighborhoods, and few gangs. Buffalo Grove is a place where young children get a good education, and teenagers just want to get the hell out.

David and Bridget invited me to drop by for dinner whenever I was in Buffalo Grove. Since I couldn't imagine a circumstance that would ever bring me to Buffalo Grove, I had to make a special trip. Their house was a split-level ranch on a dark street one block away from one of those eight-lane arterials that slice through the Chicago suburbs. Their house is about forty years old, solid and squat, built with the dark orange and khaki-yellow bricks. It's the kind of house that drives urbanists nuts—the driveway and the garage dominate the front of the house, there's no porch, no front stoop, and the front door faces the driveway, not the street.

Bridget meets me at the door, takes my coat, and asks me if I'd like a glass of wine. I grew up a few miles away from Buffalo Grove, in a Chicago neighborhood that was half Jewish and half Irish Catholic—just like David's and Bridget's three boys, who come running up the steps from the basement. David is putting the finishing touches on dinner, so Bridget asks the boys—aged nine, seven, and four—to show me some of their toys. The boys lead me down a flight of carpeted stairs into a huge basement rec room. An enormous television sits at one end of the room with three couches arranged around it; a cocktail bar built by the home's previous owners sits at the other end. And the half acre of beige carpeting that stretches between the couches and the cocktail bar is covered with toys.

Noah, the oldest, plops down on one of the couches by the television set and plays with his Game Boy. The two younger boys, Joshua and Aaron, show off their awesome collection of Rescue Heroes, a popular line of action figures. My son is obsessed with Rescue Heroes, too, so I'm familiar with most of the plastic cops, firemen, and paramedics Joshua and Adam hold out for me to inspect. Rescue Heroes have ridiculously broad shoulders, huge lats, enormous pecs, Popeye forearms, and massive thighs. Most have mustaches, and they all have enormous feet. They look like porn-star action figures.

Dinner is salmon steaks for the grown-ups and cheese pizza for the kids, and the conversation is all Judaism, all the time. Because it was the Friday night Shabbat dinner, there were candles on the table and prayers said in Hebrew before we ate. There was also a song, a blessing for the children, a poem, and finally a prayer for peace. I felt like I was at an open mic performance at a coffee shop for hyperobservant Jews. Like most Americans, I got something of a crash course on Judaism during the 2000 presidential campaign, thanks to Joe Lieberman, whose orthodox Jewish faith prevented him from driving on Fridays. But I must have missed the *Nightline* that covered Shabbat, so I asked David to explain the importance of the meal to me.

"Well, it's the day that's important, not just the meal," David said. "The meal is intended to celebrate the day, which is kept holy according to the Fourth Commandment. Shabbat is the most important Jewish holiday."

I interrupted. The most important Jewish holiday comes once a week?

"Well, Yom Kippur is the most important holiday, but it is called the Shabbat of Shabbats. But, yes, the most important Jewish holiday does come once a week. Think of food, water, and air," David continued. The boys squirmed—they'd heard this one before. "We have plenty of all three, as God created enough air, food, and water for the whole word, provided we use it properly. You can live for weeks without food, and days without water. But you can't live for more than a few minutes without air. So which is the most important of those three things?" David asked me.

Uh . . . air?

"That's right, air is the most important. It's also the most abundant. It surrounds us, it's everywhere, all over the earth, and a mile up into the sky. And we take it for granted until we don't have it. It's the same with Shabbat. It's the most important holiday and the most abundant. Once a week we pause as a family and come together and remember what family is. It surrounds us, it gives us life, and we remind ourselves not to take family for granted. Family is the air we breathe.

"God," David continued, "*breathed* life into Adam, he didn't give him a glass of water or hand him a sandwich."

One thing runs through my mind while David talks: *Bill Bennett would eat this shit up.* David and Bridget are devoted to each other, committed to their children, religious, and observant in an open, moving, thoroughly genuine way. What's for a conservative not to like about these two?

The swinging, of course. The parties, the conventions, the extramarital outlets. To Bennett and other one-size-fits-all moral scolds, David and Bridget's faith, their well-behaved boys, the hours they spend volunteering at their synagogue, and their loving, egalitarian relationship won't get them out of the "moral collapse" column on Bill Bennett's good family–bad family ledger.

After dinner ended and the boys went back to the basement, I asked David and Bridget if we could talk about swinging. Bridget got up from the table and bent to look down the stairs that lead to the basement. She called down to the boys, telling them they could put a tape in the VCR, and a small cheer went up; television is strictly rationed in this ranch house. Once she was satisfied that the boys couldn't hear us, Bridget returned to the table and nodded.

But I somehow already know the answer to my first question: Do the boys know?

David and Bridget have decided not to tell their kids about their sex lives for the time being—now it's their sex lives and not their "lifestyle." They certainly weren't going to tell them now, while the boys were so young. They probably would never tell them.

"It's not that we don't talk to our kids about sex," Bridget said. "We want them to grow up to have healthy attitudes about sex, and we want them to have all the information they need. I've talked to my older son about masturbation. But I don't think we would tell them about this."

"I look at it this way," David said. "I wouldn't want to know all the details of my parents' sex life. I mean, if your parents had been swingers, would you want them to tell you about it?"

That's a big, fat no.

"Right," said David. "So why tell our boys something they would rather not know? We can't really see how it would ever even come up."

But what if one of the boys heard something about swinging on TV or read something about the lifestyle—his parents' lifestyle—on the Internet and asked them about it?

David and Bridget looked at each other, then back at me.

"We would lie," Bridget whispered—actually, all three of us were whispering. "People say very disparaging things about swingers. It's so countercultural that people have a hard time understanding it. We wouldn't want to tell the boys for some of the same reasons we couldn't tell the neighbors or our rabbi. Swingers are discriminated against, and the way the media portrays swingers is hateful. The public image is that all swingers are sex-crazed lunatics whose lives revolve around sex."

"People say such hateful things about swingers," David said. "We spread diseases; we have no self-control. But we're very safe, and a swinging environment is controlled and respectful. But you would only know that if you went to one with an open mind, and you saw that people were using condoms, very cautiously, and that everyone was friendly and respectful of each other."

Bridget especially hates the idea that wives are forced into swinging by controlling husbands.

"The truth is, most women go to their first party because their husbands want to go," said Bridget. "And most couples don't do anything at their first party. But it's also true that it's the wives who insist on going to more and more parties. Here's this place where you can be totally sexually free and open in public *and* completely safe at the same time. How many women get to experience that in their lives? And to share that experience with my husband is a joy."

David and Bridget are quick to admit that they're part of the problem. The myths about their lifestyle will be dispelled only when swingers who don't fit the stereotype come out. Just as pot-heads with dreads are likelier to be open about smoking marijuana, it's the sex-crazed lunatics whose lives revolve around sex who are likelier to be open about swinging. If couples like David and Bridget never come out, then their rabbis, priests, friends, family, and neighbors will never reexamine their preconceptions about swingers. It's a catch-22: Until the Davids and Bridgets come out, it won't be safe for the Davids and Bridgets to come out.

The nightmare scenario in this catch-22, of course, is that their own children may grow up to believe all the hateful things that are said about swingers—they're sex-crazed lunatics, wives are forced into swinging by controlling husbands, they spread diseases—and then find out their own parents are swingers. All it would take is a club newsletter, a piece of e-mail, an explicit phone message . . .

And it's not just their kids David and Bridget worry about. They were on the dance floor at a club near their home once when someone tapped Bridget on the shoulder.

"I turned around and there was this cousin of mine," said Bridget. "It was a distant cousin, not someone I knew that well, but I was flipped out. He told David his date thought he was cute, like the four of us should go off somewhere together. That was way too incestuous for me." They've never returned to the club where they ran into Bridget's cousin.

The club they usually attend is in another Chicago suburb. The club is in a private home, and it's an elaborate setup, with a dance floor, a bar, half a dozen bedrooms, an orgy room, and room for light—very light—bondage and S&M. It sounds like a straight version of a gay bathhouse, but while there are maybe three gay bathhouses in the Chicago area, there are at least nine straight swingers clubs.

David goes up to his office and brings back the newsletter for the club they frequent. There's a party tomorrow night that David and Bridget will be attending. According to the newsletter, I missed a talent contest held at the most recent party. ("You can sing karaoke, do a dance, or strip, or tell jokes—whatever you'd like!") The newsletter included a list of upcoming theme parties (Back to School, Talent Contest II, Sci-Fi Night, Oktoberfest Party), a list of birthdays of clubs members, some bad clip art, and a funny story someone found on-line about Saint Peter trying to explain the "suburban tribe" to a perplexed God. I assumed the story was about the tribe of suburban swingers who frequent the club but it turned out to be about suburbanites and their *lawns*. On the back of the newsletter were the names and addresses of nine other swingers clubs in the Chicago area, clubs with nudge-nudge names like Private Affairs, Couples Hideaway, Club Adventure.

David and Bridget usually attend two parties a month. David's mother, who lives nearby, baby-sits on those Saturday nights.

"It's her time with the boys, and it's our date night," said Bridget. "She thinks we're going to dinner and a movie. She's asleep in the guest room when we get come home. We don't bring people home, and no one is the wiser."

"We are always having to pretend we've seen all these movies we haven't seen," laughs David. "Mom thinks we see two movies a month, so we're always 'up' on movies, you know? She calls us from video stores. 'You saw *Bicentennial Man*, didn't you? Was it good or bad? Should I rent it?' And I have to say, 'What was that, Mom? *Bicentennial Man?* Uh, two thumbs up, Mom.' "

They've worked out a system to silently communicate with each other at a club, whether they're on the dance floor or in an orgy room. They make eye contact with each other constantly ("nonverbal checking in"), and if they wind up on opposite sides of the room a tug on the ear means "come back and be with me." In an orgy room or during a group-grope on the dance floor, three taps on the shoulder or thigh means, "I'm uncomfortable, let's take a break."

But it's been a long time since they've had to use the three taps.

"We almost never feel uncomfortable," said Bridget.

"The last time she had to tap me three times was when we ran into her cousin," said David. "Those three taps just about dislocated my shoulder."

David and Bridget laughed. We'd moved into the living room, onto the couch, and Bridget was sitting next to David, leaning into him.

"When we're at a party," David continued, "we'll sometimes look at each other and say, 'Who has more fun than we do?' Because no one does." David looked at Bridget. "We've been married ten years, and no couple has more fun than we do."

"There are times when I'm walking up the block waving to people, and I think, 'Oh, if the neighbors only knew!' " Bridget said. "People would be shocked."

But isn't it possible that some of your neighbors are swingers? Couldn't they be sitting in their living rooms in Buffalo Grove, saying the exact same thing?

"That's possible, that's possible," David said, his eyes twinkling. "I guess it just goes to show that you can't take people at face value."

"All people have secrets." Bridget nodded. "But some people's secrets are more fun."

The thrill of keeping a secret may be the penultimate reason

David and Bridget don't plan on coming out, running a very close second to the disapproval of their friends and family. Like a businessman who gets a secret charge out of wearing panties under his power suit, David and Bridget get a little if-they-only-knew charge when they wave to neighbors. They're a married couple in their forties with one mortgage, two cars, and three kids; they're adults with responsibilities and big-time jobs—and they lie to David's mother about where they've been like a couple of horny teenagers. Twice a month they get to be accomplices and coconspirators, sinning in secret so as not to scandalize their friends, families, neighbors, and rabbi.

"Having a secret is fun. But the important thing is we feel closer as a couple thanks to the parties," said Bridget. "It puts some extra zest into our sex life, the sex life we share with each other."

David and Bridget emphasized that they do have a sex life outside of the parties.

"We make love just about every day," Bridget said, "whether we go to a club or not."

"There are times when I can't believe how lucky we are," David said. "She'll be on her knees, kissing another woman, while I'm fucking her from behind—"

David stopped when he saw the startled look on my face. For all the talk about sex, this was the first even remotely graphic thing David or Bridget had said, and I was taken aback. Seeing them going through all the parenting motions that evening—feeding their kids, correcting their kids, running herd on their kids—I had come to see them through the lens that strips known parents of all sexual energy and agency. Despite all the talk about sex and secrets and parties, David and Bridget were a mom and a dad in my mind's eye, not sexual adventurers, and to have David suddenly create a mental image that was so specific and overtly sexual—well, I giggled a little nervously and instinctively looked around for the boys. Our voices had been getting louder and louder after we moved to the couch in the living room. Bridget followed my eyes and then got up and walked over to the top of the stairs, just to make sure the boys were still anesthetized in front of the TV.

"Where I was going was—," David whispered.

"Try not to shock the sex-advice columnist, honey."

"—in a normal marriage, if you're attracted to someone else, you can't mention it to your partner. But because we can be honest with each other, we can really share our fantasies and desires, and that brings us closer together. All of my fantasies involve my wife—how many married men can say that?"

I ask them the obvious question, the one that's inevitably put to swingers: Don't they get jealous watching each other mess around with other people?

"Married people who aren't in the lifestyle sometimes get jealous," Bridget said. "You can't avoid feeling jealous from time to time. All married people are attracted to people they're not married to. It happens to all couples. But we can talk about it. Our feelings of jealousy, they arise because we can be honest with each other about sex in ways that nonswinging couples can't. Being in this environment makes you communicate more, and more honestly, than most couples. We don't have to lie and pretend that we don't find other people attractive."

Swinging is not for everyone, as all swingers are quick to emphasize. By contrast, according to Bennett, Bork, Buchanan, Dr. Laura, Alan Keyes, et alia, monogamy is for everyone—whether we like it or not. Swinging has allowed David and Bridget to incorporate normal, healthy lust, one of the natural sins, into their marriage. Rather than seeing their attraction to other people pull them away from each other, David and Bridget have made lust something they do together and share and, most important, control and police.

"I don't feel like we're doing anything wrong," said David. "The Torah says a man should leave his parents and cling to his wife. Well, we've been together for ten years and in the lifestyle for four years, and we're still clinging to each other."

"This may sound crazy, but what we're doing feels to us like the most natural thing in the world," said Bridget.

And so it is.

This may come as shock to some—David's mother, my mother, the pope in Rome—but humans didn't evolve two-to-a-bungalow. We evolved in sprawling, multigenerational tribes, like apes or hippies, our sex lives messy and communal, with little privacy and no rules. Early humans made it up as they went, since God didn't see fit to deliver the Commandments for the first 37,000 years of our species' existence. (And it was another 1,200 years before he sent his son down for a lynching, Roman-style.) Without Commandments or virtuecrats to tell us what to do—or who to do it to or how often to do it to them—early humans pretty much did whatever they liked. In evolutionary terms, monogamous coupling is a recent development, one that's virtually unheard of in the animal kingdom. The supposed monogamous behavior of certain animals—one kind of primate, a couple of species of birds—turned out, upon closer examination, to be so much wishful thinking on our part.

To his credit, Bennett admits monogamy is unnatural. As with global warming, the scientific evidence against monogamy being "natural" is so vast that only the most dishonest of conservative pundits pretend otherwise. In *The Broken Hearth* Bennett admits to something many conservative critics wouldn't admit under torture: "Evolutionary biologists tell us that both women and men, but especially men, are naturally promiscuous," Bennett writes. "They also assure us that a sexually exclusive, lifelong commitment is unnatural."

Maybe he's trying to be chivalrous, but Bennett doesn't tell the whole truth. Contemporary research into human sexuality is showing that women aren't any less "naturally promiscuous" than men. Indeed, women may be more naturally promiscuous.

In *The Lifestyle,* Terry Gould cites the work of groundbreaking sex researcher Mary Jane Sherfey. In the 1960s, Sherfey discovered that "the female's clitoris was an internal system as large and as refined as a male's penis." Orgasms derived from clitoral stimulation alone had long been dismissed as "immature," and women who thought twice about their clitorises were labeled nymphomaniacs. The vaginal orgasm was considered appropriate, desirable, and "mature"; the clitoral orgasm—indeed the clitoris itself—was dismissed as lesser, base, and "vestigial." But Sherfey discovered that there was no such thing as a vaginal orgasm. Some women could climax from vaginal intercourse alone because their internal clitoral tissue—the majority of their clitoral tissue—was being stimulated. But most women needed stimulation of the "head" of the clitoris, the exposed part, in order to climax—just as most men need stimulation of the head of their penises to climax.

It was Sherfey's research, published in 1966, that first demonstrated that the clitoris was as central to a woman's experience of sexual pleasure—and to her ability to orgasm—as a man's penis was to his.

What does this have to do with female promiscuity? Well, in studying female and male sexual response cycles, Sherfey documented a shocking difference: "Whereas in males the engorged blood drains back from [the penis]," writes Gould, "resulting in a comparatively long recovery time, in a woman each orgasm is followed by an almost immediate refilling of the erectile chambers. This subsequent engorgement is in no way diminished from the first and produces even more arousal in the tissues. Consequently, the more orgasms a woman has, Sherfey wrote, 'the stronger they become; the more orgasms she has, the more she *can* have. *To all intents and purposes, the human female is sexually insatiable. . . .*'" (The emphasis is Sherfey's.)

It's a staggering thought for straight men: No woman can ever— *ever*—be truly satisfied by just one man. Ever, ever, ever. That may be overstating it a little. One man could conceivably satisfy one woman—provided he's willing to bring her a dozen or more or-

gasms *before* he enjoys his one comparatively pathetic and brief little orgasm. Or, if he comes too soon, he may be able to satisfy her
if he's willing to continue stimulating her with his tongue and fingers—or her vibrator—until he's ready to go again. And again and
again and again. (Straight guys can say what they like about male
homosexuality but, hey, at least I can roll over and go to sleep with
a clear conscience after my partner has one orgasm.)

While most women are, as Sherfey wrote, "unaware of the extent of [their] orgasmic capacity," the same can't be said of women
in the lifestyle. Like Bridget, most women attend their first swing
events at the request of their husbands. And many of these women
soon discover that it's female sexuality, not male sexuality, that finds
its ultimate expression at swing clubs. Which may explain why, as
Gould points out (and Bridget concurred), husbands may bring
wives to their first party but it's wives who drag husbands back
again and again.

So what's in it for the husbands? The wives in swinging couples
get multiple partners and an evening of orgasms too numerous to
count. Beyond the obvious (and not insignificant) perks of variety
and novelty, why would a man want to watch other men bring his
wife to orgasm after orgasm? Especially when he can have only one
himself?

Sperm competition.

Back to the science of swinging: Males of a primate species have
large testicles if other males are mating at the same time with the
same females. Gorillas, to take one example, live in cohesive
groups comprising one adult male, two to three adult females, and
their offspring. When a gorilla female is ready to mate, normally
only one adult male is there as a partner. Since one alpha male mo-
nopolizes all the females, the four-hundred-pound male gorilla has
relatively tiny testes (relative to his body size), *because his sperm
doesn't have to compete with the sperm of other males.*

Compared to gorillas, chimps live in more loosely structured social groups, with a lot of males and females, and when a female

chimp is in heat, she typically mates with every male in her group—and some sneak off at night to mate with males in other groups. And she does all this mating in a twenty-four-hour period. So there's an awful lot of sperm sloshing around inside her the next day, all of it racing to get to her one egg. The male with the biggest testicles produces the most sperm, making his sperm the likeliest to win the competition, fertilize the egg, and pass his genes—including the one for big balls—on to the next generation of chimps.

So how do the testicles of *Homo sapiens* measure up? The balls of the human male are larger compared to our body size than they would be if *Homo sapiens* had evolved with some expectation of female faithfulness. The size of our balls tells us that human sperm, unlike gorilla sperm, evolved to compete with the sperm of other males, presumably in the vaginal canal. The balls of human males aren't as big as the balls of male chimps—relative to our respective sizes—because female humans don't fuck around as much as female chimps. But human females were still designed for fucking around.

But what's in swinging for men? Researchers have discovered that human males are programmed to ejaculate more sperm when they know or suspect that their female partners have recently been with other males. To ejaculate more sperm, males have longer-lasting, more intense orgasms. Gould calls it "sperm competition syndrome," and in most men it's a subconscious response to a long absence or a suspected infidelity. When a husband returns from a business trip (or the wife returns), the husband is anxious to make love to his wife. Sure, absence makes the heart grow fonder. But absence also triggers a physiological response, an evolutionary stratagem, that prompts the man to have sex with "his" woman. His body assumes her body has some other male's semen in it. He may think he wants to have sex with his wife right away because he's happy to see her, but his body wants to have sex right away because it wants to "flood out" the semen of any other males who mated with his woman while he was away.

At a swingers' party, where no one is in competition for the affections and loyalty of his spouse, the men are free to enjoy the feeling of sperm competition without having the abandonment worries that usually accompany an infidelity. In other words, Gould writes, men subconsciously cultivate and savor the longer, more intense orgasms induced by the sperm-competition response. In *The Lifestyle* and other writings about swingers, husbands are described as literally beaming as they wait their turn to mount their wives—their naturally insatiable wives—while their wives have sex with one, two, three or more men. Then the husbands mount their wives for one long-lasting, mind-blowing, ultraintense orgasm. And then he goes to sleep. Or, if the husband had an orgasm with someone else's wife, when he gets his wife home from the party or early the next morning he wakes up and has a mind-blowing sperm competition orgasm, his body instinctively attempting to flood out the other men's sperm. (No sperm, I should note, is actually left in his wife. Swingers are strict about sexual safety, so men wear condoms without question or complaint. Also, not every couple who attends swingers parties and conventions has intercourse. Some couples come to enjoy the sexually charged environment, and some limit their sexual play with others to masturbation or oral sex, reserving intercourse for their spouses.)

So while many straight men might think swinging husbands have to be crazy to share "their" wives with other men, these husbands may actually be the sanest and most rational men around. Aware that he can never completely satisfy his wife—no man can—the swinging husband enlists the services of other men he can trust in getting the job done. It's like a bunch of Amish guys getting together to build a barn.

While Bennett acknowledges that monogamy isn't natural—and he deserves nothing but praise for his honesty—he fails to draw the obvious conclusion: Only fools would build marriages with monogamy as their foundation (and only a foolish society would demand such behavior). Instead Bennett recommends men and women do the *unnatural* thing: "If we hope to preserve the humanly ennobling qualities associated with marriage and family life—monogamy, lifetime commitment, child-centeredness—we have to be prepared to repel assaults, including those mounted under the banner of 'nature.' " To make marriage stronger, Bennett would have married men and women engage in a lifelong battle against their own sexualities. (I expect Bennett to leap to his feet in my defense the next time someone condemns homosexuality for being "unnatural." If unnatural is good enough for straight, then, godammit, unnatural is good enough for me!) Lust is a powerful and, at times, irresistible force in our lives. To make the survival of a marriage hang on the ability of both husband and wife to control their natural, lustful, extramarital urges for decades seems foolish in the extreme.

Before I go any further I want to say that I'm a fan of marriage. I would like very much to get married myself, which Bennett would object to, but if anything I've written in this chapter gives Bill Bennett a nosebleed, it will probably be this: I consider myself a conservative when it comes to marriage. I agree with Bennett when he says that divorce is too easy to obtain; I agree that some couples get divorced for selfish reasons; I think couples should be encouraged to stay together for the kids; and I know from personal experience just how painful divorce is for all involved. I think marriage is so important that no one should rush into it—and so important that no one should rush out, either. I also believe that children are better off with two married parents in the house. (That's why I would marry my son's other father, if that option were open to us.)

And it's precisely because I'm conservative on this issue that I believe we need to take a more realistic—and relaxed—attitude towards lust and adultery.

We conservatives are supposed to be the realists, right? It's those liberals who are dreamy idealists, always trying to "improve people." So my fundamental conservatism compels me to point out that putting monogamy first—"monogamy, lifetime commitment, child-centeredness"—undermines and destabilizes more marriages than it saves. Adultery "touches" 80 percent of all marriages; married people lust after people who aren't their spouses because that's how our creator made us. We're wired to cheat, we're tempted by thoughts of cheating when we're awake, and we dream about cheating when we're asleep. Hell, we think about cheating while we're having sex with our *spouses*. And in almost every marriage, the husband or the wife—*or both*—eventually cheats.

As that's the case, telling people that monogamy comes first—making adultery the ultimate betrayal—sets millions of serviceable, salvageable marriages up for failure. Any true conservative would, I believe, prepare people for marriages as they are, not as we would like them to be, and should help people construct their relationships in such a way that they routinely survive routine adulteries. If adultery touches 80 percent of marriages, then we shouldn't encourage people to harbor unrealistic expectations of lifelong fidelity. Nor should we encourage people to view adultery as a marriage-ending betrayal, a violation so severe that the wronged party can only regain his or her self-respect by divorcing the cheating (son of a) bitch. Instead, conservatives should encourage people to regard adultery as perhaps sad and, yes, a betrayal, but a common sort of betrayal, one that's natural, understandable, and one that any decent relationship should be able to survive.

In his chapter on the state of marriage, Bennett identifies unrealistic expectations as one of the challenges we pro-marriage conservatives face. "Pastoral counselors tell me of a recurring problem they confront: extremely high, unrealistically high, expectations surrounding marriage and family life." My point exactly, only Bennett is one of the people pumping up unrealistic expectations, promoting the idea that monogamy, something we humans aren't very good at, is a rock on which we should build marriage and family life.

My hard-assed, realistic, soft-on-adultery position is deeply conservative because it takes people how they are (or how they evolved) and not how they ideally should be. To make a behavior humans did not evolve to be very skilled at the foundation and cornerstone of an institution as important as marriage is unwise in the extreme. Yet in *The Broken Hearth,* Bennett thoughtlessly suggests that some marriages "ought to end in divorce," as they are "irretrievably broken, destroyed by infidelity . . ." But if adultery is common and divorce is undesirable, then no man who calls himself a conservative should endorse the idea that a marriage ought not survive an infidelity. The true conservative would encourage couples to regard adultery as an unfortunate event that can be endured and forgiven. Or, as David and Bridget demonstrate, celebrated.

As things stand now, we've made the survival of a marriage contingent upon the ability of one man and one woman to do something neither evolved to do and consequently aren't very good at—and, thanks to our ever-expanding life expectancies, we ask them to keep it up for forty, fifty, or sixty years! And if either slips up—just once—we tell both that the marriage is over. This is madness. It's like telling couples they're only obligated to stay married for as long as they can both breathe underwater. From Jenny "No woman should stay with a man who steps out on her!" Jones to William "Destroyed by infidelity!" Bennett, our culture practically orders the cheated-on spouse to call his or her lawyer. We encourage naturally nonmonogamous human beings to view divorce as the only way to salvage their dignity and self-respect if (or when) their partners cheat and then we wonder why the divorce rate is so high.

I'm not advocating that conservatives like me run around telling people that adultery is no big deal. Adultery *is* a big deal, particularly when someone has promised to be faithful. (Yes, everyone who gets married promises to be faithful—they also promise to love, honor, and obey, but we don't tell people they should call their lawyer the first time the spouse dishonors or disobeys.) So by all means let's tell people that adultery is a big deal. But let's add that a good, solid marriage can survive an isolated adulterous incident. Better yet, let's tell people that we *expect* marriages to survive an isolated adulterous incident.

I realize that even suggesting that a marriage be flexible enough to accommodate a little adultery now and then is heretical in the extreme. (I fully expect *Oprah's* Dr. Phil to kick my ass if we ever bump into each other in an airport.) But what choice do we have? People cheat—people evolved to cheat, and people are going to go right on cheating despite Bill Bennett's best efforts to stop us. There's a right way to commit adultery (with your partner's permission, in your partner's presence), and there's a wrong way to commit adultery (behind your partner's back, in front of the international press). To reduce the harm of divorce, we should promote more realistic attitudes towards adultery. Otherwise we're going to go on seeing lots of perfectly good, perfectly stable, perfectly serviceable marriages end because we've convinced ourselves that they must. In this case, a little heresy might save more than a few marriages.

But won't tolerating adultery undermine marriages? After all, if we tolerated adultery, more people will commit adultery, right?

It's the old if-you-make-getting-high-legal-everyone-will-want-to-get-high argument applied to sex. But in the same way that not everyone wants to get high, not everyone wants to cheat. And with half of men and a third of women already cheating, well, it hardly seems like our current attitude towards adultery is restraining very many people. People are already committing adultery. They're just committing it in a culture that tells them the desire to do so means their marriages are a sham and tells their spouses that divorce is the only answer. Even in a culture that tolerated some amount of adultery, most individual couples would still regard it as a big issue and, absent an understanding, deeply problematic. But if we want to preserve marriages, we shouldn't encourage them to regard it as automatic grounds for divorce.

Allowing for outside sex under certain circumstances is not the same thing as allowing for outside sex under any and all circumstances. Being nonmonogamous is not the same thing as being out of control. And if a couple sets strict limits governing outside sex (only on other continents, only at swing clubs, only Russell Crowe), just knowing that there are circumstances that might come together that would allow you, at some point in the future, to have sex with someone else would go a long way towards alleviating one element of lifelong monogamous commitments that is rarely discussed: Despair.

I'm not advocating that all married couples become swingers. Although that works for David and Bridget and other playcouples, the lifestyle isn't for everyone. Indeed, I find the gay version of the lifestyle—gay bathhouses—revolting. Heaps of people on mattresses, all male or of mixed genders, just doesn't do it for me. Group sex is a minority taste and always will be—it's even something of a minority taste among swingers. Many couples involved in swinging prefer to make connections with one other couple and head for a private room.

But it's time to admit the obvious: Lust can't be contained in the box we've built for it. How many times are we going to watch someone come tumbling out of the box—Bill Clinton, Meg Ryan, Jesse Jackson, Newt Gingrich, Henry Hyde—before we stop condemning the men and women falling out of the box and reexamine the size and shape of the box itself? I'm not in favor of a world without boxes—it's just clear that men and women need a slightly bigger box, one with a little more room to maneuver, one in which there's more than one "understanding" that a loving, committed, child-centered couple can come to.

SLOTH

I Am Not a Pothead

My kid doesn't smoke pot. He's either at school, soccer practice, piano lessons, or at a friend's house. —Smiling, middle-class mother in a Partnership for a Drug-Free America ad

I usually get stoned at school, after soccer practice, before piano lessons, or at my friend's house. —Her smiling, middle-class kid, in the same ad

A lengthy chapter devoted to sloth, one that was thorough and exhaustively researched, would surely violate the spirit of this project. Sloth is a sin that makes few demands on the sinner (do nothing and you've mastered it), and it was my stated intention to indulge myself in each of the seven deadly sins. I'm tempted to end this chapter right here, declare victory, and move on to my next sin—but I was raised a good Catholic boy, and I feel guilty if I don't do what I'm supposed to do, especially if I'm getting paid.

According to the *American Heritage Dictionary*, sloth is "an aversion to work or exertion; laziness; indolence." To the monks, saints, and popes who pulled the list of seven deadly sins together, sloth was primarily seen as spiritual sloth, a weakness of faith, rather than general laziness. (The most popular medieval example of sloth is the cleric who is negligent in performing his duties.) Being spiritually slothful, according to Saint Augustine, left a person open to temptation. (Nowadays, of course, giving into consumerist temptation is believed to be our solemn duty as patriotic American consumers—thanks, Osama!) In its most dire form, sloth becomes despair: the belief that you're so steeped in sin that it's impossible to get back on God's good side.

In some significant ways, modern, secular sloth—simple laziness—is unique among the seven deadly sins. Unlike pride, anger, envy, lust, and greed, a person can be slothful without doing or feeling much of anything. Someone who acts on her anger is usually acutely aware of her emotional state: she's been swept away by powerful feelings she can't control. Someone who gives himself over to lust is usually aware that he has an erection. In contrast, it's possible for someone to be unwittingly, blissfully slothful. The slothful person can be lazy and unproductive without feeling any particularly acute emotions; the slothful person may be too lazy for serious introspection, and be unaware that he's even being slothful. And unlike gluttony, the only sin that requires action (you have to feed your face, not just want to feed your face), a person can be slothful without doing anything. And since sleep is the purest expression of sloth, it's the only deadly sin that we can commit while unconscious.

Lust and gluttony, as I pointed out in the first chapters, were considered "natural" sins, since people have to do a certain amount of fucking and eating in order survive. Sloth should also be considered a natural sin, a sin that is both necessary and desirable.

Here's how sloth is necessary: While some of us can get through a twenty-four-hour day without feeling greedy or angry or envious or lustful, only speed freaks can get through twenty-four hours without a little downtime. Human beings need sleep; we also need to stare off into space, look out the window, daydream, pick our noses, surf the Net, and spend some time every day being indolent and useless. When we work too much and sloth too little, humans get physically sick. By contrast, no one ever got sick from too little envy or too little greed.

Sloth is desirable because it's scarce, as scarcity creates desire. While we all want more sleep and longer vacations, very few of us are in a position to have either. In a consumer culture, the scarcity of something is directly related to its desirability. The rarer something is, the more status accrues to the person who possesses it. And unless you happen to be the forty-third president of the United States of America, who before September 11, 2001, had spent 40 percent of his time in office on vacation (including the entire month of August[1]), you probably haven't had much time away from work in the last decade or so. In a survey conducted in 2001 (after our current economic downturn began), 20 percent of Americans said they never went on vacations, 33 percent had too much work to take any time off, and 11 percent were worried that, if they did take a vacation, they would lose their jobs. This survey was conducted before thousands of people were laid off in the wake of September 11; no doubt the numbers of people who won't or can't take a vacation for fear of losing their jobs is higher today.

A recent United Nations report found that Americans work harder and longer hours than the citizens of any other industrialized nation. According to the UN's International Labor Organization (ILO), our lead over Japanese workers, who were once the hardest-working people on the planet, grew by nearly a full week during the 1990s. The average American worked 49½ weeks in the year 2000, 6½ more weeks per year than British workers, 3½ more weeks per year than Japanese workers, 12½ more weeks per year than German workers. (Who won that war again?)

"It's unique to Americans that they continue to increase their working hours, while hours are declining in other industrialized nations," Lawrence Jeff Johnson, an economist with the ILO, told

---

1. Can you imagine the howls from right-wing nutcases had Bill Clinton spent the entire month of August on vacation and then terrorists attacked the United States in early September? Especially if Clinton had been warned *during* that vacation that Osama bin Laden was planning to hijak American planes inside the United States. Far from rallying around "our president," right wingers would've seized on the tragedy as another chance to force Clinton from office. Clinton would've been accused of goofing off when he clearly should've been hunkered down in the Oval Office. And if Clinton made the missteps Bush did in the days immediately after the attack (running, hiding, mumbling, stumbling, sending his press secretary out to lie about "credible threats" directed against Air Force One), Ann Coulter would've spontaneously combusted—boom!—right there on *Politically Incorrect.*

the *New York Times*. "It has a lot to do with the American psyche, with American culture. American workers are eager to make the best impression, to put in the most hours."

While it may be true that some workers put in longer hours to make the best impression on their employers, labor organizers have documented hundreds of cases in which management simply refused to schedule vacations for employees who requested time off that they had coming. And let's not forget the "working poor." Companies that don't pay living wages or provide health-care benefits certainly don't give their employees paid vacation days. The problem of an overworked, underslothed America is likely to get worse: again, in the aftermath of September 11, hundreds of thousands of workers were laid off all over the country. People who fear losing their jobs are unlikely to ask for time off—no matter how often George W. Bush exhorts Americans, as he did during a press conference, "to fly and enjoy America's great . . . uh . . . destination spots."

Perhaps more Americans would take their kids to Disney World, Mr. President, if American workers were entitled to as many paid vacation days as workers in other industrialized nations. While the average American worker earns a measly thirteen paid vacation days per year (and not everyone who earns 'em takes 'em), the average worker in Japan or Korea gets twenty-five paid vacation days per year. Canadian workers get twenty-six paid vacation days; British workers get twenty-eight; Brazilian workers get thirty-four; German workers get thirty-five; and French workers get thirty-seven.[2] The European Working Time Directive mandates four weeks of paid vacation every year, and a maximum forty-eight-hour workweek. In France, workers are obliged by law not to put in more than thirty-five hours of work per week.

In addition to being the most overworked people on the planet, Americans are also the most productive—clear evidence that, how-

2. Maybe George W. Bush thinks he's the president of France?

ever overworked and stressed-out we are, very few Americans are slacking off at work. Indeed, 32 percent of American workers eat lunch and work simultaneously; 32 percent of us never leave the building once we arrive at work; and 18 percent say that they can't use the vacation days they've got coming because they're simply too busy. Which may be why the ILO ranked the American Worker first in productivity. Productivity per American worker in constant 1990 dollars was $54,870 in 2000, $1,500 more per year than Belgium, the number-two nation. According to the ILO, productivity per worker in the United States was $10,000 higher than in Canada last year and $14,000 higher than in Japan. So while we may be stressed-out and exhausted and chained to our desks and cheated out of the few vacation days we've got coming, hey, at least we're number one.

How do we do it? How do Americans take shorter vacations or none at all, work longer hours, work harder, and produce more, all with no time for restorative, restful sloth? How do Americans (excluding President George W. Bush[3]) manage to survive without monthlong vacations?

Well, like that poor, stressed-out kid in the Partnership for a Drug-Free America ad, a lot of us smoke pot.

I want the American people in general, and my mother in particular, to hear this. I'm only going to type it once: I am not a pothead.

But I do smoke pot. Sometimes. Occasionally. Cautiously.

Many of us who don't fit the pot-smoking stereotype are reluctant to be open about our pot use; we don't want people to think we're irresponsible potheads. But so long as only white college kids with hemp T-shirts are willing to admit to smoking pot, well, then the public image of pot smokers will never improve. Like swingers who won't come out to their families, friends, and neighbors, the

3. Footnotes are fun, aren't they?

silence of pot smokers like me perpetuates the stereotypes about pot smokers and keeps the War on Drugs roaring. So I'm going to risk telling the truth: I am a pot smoker—and I don't fit the stereo-type. I don't wear hemp; I don't have dreads; I don't think deodor-ant is a bourgeois plot; I don't smoke pot on a daily basis; I don't have glaucoma; and I didn't vote for Ralph Nader. And unlike most people who've "experimented" with pot, I didn't start in my teens. I didn't smoke pot for the first time until I was in my thirties. And, finally, I don't even smoke that much pot.

This is how I'd describe my pot use: Every once in a very, very great while, when my son is spending the night with his grandpar-ents or sleeping over at a friend's house, my boyfriend and I rent some videos, lay in some chips, and obtain one—just one—measly little joint from someone who is forever in our debt, at least where pot is concerned. (More on that in a moment.) We put in a video, crawl into bed with our joint and our bags of chips, and we get really, really baked, and attempt to watch a movie. *We do this once or twice a year.* Did I say I don't smoke pot daily? It would be more accurate to say that I sometimes don't get around to smoking pot semiannually. In between our very rare pot nights, my boyfriend and I don't smoke pot, buy pot, grow pot, and we don't keep pot in our home.

Well, that's not entirely accurate. We were recently keeping a huge amount of pot in our home. You see, Officer, when our wash-ing machine broke down, my boyfriend took our dirty clothes to a Laundromat. When he pulled our clothes out of the washing ma-chine, everything was covered with what looked like oregano. But it wasn't oregano—it never is oregano, is it? Apparently, the hippie who used the washing machine before my boyfriend had left a huge bag of pot in his clothes. His huge bag of pot must have fallen out of whatever pocket it was in, and the hippie left his huge bag of pot in the washing machine. My boyfriend came along and put our clothes in the washing machine with the hippie's huge bag of pot. When our clothes were being washed, the huge bag of pot opened up and pot got all over our clothes. After my boyfriend pulled our clothes out of the washing machine and discovered they were covered with what looked like oregano, he launched an investigation into the oregano's source. That's when he found the huge bag of pot in the washing machine.

A woman was waiting to use the washing machine after my boyfriend, which presented him with a quandary: If he left the huge bag of pot in the washing machine, the woman would find it and think it was *his* huge bag of pot. He didn't want this woman— or anyone—to think he was the kind of person who owned a huge bag of pot, so my boyfriend put the huge bag of pot in our laundry basket and brought it home. Which meant, of course, that to prevent some woman from thinking he was the kind of person who owned a huge bag of pot, we were now, problematically enough, the proud owners of a huge bag of pot.

When we weighed our huge bag of pot we discovered to our horror that it was heavier than a Quarter Pounder with Cheese. Twice as heavy. (It was still damp when we weighed it, *but it was still a huge bag of pot.*) We figured that it would take us about twenty-five years to life to smoke all the pot in the bag my boyfriend brought home. In the meantime, of course, drug-sniffing dogs three counties over would be howling in the direction of our house, and if the police ever found this huge bag of pot in our house, well, we'd look like a couple of drug lords. Since we would never be able to smoke all of this pot, and since we couldn't risk keeping it in the house, we decided to give the huge bag of pot away—that's right, Officer, we *gave* it away. We didn't *sell* it. Selling a huge bag of pot would be *wrong*. It might even be illegal. So we found a loving home for our huge bag of pot, one where it wouldn't last twenty days. And when I handed the huge bag of damp pot over to a friend who smokes more dope than a DEA incinerator, he shook my hand and told me he would be forever in my debt. And once or twice a year, when my son is at his grandparents' or sleeping over at a friend's house, I call the incinerator and remind him that, as time has not ended, he is still in my debt.

According to the National Household Survey on Drug Abuse, 20 million Americans use marijuana at least once a year, 6 million use it at least once a week, and 3 million Americans smoke marijuana daily. The Household Survey put current national consumption of marijuana at 7 to 10 million joints *per day,* or 1,200 to 1,800 metric tons per year. These figures may be low, since most researchers believe the Household Survey underestimated actual drug use. ("Hello, I'm from the government. How much dope are you guys smoking lately?") Other attempts to measure American consumption of marijuana put the figure anywhere from 2,700 metric tons to 4,700 metric tons. To put these figures in some sort of perspective, a metric ton is 2,204.6 pounds; 4,700 metric tons is 10,361,620 pounds of pot, or roughly 46,000 Oprahs. The street value of a pound of pot is about $5,000, so 10,361,620 pounds of pot represents an annual gross sales of $51 billion.

Americans smoke more pot than the citizens of any other industrialized nation: 7.2 percent of U.S. population regularly smokes pot, compared with 5.4 percent in Europe and 2.1 percent in Asia. Marijuana is the fourth largest cash crop in the United States, behind corn, soybeans, and hay. It's the biggest cash crop in Alabama, California, Connecticut, Hawaii, Kentucky, Maine, Rhode Island, Tennessee, Virginia, and West Virginia. Which may explain why drug warriors haven't proposed spraying toxic defoliants or funding right-wing death squads in an effort to "cut off" the supply of pot to American consumers. (Defoliants and death squads are integral aspects of Plan Colombia, our federal government's effort to halt the cultivation of coca in that miserable South American country. Somehow what's good for Colombia isn't good for Oregon or Alabama. Perhaps Colombia would come in for gentler treatment if it had a congressional delegation and a handful of votes in the electoral college.) Despite a decades-long drug war, billions spent to fight marijuana cultivation, and thousands of Americans tossed in prison for marijuana possession, "marijuana is the most commonly used illicit drug in America today and is readily available throughout all metropolitan, suburban, and rural areas of the continental United States," according to the U.S. Department of Justice.

If the sale of pot were legalized in the United States today—and strictly regulated, like other widely available and infinitely more destructive mood-altering substances (cigarettes, alcohol, cable)—the federal government might be able to fund a new round of tax breaks for the wealthy. (Think about it, George.) Here's another attractive aspect to marijuana legalization for right wingers: Legalization would take the immensely profitable marijuana business out of the hands of urban African Americans, Hispanics, and poor whites—the folks who deal and distribute marijuana—and put it in the hands of huge multinational corporations controlled by white men in suits.

According to a Substance Abuse and Mental Health Services Administration study, 33 percent of all Americans have used pot; other estimates range as high as 60 percent—which means more Americans have used pot than voted for George W. Bush. Again, "official" counts of American pot smokers are believed to be low; I personally don't recall anyone from the government asking me if I smoke dope. (And wouldn't most Americans, if asked about smoking pot, lie to the government *since the government is in the habit of arresting pot smokers?*[4]) And yet despite all the dope we're smoking,

---

4. In 2000, the number of Americans arrested for pot-related charges was 734,498; most were arrested for possession, not dealing. Canada and Great Britain, meanwhile, are well on their way to decriminalizing marijuana use, medical and otherwise. A sane person might think that, in the wake of September 11, the federal government would have better things to do than go after pot smokers. After all, we have a real war on our hands now, against a real enemy. Maybe it was time to call off the fake war against American citizens who smoke pot? The Bush administration, however, began cracking down on pot smokers the month *after* September 11, raiding the suppliers of medical marijuana in states that passed medical marijuana initiatives. Didn't George W. Bush run partly on a state's rights platform?

Americans are the most productive, hardest-working people on the planet. We may be higher than the workers in every other industrialized nation, but we work longer hours, we take fewer vacations, and we produce more than the better-rested, better-paid, and less-stoned workers in other industrialized nations.

Bear that in mind.

One common argument against drug legalization—a highly controversial move that would make it more difficult for many Americans to buy recreational drugs—is that drug use negatively impacts the productivity of American workers. Drug warriors claim that productivity loss attributable to pot smoking alone costs American businesses $100 billion a year. That's one hundred *billion,* with a *b*—and what a nice round number it is. One hundred billion. $100,000,000,000. So many zeros, all in a neat little row. The number is so round and so large, in fact, that it immediately makes any thinking person suspicious and every pot smoker paranoid.

As an admitted semiannual pot smoker, I have an obvious pro-pot bias. (This admission has dashed my childhood dream of obtaining a haz-mat trucking license.) Nevertheless, it seems impossible to me that all three of the following things can be true: (1) American workers smoke *more* pot than the workers in any other industrialized nation. (2) Pot use has an *enormous* negative impact on the productivity of the American worker, to the tune of $100 billion every year. (3) American workers are the *most productive workers on the goddamned planet.* How can we be the most productive workers *and* the highest workers if pot smoking is so harmful to our productivity? And even if all the pot smokers in the United States stopped smoking dope tomorrow (think of all the family farmers in Oregon that would put out of business), how much more productive can the American worker possibly be? Barring an act of God, there is a limit to the number of hours in the day, the number of days in the week, the number of weeks in the year.

Since we know that the first two premises are facts—we smoke more, we're more productive—I think it's clear that federal drug warriors pulled that $100 billion figure out of their asses. So what impact does pot have on job performance? Very little, I should think, since the vast majority of pot smokers, like the vast majority of beer drinkers, are only interested in indulging themselves after work. They're called recreational drugs for a reason—to wit, most people who use them do so when they're recreating, not working. Drug warriors don't want to talk about pot smokers who want to indulge at home, since most Americans believe that what people do when they're not at work isn't anyone's business. Whenever legalizing marijuana is discussed, drug warriors raise the specter of people smoking pot at work, calling to mind terrifying images of stoned surgeons and airline pilots. It's a bullshit, let's-change-the-subject nonargument: very few pot smokers believe people should get high at work—or drunk at work, for that matter. That some people get drunk and go to work is not held up as a reason to prohibit the sale and consumption of alcohol. (And arguing against legalizing pot because some people get high at work presupposes that pot's illegality is somehow keeping it out of the hands of people who get high at work. Pot is currently illegal and widely available; anyone who wants to get high and go to work is doing so already. Just take a look at your local barista, CD-store employee, and pizza delivery driver.)

Having come out boldly against stoned people performing surgery and flying airplanes, I feel obligated to note that while the federal government hasn't funded many studies looking into the effects of marijuana on job performance, what little research has been done was inconclusive. Researchers who attempted to measure pot's impact on job performance have found that people have a hard time performing sequential addition/subtraction problems while high. Addition and subtraction is not a task many of us perform at work, but clearly CPAs should not smoke dope on the job. Researchers have also found that some people have difficulty judging distances and difficulty with visual tracking while high. Finally, researchers have found that pot smokers are able to "suppress the marijuana high" when they need to, which may be why studies that dealt directly with actual job performance while high have shown no—repeat, *no*—difference between people who are high and people who are not high.

If I were a pot fanatic, I would point to this last bit of data and insist that people should be able to get high at work; a pot fanatic might argue that a high surgeon doing a quadruple bypass should be able to "suppress the marijuana high" long enough to close up your chest. My personal experiences with marijuana, however, prevent me from making that argument. In research conducted on myself, I've documented that I'm not a very productive person when I'm high. This might have something to do with how late in life I began "experimenting" with marijuana, or how infrequently I use the drug. While the vast majority of my fellow pot-smoking Americans began experimenting with dope when they were teenagers, I didn't smoke dope for the first time until I was thirty-two years old. My late start coupled with the infrequency of my indulgence has kept my tolerance for pot low; one or two puffs, and I'm pretty much useless. I'm one of those pot smokers who gets lost on the way to the bathroom, so I'm no more comfortable with the idea of high pilots or surgeons than the average drug czar.

When discussing pot and productivity, at some point it has to be acknowledged that pot smokers make easily verifiable contributions to our legitimate economy. First, most of us are employed, we pay taxes, and we stay out of trouble. Pot smokers also support the small farms in places like Alabama, West Virginia, and Kentucky that grow and sell pot. Finally, let's not forget the snack food industry. According to PepsiCo's 2000 Annual Report, the company sold $1,782,000,000 worth of Doritos in the United States and Canada that year. You don't have to be high to eat a bag Doritos, I realize, but it helps. State and local governments take in tens of millions of dollars every year in Doritos-related sales tax, while the more than 45,000 people employed by PepsiCo to make and distribute Doritos pay income taxes to the federal government. It seems to me an appalling act of ingratitude for the federal government to use money collected from PepsiCo's employees to jail some of PepsiCo's best customers.

I'd like to take a moment here to reassure my mother. I don't hang out with a lot of dope smokers, Mom, nor do I see myself as a member of a dope-smoking underground, subculture, or community. I don't even like Doritos that much. I'm just a regular, working parent who smokes dope from time to time. I suppose I could have played it safe and found some other pot smoker to profile in this chapter, but I felt that it would be dishonest to write about pot smoking without coming clean about my own pot use. Furthermore, profiling myself was the slothful thing to do—I didn't have to leave the house to find a pot smoker, and I was always available for interviews.

Though I don't count myself a wild-eyed marijuana booster, I am, however, grateful to *High Times* readers and hemp wearers for ensuring the continued supply of dope in this country, and its constantly improving quality. Even so, you're never going to see me in a marijuana leaf T-shirt, Mom, I swear to God.

Now I'd like to go one step further and argue that pot not only doesn't have a negative impact on the productivity of the American worker, but that pot also makes it possible for the American worker—the pot-smoking ones, at least—to be as productive as we are.

While the workweek shrinks and vacation time grows for European workers, the amount of time Americans spend at work continues to grow (at least for those of us who have jobs). How do we do it? How do we work like crazy without going crazy? I think pot has a lot to do with it. It's a just hunch, I'll admit, and since I'm not a drug czar, I don't expect the things I say to be taken at face value. Unlike William J. Bennett, Gen. Barry McCaffrey, or our current drug czar, John Walters, I don't think every fool thing that pops into my head is God's revealed truth. So I'm eager for social scientists and researchers to look into my theory, and if they can prove that I'm wrong, I will do something very unlike a drug czar (or Bill O'Reilly) and *admit* that I'm wrong. Until someone provides me with proof, however, I will go on believing that smoking pot isn't a $100 billion-per-year threat to American productivity—indeed, pot is one of the chief pillars of American productivity.

Like other American workers, I've worked fifty-two weeks per year, year in, year out, for the last decade. Since 1991, I've worked ten- and twelve-hour days, nonstop. I work at work, I work at home, I work on weekends, I work at night, I work during my commute. When I have to travel for work, I work on planes, I work in hotel rooms, and I work in cafés, bars, and restaurants. (I'm typing these words in a coffee shop in Chicago filled with other people working on their laptops.) Work, work, work, all I do is work. There's no time in my life for restful, restorative sloth, no time to stare off into space or let my mind wander. I haven't been indolent since the first President George Bush was in office, and looking ahead, I don't see much downtime coming my way. How can I live without sloth and retain my sanity? How can I, like other American workers, be so ridiculously productive? How can I work this hard and without snapping and, for example, beating to death the man sitting next to me in this café yakking into his cell phone about his hair transplants and dinner reservations?

I smoke pot.

Research has shown—actual scientific *research,* not I'm-the-drug-czar-and-I-said-so fairy tales—that marijuana interferes with a pot smoker's ability to judge correctly the passage of time. The active ingredient in pot, THC, enters the bloodstream through the millions of alveoli in the lungs. THC mimics the actions of a naturally occurring neurotransmitter called anandamide, which binds with certain receptors in the brain, filling the gaps between synapses. The synapses affected by THC in the hippocampus, a thumb-shaped lobe under the pituitary gland, *interfere with the normal function of short-term memory.* In other words, pot slows stuff

down—way, way down. The better the pot, the slower time seems
to pass, and the potency of pot has greatly increased in the last
twenty-five years. Thirty years ago, people were smoking *Cannabis
sativa,* with a THC content of 0.5 to 2.0 percent. The pot we smoke
now is *Cannabis indica,* which has a THC content of 8 to 10 percent. Why the switch? More potent pot facilitates smuggling and
transportation; the stronger the stuff is, the less of it has to be
moved from place to place, and the more you can charge for it. Potent pot is better for pot smokers, too, since we don't have to
smoke as much to get high. (Smoking is bad for you, you know.)
When you're high, five minutes feels like a lazy afternoon, and six
hours feels like a week at the beach. The morning after one of my
infrequent pot nights, I wake up feeling like I just got back from a
week's vacation. I'm rested, content, and ready—ready to go back
to work and kill myself. Pot gives me biannual, concentrated doses
of restful, restorative, fattening sloth. Thanks to THC's ability to
slow down the passage of time, pot is as close as many pot-
smoking American workers ever get to a week off. Two nights high
= two weeks off. Three nights = three weeks off. Four nights high
and, hey, *you're the fucking president of France.*

I would estimate that millions of American workers (perhaps
even as many as 100 billion) would love nothing more than a
month of paid vacation or, at the very least, the two weeks' paid vacation they have coming to them. But no one gets a month off in
George W. Bush's America—no one except George W. Bush. So
overworked, underslothed Americans take a month off the only
way they can get it: one puff at a time. Millions of Americans who
can't get away from work physically get away pharmacologically.
And if our political leaders want the American worker to remain
the most productive on the planet, well, then perhaps it's time to
can the guilt trips about our drug use and legalize pot.

My sister Laura is a drug-abuse counselor, and I don't doubt
that she's a very good drug-abuse counselor. Laura is opposed to

drug legalization, she says, because she's seen what drugs can do to people. I've pointed out to her on many occasions that drug-abuse counselors only see the bad things drugs do to people, since people who don't have a problem with drugs don't go (or get sent) to drug-abuse counselors. Nevertheless, my sister has an "issue," as drug-abuse counselors like to say, with anyone advocating the use of any drug, even marijuana. My sister has helped a lot of people who have problems with drugs, and I think that's just swell. Really. People who are addicted to drugs—including nicotine and alcohol—need all the help they can get. The problem I have with my sister, though, is that I don't have a problem with drugs and yet my sister insists on trying to help me.

When the subject of my marijuana use comes up at family gatherings, she purses her lips and looks at me with pity in her eyes. "All drug use is abuse, Danny," she usually says, slowly shaking her head.

"Not my drug use," I usually respond. "I don't abuse drugs. I use them. Very occasionally, very responsibly."

"That's what *all* addicts always say," she serves. "They all say, 'I don't *abuse,* I *use.*' And it's *always* a lie."

"It may be a lie when an addict says it," I volley, "but *I'm* not an addict, so it's *not* a lie when *I* say it." (We *abuse* italics in my family; it's a bad habit we picked up from our *mother.*)

Whenever my sister starts to lose the argument about drug legalization, which she always does, she resorts to the I'm-a-drug-abuse-counselor look. She cocks her head to one side, pulls in her chin, purses her lips, and raises her eyebrows. The look says, "Suuuuuuuuure, Danny, you're not a drug addict." I think my sister took three graduate-level seminars to master that sure-you're-not-a-drug-addict look. The look makes me defensive. ("I am *not* an addict! Mom! Tell Laura to *stop* calling me an addict!") That's the whole point of the look: In the batty circular logic of American Twelve Step programs, defensively denying that you're an addict is rock-solid proof that you are, in fact, an addict. Insisting that you have a right to be defensive since you're defending yourself against a charge that isn't true just digs you in deeper. Denying something that isn't true only proves you're in denial, and all addicts are in denial until they admit they're addicts, at which point they're in recovery. Which is where my sister would like to see me.

My sister and I live thousands of miles away from each other, so for all she knows I lie around my house all day long with a needle in my arm, covered in my own excrement, and clean myself up only for the occasional family visit. When I describe to her the circumstances of my pot use—twice a year tops, at home, in bed—she accuses me of minimizing my problem in order to win the argument. If I came clean and told the whole family how much pot I really smoke, then everyone would know what my sister instinctively knows: I'm an addict.

But if I'm an addict, how come I'm able to hold on to my job, meet my various deadlines, and keep up with a strict personal hygiene regimen?

The last time we had this argument, my sister, under pressure from my mother ("Laura, would you *please* tell your brother he's *not* an addict!"), finally conceded that it was possible that I just might not be a drug addict.

"You're still *abusing* drugs," she insisted, "which you get away with because you're what we call a '*highly-functional*' drug abuser."

Which brings us back to the kid in the Partnership for a Drug-Free America ad.

School, piano lessons, soccer practice, that boob of a mother—if that kid didn't have access to marijuana, I would be tempted to buy him a huge bag of pot myself. (The kid and his mother are, I realize, entirely fictional. And honestly, Officer, I would never buy a child a bag of pot. That would be wrong and illegal. And all the stuff in this chapter about me smoking pot? Made it up. Didn't happen. Never touched the stuff. Didn't lick those doorknobs either.) Not satisfied with working herself to death, that kid's parents are working him to death—and he's not alone. Our kids may not be making shoes in Nike sweatshops, but American kids have as little time for sloth as American parents. We march our kids from school to piano lessons to soccer practice to scheduled "play-dates" at the homes of vetted, screened, preapproved "friends." The kid in the ad is as busy as his parents, with just as little time for sloth.

At the end of a day like that—school, piano lessons, soccer practice—that kid deserves a little sloth, doncha think? I'm not in favor of young people smoking pot; like beer, pot is for grown-ups. But if we're going to eliminate sloth from the lives of young people—if we're going to work our kids to death, too—who can blame them for taking sloth in concentrated doses? If this particular kid can get high and keep his grades up and make it to piano lessons and remember which end of the field to kick the soccer ball to and pull the wool over his mother's eyes, then he must be a "highly functional" pot smoker, just like I am.

No one wants to see young people using drugs, of course. I believe that pot, alcohol, cigarettes, caffeine, sex, and air travel are for adults only. I hate walking to my local coffee shop and seeing all the teenagers out front abusing the legal drugs in coffee and cigarettes. But if a kid is going to abuse a substance, however, he's much better off smoking pot than he is drinking beer or smoking cigarettes. Marijuana is less addictive than alcohol and nicotine (and caffeine), and the long-term health consequences of moderate pot use are infinitely less deadly. Fifty thousand people die in the United States every year from alcohol poisoning; four hundred thousand die every year from cigarette-related illnesses. Despite what the Partnership for a Drug-Free America would like us to believe, it's simply impossible to overdose on marijuana. According to *The Lancet,* a European medical journal, "the smoking of cannabis, even long-term, is not harmful to health. . . . It would be reasonable to judge cannabis as less of a threat than alcohol or cigarettes."

Will kids who smoke dope become addicted to pot or other hard drugs? Most likely not. According to the U.S. Institute of Medicine, fewer than one in ten young marijuana smokers become regular users of the drug, and most who do become regular users voluntarily stop using marijuana in their thirties. While pot smoking isn't good for growing lungs and brains, it is clinically proven to reduce feelings of aggression, which is a serious problem among adolescent males in the United States. (Maybe if we called pot *Ritalin,* people would be more comfortable with it.) Personally, I would rather see a stressed-out teenage boy pick up a bong every once in a while than pick up a gun and shoot his parents, teachers, classmates, soccer coach, and piano teacher to death.

One reason we're told we can't legalize pot is because it would send a "mixed message" to kids. I don't understand why we can't tell kids the same thing about pot that we tell them about beer: It's for adults. That might make pot seem like a "forbidden," grown-up pleasure, but I don't see how "for adults only" makes something any more alluringly forbidden than "so much fun it's illegal." Maybe our message to kids should be the facts: Recreational drugs can be hard on your system, they aren't good for growing bodies, and some drugs are infinitely more dangerous than others. Of all the drugs you shouldn't be using—which includes booze—pot is the least dangerous. While we would prefer you not to use drugs while you're young, if you're going to use drugs, please use them in a safe place, don't drive on drugs, and drugs are no excuse for engaging in risky behaviors you wouldn't otherwise perform.

Or we could teach kids that soft drugs like pot, much like booze, is something that can be safely enjoyed in moderation. In an editorial about drinking, the *Wall Street Journal*'s Michael Judge complained about local governments and universities banning happy hours, two-for-ones, and other drink promotions. "The problem," Judge writes, "is that many Americans see boozing as somehow immoral. . . . Studies by the Berkeley Alcohol Research Group and a host of others find that nations that teach children moderation over abstinence, such as France, Spain, and Italy, may have higher overall rates of alcohol consumption, but far lower rates of alcoholism and alcohol-related disease." Encouraging responsible indulgence, Judge concludes, "is a sure way to guard against excess than preaching abstention." Why can't we take—and why isn't the *Wall Street Journal* promoting—the same approach when it comes to pot?

Yes, it might mean delivering the dreaded "mixed message," but the truth is often a mixed message. Right wingers always and left wingers often want all or nothing, black or white, when it's often neither or both. The truth is, not all drugs are created equal, and the mix of different drugs available in American schools requires a mix of messages. Again, I'm not in favor of encouraging kids to use drugs. Kids do use drugs, though, and they're familiar with drugs, and that means messages we send them about drugs must have something to do with reality or the kids will tune them out. Currently the only message virtuecrats want people to give kids is that all drugs are equally bad, equally harmful, and equally deadly. It's a lie, and they're on to us. We've been giving kids this unmixed message for decades, and kids go right on experimenting with drugs, hard and soft. Why? Because kids are likelier to believe their own eyes and their friends than the lies of drug czars (not that kids watch a lot of C-SPAN) and "educators" who've made it their mission to misinform them.

Here's a case in point: cartoonist/illustrator Ellen Forney drew a one-page comic that appeared in *The Stranger,* the weekly newspaper I edit in Seattle, Washington. Her comic, "How D'Ya Smoke Pot and Stay Out of Jail?," was full of tips for potheads from a criminal defense lawyer. Two weeks after the comic appeared in *The Stranger,* a package arrived at our offices for Ellen.

"The 6th Grade students in room 9 at Bow Lake Elementary value the core principles of freedom of speech and press," wrote Jason J. Dodge, a teacher at Bow Lake. "At the same time, we also value productive freedom of press and speech. Interestingly, we ask our children to steer away from things like drugs, alcohol, and other choices that lead to negative experiences. So why, then, do adults write articles informing people how to use drugs without getting caught? My students and I just couldn't figure why some-one would write an article supporting the use of illegal drugs."

Enclosed with Mr. Dodge's letter were more than twenty letters from his sixth-grade students:

"When my teacher showed us your article I was surprised that anybody would write a stupid and useless article," wrote Amy.

"I'm writing this letter because of how to pot smoke and get away with pot smoke. I think about this article that is bad because it is helping people how to pot smoke but I think it is bad to pot smoke," wrote Josh, barely.

"Do you know that drugs can take away 20 or 30 years of your life? Also they can kill you or you can become high and drive and kill other people, and they can become addicted," wrote Nicole.

"You have the right to freedom of the press but you also have the right to remain silence," wrote Artem.

"If you wrote this in a different country, you would get your hands cut off and be sent to jail forever," wrote A Concerned Sixth Grader.

"All people who smoke pot grow up to be criminals. They go to jail," wrote Galib.

"If you had a child in the sixth grade, would you want him/her to read the article you wrote?" wrote Sammy.

Where do I start?

First of all, Ellen Forney didn't give her comic to a room full of children in the sixth grade. Mr. Dodge did. (Now all of them know how to smoke dope without getting caught—good work, Mr. Dodge!) Second, kids say the darnedest things, don't they? Espe-cially when an authority figure is standing at the front of the class-room and orders them to say the darnedest things. Clearly the children in Mr. Dodge's class don't know the first thing about mar-ijuana—the first true thing, I should say. What they do know about marijuana—it shortens your life by twenty years, you'll die, you'll go to jail, you'll be a criminal—is nothing but a bunch of lies drilled into their little heads by Mr. Dodge and police officers from the Drug Awareness Resistance Education (DARE) programs.

Mr. Dodge and DARE may be able to fool a room full of sixth graders into believing that people who "pot smoke" are all criminals who wind up in jail or dead. But what's going to happen to Mr. Dodge's students when they get into high school or college and start meeting other kids and adults who've smoked pot and weren't harmed by it and refuse to "remain silence" in the face of DARE hysteria and scare tactics? I wonder how Mr. Dodge's kids will react to the news that former President Bill Clinton smoked pot. Can you imagine the looks on their little faces when they find out that former Vice President Al Gore smoked pot, as did former Senator Bill Bradley, Supreme Court Justice Clarence Thomas, former House Speaker Newt Gingrich, New York City Mayor Michael Bloomberg, and New York Governor George Pataki? George W. Bush refuses to deny that he ever smoked pot, which strikes the high school students I know as an admission of guilt.

What happens when kids who have been lied to about drugs grow up and discover the truth?

"In junior high, the drug-free group was the place to be," writes Marissa K. Kingen, a freelance writer. "I was an enthusiastic member." When Kingen got to high school she learned that, "the Red Ribbon anti-drug week was a joke, and only stoners wore DARE T-shirts. (Many of our teachers had to look up 'irony' in the dictionary.)" At college, Kingen's eyes were opened to the reality of marijuana. "When you get to college, no matter what college, it's pretty easy to look around your hall and find someone who smokes pot casually and has not ruined his or her life. This undermines the entire extremist message [of] our government-run 'education' programs. . . . Once it's clear that you've been had, it's easy to ignore the whole spiel."

Most researchers who have looked into the effectiveness of DARE/scare programs have shown them not to have any impact on whether or not kids use drugs later in life; some researchers have even found that DARE actually backfires. The U.S. Surgeon General and the National Academy of Sciences have issued reports that describe DARE programs as ineffective. A University of Kentucky study found DARE had no measurable impact on drug use; a six-year study at the University of Illinois found that children who had been subjected to DARE's scare tactics were more likely to use drugs in high school.

"DARE participants are likelier to use drugs in the future than students who haven't participated in the program," wrote *Chicago Tribune* columnist Salim Muwakkil, referring to the University of Illinois study. "[DARE presents students] with kindergarten stories about the demonic evils of drugs and the despicable characters who use them. In such a cardboard world, drug users can't grow up to be presidents."

But pot users do grow up to be presidents—they also grow up and win gold medals. Canadian snowboarder Ross Rebagliati won a gold medal at the 1998 Olympics in Nagano, Japan, a medal that was almost taken away from him when he tested positive for marijuana (a performance *de*-hancing drug). When Rebagliati tried to enter the United States for the 2002 Winter Olympics in Salt Lake City, Utah, American immigration officials, perhaps busy with Mohammad Atta's student visa application, refused to let Rebagliati enter the United States. During the controversy over his drug test in Japan, Rebagliati had admitted to smoking marijuana in the past. (Rebagliati claimed he tested positive for marijuana at the Olympics after inhaling secondhand pot smoke at a party. Sure you did, Ross, sure you did. . . .) Rebagliati got to keep his medal, but because he was now an admitted pot smoker, the government of the United States regarded him as a dangerous criminal.

"If Ross Rebagliati is forbidden from entering the U.S.," said Keith Stroup, Executive Director of the National Organization for the Reform of Marijuana Laws (NORML), "how is it that Paul McCartney—an outspoken marijuana activist and convicted pot smoker—was allowed entry to this country to perform at [the 2002] Super Bowl?"

If past pot use is enough to keep Ross Rebagliati out of the country, how is it that Clarence Thomas gets to sit on the Supreme Court? How is it that more people voted for Al Gore than voted for the son of the man who appointed a pothead to the Supreme Court? How is it that Bill Clinton and George W. Bush get to be president? How is it that Willie Nelson, who once told ABC News that he smokes pot on a daily basis, gets to sing "America the Beautiful" at patriotic rallies after September 11? Young people have finely tuned bullshit detectors, and nothing annoys young people more than adult hypocrisy, and on the issue of pot, adults, teachers, DARE educators, and politicians positively reek of it. We know marijuana, used in moderation, is harmless, and millions and millions of Americans know it from personal experience— and that includes lots of Americans who are currently running this country.

When it comes to marijuana, the scare tactics don't work, they don't keep kids off drugs, and every time a kid turns on the television set or looks at a newspaper, he sees proof that marijuana users don't go directly to jail. What's worse, the use of scare tactics around a relatively harmless drug like marijuana undermines the best arguments against the use of harder, more addictive drugs. Heroin and crack and methamphetamines really are addictive, they really do kill people, and people who use these drugs really do wind up in jail or in hospitals or in psych wards. But if adults and politicians and parents cry wolf over pot, skeptical teenagers angry about being lied to and manipulated wind up tuning out truthful messages about drugs that *are* scary. ("Once it's clear that you've been had, it's easy to ignore the whole spiel.")

Which is exactly what kids are doing. According to the *New York Times,* between 1991 and 2001 the number of twelfth graders who have used pot jumped from 37 percent to 49 percent, while the number of tenth graders who used pot jumped from 23 to 40 percent, and the number of eighth graders who have smoked pot doubled, from 10 percent to 20 percent. Again, I'm not in favor of kids smoking pot, but I'd rather my twelfth grader smoked pot than drank beer—and I can't imagine that I'm the only parent in America who feels that way.

Predictably, social conservatives look at these numbers and conclude that the rise in pot use by kids is All Bill Clinton's Fault (ABCF). Clinton was soft on drugs, they insist, and the federal government under Clinton failed to prosecute the drug war vigorously, which led to these upticks in pot use among kids. As with most ABCFs, this one doesn't hold up under scrutiny. "Approximately 1.5 million Americans [were] arrested on marijuana charges during the first three years of Clinton's administration," according to NORML, "84% of them for simple possession. The average number of yearly marijuana arrests under Clinton (483,548) is 30 percent higher than under the [first] Bush administration (338,998)."

The government's latest scare tactic was rolled out during the 2002 Super Bowl.

The White House Office of National Drug Control Policy spent $3.4 million to air two thirty-second anti-drug spots during the Super Bowl. The campaign alleges that the illegal drug trade funds terrorism, and that Americans who use drugs are aiding terrorists. The ad campaign was paid for out of a National Youth Anti-Drug Media Campaign, a five-year, $1.5 billion program funded by Congress in 1997 to allow the drug czar's office to purchase advertising on various media outlets. Not being a big fan of pro-football, I missed the commercials on television. I did, however, catch the print ads in the papers.

"Last weekend," read text superimposed over a young man's face, "I washed my car, hung out with a few friends, and helped murder a family in Colombia. C'mon, it was a party."

At the bottom of the ad, the copy reads, "Drug money helps support terror. Buy drugs and you could be supporting it too."

The ads direct readers to a Web site, theantidrug.com, where I found this: "If you're using drugs in America, whether you're shooting heroin, snorting cocaine, taking Ecstasy *or sharing a joint in your friend's back yard,* evidence is mounting that what you're doing may be connected to events far beyond your own existence." (Emphasis added.)

There's one big problem with this campaign (well, there are dozens of problems with it, but I want to talk about pot): American pot smokers don't buy marijuana from terrorists. Eleven of the twelve groups on the government's list of terror organizations with links to drug trafficking are based in the Middle East and Colombia, which are not pot-growing regions. The twelfth is a Basque terror group known to traffic in heroin, not pot.

"The majority of America's illicit drug users are solely marijuana smokers, and do not use other drugs such as heroin or illegal opiates," said Keith Stroup, Executive Director of NORML. "It is patently absurd to suggest that marijuana smokers are in any way supporting terrorism. The overwhelming majority of marijuana consumed in this country is domestically grown or imported from Mexico, Jamaica, or Canada."

Americans are going to keep using drugs—we always have and we always will. "The drive to alter consciousness is as ancient as humanity itself," Salim Muwakkil writes in the *Chicago Tribune.* "Some anthropologists argue that psychoactive substances are so common to so many cultures, their use may have some evolutionary benefit."

The human desire for psychoactive drugs is never going away—the war on drugs, however, can and should go away. If the government is truly interested in cutting off the flow of drug money to terror groups, then George W. Bush should be talking about legalizing drugs, which is possible, and not halting drug consumption, which is impossible. At the very least, the government should be encouraging Americans who want to alter their consciousness to stick to home-grown pot, and not imported coke or heroin. Again, most of the pot smoked in the United States is grown in the United States, and legalizing pot—legalizing all illegal drugs—would get the profits out of the hands of crooks and terrorists and into the hands of big business people and the politicians they support. For Republicans, drug legalization is a win-win.

In keeping with the theme of sloth, I would like to lift seven wonderful arguments in favor of legalizing pot from a brilliant piece I stumbled across in a national magazine.

1. "Marijuana is widely used, and for the vast majority of its users is nearly harmless. . . ."

2. "Most people who use marijuana, even people who use it with moderate frequency, don't go on to use any other illegal drug. . . . 'There is no evidence,' says [the National Academy of Sciences], that marijuana serves as a stepping stone [to harder drugs]."[5]

3. "Two researchers in 1991 studied the addictiveness of caffeine, nicotine, alcohol, heroin, cocaine, and marijuana. Both ranked caffeine and marijuana as the least addictive. [One] ranked marijuana as slightly less addictive than caffeine."

4. "A small minority of people who smoke it may—by choice, as much as any addictive compulsion—eventually smoke enough of it for a long enough period of time to suffer impairments so subtle that they may not affect every day functioning or be permanent. Arresting, let alone jailing, people for using such a drug seems outrageously disproportionate."

5. "For the overwhelming majority of its users marijuana is not the least bit dangerous."

6. "If it's on the basis of effect—namely, intoxication—that [drug warrior] William Bennett considers marijuana immoral, then he has to explain why it's different from drunkenness, and why this particular sense of well-being should be banned in an

---

5. Hey, another footnote: I used cocaine, acid, and mushrooms in college, more than a decade *before* I smoked pot for the first time. So much for that "stepping stone" theory, huh? Pot was the last drug I got around to trying.

America that is now the great mood-altering nation, with millions of people on Prozac and other drugs primarily meant to make them feel good."

7. "Drug warriors recently have tried to argue that research showing marijuana acts on the brain in a way vaguely similar to cocaine and heroin—plugging into the same receptors—proves that it somehow 'primes' the brain for harder drugs. But alcohol has roughly the same action, and no one argues that Budweiser creates heroin addicts."

What lefty publication did I find this pro-pot piece in? *The Nation? The Progressive? The American Prospect?* No, I found it in *National Review,* the hard-right home of William F. Buckley Jr. ("Weed Whackers: The Anti-Marijuana Forces and Why They're Wrong," Richard D. Lowry, *National Review,* August 20, 2001). Do not despair, right wingers: *National Review* hasn't gone soft on us. In the same issue that Lowry, the magazine's editor, came out swinging for pot, the president of the conservative Family Research Council, Kenneth L. Connor, wrote, ". . . even in a system of representative self-government, the people do not have a right to do what is wrong." And who gets to determine what is and isn't wrong? Connor didn't say, and *National Review*'s get-the-government-off-our-backs editors didn't challenge him on the point.

Nevertheless, on account of the Richard Lowry piece on pot, I am now a proud subscriber to—and the occasional ripper-upper of—*National Review,* a magazine that hates only trial lawyers and Susan Sontag more than it hates homosexuals. (If Susan Sontag spoke before an organization of gay trial lawyers, well, that might give the editorial board of *National Review* brain aneurysms all around.) But, hey, politics makes strange bedfellows, and why should the politics of pot be an exception? In the spirit of strange bedfellows, Richard Lowry has a standing invitation to crawl into bed with me, my boyfriend, a bag of chips, and a single joint. We'll get baked, and watch *Showgirls* on video. Lowry is a busy man, and he could probably use the occasional pot getaway just as much as or more than I can. This bud's for you, Rich.

But Lowry's voice is a lonely one on the right—and on the left, for that matter. Marijuana came no closer to being legalized under eight years of Bill Clinton, who didn't inhale, and Vice President Al Gore, who is rumored to have spent a few years doing little else. Bill Clinton's drug czar, Gen. Barry McCaffrey, was something of a pathological liar. "The murder rate in Holland is double that in the United States," McCaffrey said on CNN. "That's drugs." In reality, the Dutch homicide rate is one-fourth that of the United States. "The most dangerous drug in America is a twelve-year-old smoking pot because they put themselves in this enormous statistical probability of having a [hard] drug problem," McCaffrey said on CNN in 1997. In reality, for every ten people who have used marijuana, there is only one regular user of cocaine and less than one heroin addict.

No one who smokes pot is under any delusions about George W. Bush pulling a Nixon-in-China on marijuana decriminalization, but his choice for drug czar still came as something of a shock. On the campaign trail, Bush made noises about treating marijuana more as a public health issue and less as a criminal justice issue. Once he was elected, Bush reversed course, appointing John Walters, a former deputy of William J. Bennett, as his drug czar. Walters believes in tossing nonviolent drug users in jail, and like his old boss, Bill Bennett, Walters refuses to acknowledge that there's any difference between smoking a little marijuana and shooting a whole lot of heroin. It's hard to imagine that Walters, Bennett, and Bush—all baby boomers—don't know dozens if not hundreds of friends, former college classmates, coworkers, and family members who smoked pot and lived to tell the tale.

While most politicians know from personal experience that marijuana is utterly harmless, boomers taking over all the top jobs in Washington isn't moving pot any closer to legalization, thanks to political cowardice. It doesn't help that their own drug-war rhetoric has boxed them into a corner; like the Catholic Church on the issues of birth control, celibacy, and female priests, the federal government's rhetoric on drugs has left it precious little wiggle room. "We were wrong" isn't something the feds or the Vatican have an easy time saying. At the rate we're going, matricide will be decriminalized before marijuana—at least in the United States.

Canada is moving towards decriminalization, as is Great Britain. In March of 2002, Tony Blair's Advisory Council on the Misuse of Drugs (ACMD) recommended that "all cannabis preparations" be essentially decriminalized. Unlike the United States, which arrests and prosecutes 600,000 marijuana users (not dealers, *users*) every year, Great Britain is moving towards the Holland model: the possession of small amounts of pot won't be prosecuted, and the sale of marijuana will be tolerated in Dutch-style "cafés."

"The high use of cannabis is not associated with major health problems for the individual or society," according to Britain's ACMD, "[and] the occasional use of cannabis is only rarely associated with significant problems in otherwise healthy individuals." According to the *London Evening Standard,* "[the ACMD] makes it clear that alcohol is far more damaging than cannabis to health and society at large because it encourages risk-taking and leads to aggressive and violent behaviour."

The Brits haven't discovered something we don't already know. In 1972, Richard Nixon's National Commission on Marijuana and Drug Abuse recommended that marijuana use and possession be decriminalized; in 1982, the National Academy of Sciences not only recommended that marijuana use and possession be decriminalized, "but that lawmakers give serious consideration to creating a system or regulated distribution," as well, according to NORML. In 2000, a long-term study conducted by Kaiser Permanente found that not only wasn't there a link between regular marijuana use and death but also that the marijuana prohibition represented the only real health risk to the user. (Ask anyone who was raped in a holding cell after being picked up for marijuana possession.) Kaiser recommended that, "medical guidelines regarding prudent use . . . be established, akin to the common-sense guidelines that apply to alcohol use."

American politicians, unlike their British and Canadian counterparts, refuse to wake up to reality. Pot isn't a threat to our health, our nation's productivity, or our national security.

Voters seem to get it. Medical-marijuana initiatives have passed in Alaska; Arizona; California; Colorado; Hawaii; Maine; Nevada; Oregon; Washington State; and Washington, D.C. In the fall of 2000, voters in California approved a state initiative that mandated treatment, not jail time, for nonviolent drug offenders. There is one glimmer of hope among our elected representatives; in Vermont the State House of Representatives passed a medical marijuana bill in March of 2002. (Vermont's Democratic governor plans to veto the bill if it makes it through the Vermont Senate.) As Lowry pointed out in *National Review*, "[medical marijuana] is the camel's nose under the tent for legalization, and so—for many of its advocates—it is. Both sides in the medical-marijuana controversy have ulterior motives, which suggests it may be time to stop debating the nose and move on to the full camel." Debating the camel is good for pot legalization, since all the facts support legalization. Indeed, it was examining the facts that forced the reliably conservative *National Review* to go all wobbly on marijuana prohibition. I live in hope that one day marijuana will be as legal as it is widely available.

Will some people smoke too much pot after marijuana is legalized? Sure they will—but they're the same people who *already* smoke too much pot. Countries that have decriminalized marijuana possession haven't seen a surge in marijuana consumption. Americans who want pot now already have pot. The idea that prohibition is all that stands between people who wanna get high and pot is absurd; it's one more faulty assumption heaped on the drug warrior's vast pile of faulty assumptions. The idea that legalizing pot will make us a nation of out-of-control stoners can be demolished with one word: beer. In addition to being addictive, inebriating, and potentially life-threatening, beer is also perfectly legal, culturally celebrated, and widely advertised. And yet we're not a nation of drunks. Why? Because the vast majority of us don't want to be drunk all the time. Even people who like to get drunk once in a while don't want to be drunk every day.

Robert Bork disagrees. He looks at Americans and sees a people that, but for the intervention of the state, can't control themselves. "An increasing number of alienated, restless individuals, individuals without strong ties to others, except in the pursuit of ever more degraded distractions and sensations. And liberalism has no corrective within itself; all it can do is endorse more liberty and demand more rights," Bork writes in *Slouching Towards Gomorrah*. Like most Americans, I have sought out distractions and sensations that Bork would regard as degraded. (One man's degraded distraction is another man's pursuit of happiness.) Bork assumes that a man who pursues happiness in places or with plants he doesn't care for can never be satisfied, that he must go from degraded distraction to degraded distraction. However, like most Americans, I don't need the architects of "liberalism" to instill in me a sense of control or balance. I have a corrective within myself (it's called being a sensible adult), liberalism doesn't have to stick one in me like some sort of vibrating butt plug.

You see, Mr. Bork, while I like pot, and I can get my hands on just as much pot as I want, I don't actually smoke pot all that often. Why? Because I don't want to be high all the time. Like the vast majority of Americans, I have goals, aspirations, and desires that preclude spending all my time in bed, stoned out of my mind, watching *Showgirls* with Richard Lowry. My corrective may not kick in when you would like it to—that is, it doesn't kick in at the same point yours does—but that doesn't mean I don't have one.

Another favorite tactic of drug warriors is to turn any conversation about legalizing pot into a conversation about legalizing heroin, in the same way they seek to turn any conversation about people who smoke pot at home into one about surgeons who smoke pot at work. (Drug warriors are addicted to the logical fallacy of changing the subject.) While many of the same arguments for legalizing pot can be applied to legalizing heroin, nowhere is it written that if one banned drug is legalized all banned drugs have to be legalized at the same time. The two drugs can and should be debated separately. But let's talk about heroin: Since 1989, the number of people who have used heroin in their lifetime has remained constant, according to the Substance Abuse and Mental Health Services Administration (SAMHSA). Admissions to emergency rooms for heroin-related causes, however, have almost doubled, from 38,100 in 1989 to 79,000 in 1998 (the most recent year for which figures are available). Why are heroin casualties growing while heroin use stays constant? Because the heroin available on the street is purer and stronger today than it was in 1989. Clearly, our never-ending war on drugs isn't having any impact on heroin use or consumption—unless you count making heroin more dangerous.

The increasing purity of heroin has made it easier for people who are afraid of needles to snort the drug. (How someone can be afraid of needles but not afraid of *heroin* is beyond me.) But while heroin is cheap and plentiful and pure, and while I live in Seattle, a city where the streets are practically paved with heroin, and while I am at times a restless, alienated individual, easily bored and prone to seeking out distractions and sensations that Bork might consider degraded, I've never been tempted to try heroin. Not once—and not because it hasn't been offered to me. But like most people, I don't want to use heroin for the one simple reason: I'm not an idiot. Unlike pot, heroin is wildly addictive, and it actually kills people. I don't do heroin because heroin is a dangerous drug, and people who use it are trying to kill themselves, and I'm not interested in killing myself. Even if heroin were legal, I wouldn't do it. There's that pesky internal corrective of mine again, kicking in without a nod from Hillary Clinton or Tom Harkin.

What about people who become addicted to drugs? Shouldn't we fight the drug war to protect these people from themselves? That some people have no internal correctives where drugs are concerned is not a good enough reason to deprive (or imprison!) the vast majority of us who do. The argument that we can't legalize drugs because some people are addicts is absurd. Addicts don't have any problem getting their hands on drugs *right now,* drug war or no drug war, big city or rural area, on the street or in prison, in schools or at malls. Furthermore, the some-people-can't-control-themselves argument isn't made about any other substances; people get addicted to caffeine, sugar, computers, booze, food, and sex. Some people are destroyed by these addictions. Cigarettes kill 400,000 people a year; 16,653 people were killed by drunk drivers in 2000, according to Mothers Against Drunk Driving, and 25,000 Americans die every year of cirrhosis of the liver; the fatty American diet causes heart disease, which kills 500,000 Americans every year according to the Harvard School of Public Health. I've personally known people, men and women, gay and straight, who couldn't control their sex drives and literally fucked themselves to death. By contrast, marijuana has never killed anyone; no one on earth has ever died of a marijuana overdose. And yet pot is banned and Budweiser, cigarettes, hamburgers, and sex are not.

Addicts, addicts, addicts—I get so sick of hearing about addicts. Tens of millions of Americans use drugs every year, but only a few hundred thousand Americans are addicts. That's a good indication that most people can use drugs—even addictive ones—without becoming addicted. But the only times we hear about drug use is when people who are addicted are being condemned, imprisoned, pitied, or rehabilitated. If the only time food was ever publicly discussed was in connection to some horror story about people eating themselves to death, well, the public image of food and our attitudes towards food "users" would be distorted. Some will insist that the comparison isn't a valid one because we can't live without food. As a species, we can't seem to live without stimulants and euphoria-inducing substances either. Every culture has its mind-blowers, from peyote to beer to wine to khat to pot to sweat lodges to vision-inducing fasts to Harveys Bristol Cream.

For the time being the right-wing scolds can gripe at me for smoking dope, and DARE "educators" can attempt to stuff my kid's head with lies about marijuana at his public school (lies I fully intend to debunk). But they can't stop Americans pursuing happiness (and slothful, restful, pharmacological vacation time), even if it leads us to the head shop.

"I do not believe an America that accepts widespread drug use is going to retain the spirit of optimistic individualism that has been our hallmark. Massive drug use may be acceptable in a more passive society, but it is antithetical to a free nation of self-reliant individuals." So says Newt Gingrich in his book *To Renew America*.

I hate to end this chapter by picking on poor ol' Newt Gingrich, who always was something of a slow-moving target. Picking on Newt is slothful of me, however, and for that reason I'm going to indulge myself. I spent so much time working on this chapter that I hardly feel as if I committed this particular sin, and that was supposed to be the point of this book.

I love this quote. Drug use, for many of us, induces the very spirit of optimism that Gingrich identifies as our national hallmark. And far from being antithetical to a free nation of self-reliant individuals, the right of one self-reliant individual to put in his pipe and smoke whatever he cares to grow in his garden seems to me the very picture of freedom. If some Americans want to pursue happiness in clouds of marijuana smoke, that should be among their inalienable rights. While Newt Gingrich may not believe that drug use and optimism go together, self-reliant individuals living in a free nation should have an absolute right to make that call for themselves.

GLUTTONY

Eating Out with Teresa and Tim

Their God is their belly. —Saint Paul (Phil. 3.18)

Because of the brief pleasure of the throat, lands and seas are ransacked. —Saint Jerome

As anyone who watches political chat shows can tell you, a lot of American virtuecrats have weight problems.

I'm not the first, you know, terribly, terribly serious writer to point this out. In his groundbreaking work of political scholarship, *Rush Limbaugh Is a Big Fat Idiot,* Al Franken opened America's eyes to the vast waistland (har!) that is Rush Limbaugh, the conservative talk-radio host. Robert Bork, William J. Bennett, and Jerry Falwell don't just resemble Limbaugh politically; all four men aren't exactly skin and bones, with Falwell being the most Rubenesque of the bunch. That so many conservative scolds are overweight might explain why we don't hear much from them about the sin of gluttony. Or perhaps the silence of the scolds on this issue has something to do with the fact that Republicans tend to be more obese than Democrats, as do born-again Christians, Southerners, and Bush supporters.

Nevertheless, overindulgence in food and drink was once regarded as a sin on a par with the other deadly sins; gluttony used to be right down there with adultery, divorce, and fornication.

Dante condemns the gluttonous to the third circle of hell, where a heavy, cold rain falls on their huge bodies. One Dante translator, John D. Sinclair, points out that Dante puts the gluttonous lower in hell than the lecherous because gluttony "is more simply a yielding of the soul to the flesh without any but a fleshly motive; it is a more entirely beastly sin," more beastly, in Dante's opinion, than fornication or adultery. Writing in the fourth century, Saint Jerome is even less kind to gluttons, blaming their sin for the fall of man: "[Adam obeyed] his belly and not God, was cast down from paradise into this vale of tears."

People who ate too much were believed to think too much about food and drink, which left them with too little time for God and salvation. Today, however, we have to look to secular culture to find ringing condemnations of gluttony, where the sin is no longer discussed in terms of spiritual health, but in terms of physical health—and physical attractiveness, which may explain why modern scolds leave the subject alone. Allowing people to become obese, or standing silently by while your flock porks out, may prevent them from becoming the "occasion of sin" (inspiring lust in others) and encourage other virtues scolds value, like chastity and, uh, let me see . . . heart disease?

When it comes to fat, I'm in no position to throw stones at Jerry Falwell or Bill Bennett. I may not be as fat as they are—as of this writing—but I love food just as much as they appear to. For me, a day without bacon is like a day without, well, what compares to bacon? Hands down my favorite food is cake, and my favorite cake is chocolate, and my favorite kind of chocolate cake is the kind of cheap bakery cake that's gritty with sugar and covered in frosting flowers. While I may be slightly underweight for my height, staying slim is a constant battle against my genetic makeup (most of the people in my family are heavy) and my baser impulses (I would eat bacon cake all day long if I let myself). I was fat for a few years as a teenager, so I don't think, "What a pig!" when I look at Falwell. Instead I think, "He is my destiny." My relationship with food is

deeply unhealthy, larded with fear, guilt, self-recrimination, binge-
ing, penance, and frustrated desires. (Alas, no one has yet to perfect a bacon cake.)

The battle in my head over food never seems to stop—I think
about food when I wake up, and I'm still thinking about food when
I go to bed at night. In my head, my desire to eat everything in
sight plays out as a battle between good and evil, a struggle with
distinctly religious overtones. Gluttony is the one sin I would most
like to indulge myself in, and yet I'm overwhelmed by feelings of
guilt after I eat, say, two pounds of bacon followed by a cheap
chocolate cake. When I do something like that—and, yes, I've
really, really done that—I think of myself as fallen, as a sinner, as
someone who should be punished. When I get my ass back to the
gym or on those rare occasions when I walk out of a bakery without buying myself anything or those rarer occasions when I stop
eating the bacon before it's all gone, I think of myself as saved, as
something of a saint, as someone who deserves a reward. (Maybe a
piece of chocolate cake?)

While my own inner struggle with gluttony plays out in quasi-
religious language and images, public discussions of gluttony and
obesity are now entirely secular. It's not the preachers who get after
us about our gluttony, it's the personal trainers and diet gurus—
Jenny Craig and Sarah Ferguson, not Jerry Falwell and Pat Robertson. Secular obesity virtuecrats aren't much gentler with gluttons
than Saint Paul was two thousand years ago. Fat-assed Americans
are ostracized, dismissed as unattractive and unlovable, and hu-
miliated in a thousand little ways every day. Non-fat-assed Americans may have loved John Candy and Chris Farley on television,
but who among the narrow-butts would have wanted to sit next to
Candy or Farley in coach? Every narrow-butt in the United States
of America has made "the face," what our obese fellow Americans
call the look on skinny people's faces when they see someone the
size of Chris Farley coming down the aisle. "Please, God," the face
says, "don't let that fat ass sit next to me. . . ."

The hostility fat-assed Americans are subjected to seems especially odd when you consider just how many Americans have hugely fat asses. According to the U.S. Department of Health and Human Services, the number of obese adults has doubled in the last twenty years; according to the DHHS, 61 percent of all adults in the United States were overweight or obese in 1999 (the last year for which figures are available). The numbers of overweight or obese children has tripled in the same period, to 13 percent of children and 14 percent of adolescents. American adults are obese, American children are obese—our friggin' *pets* are obese. We're in the midst of an obesity epidemic, according to Surgeon General David Satcher, who released a report in early 2002 with this appropriately bloated title, "The Surgeon General's Call to Action to Prevent and Decrease Overweight and Obesity." Sounding like Bill Bennett discussing adultery, Satcher encouraged Americans to stop thinking of obesity "as strictly a personal matter," and pointed to the social costs of obesity, from the three hundred thousand deaths per year linked to obesity, to health problems like heart disease, cancer, diabetes, stroke, arthritis, and breathing problems. The Centers for Disease Control and Prevention recently announced that more than one in five American adults—47 million people—suffer from metabolic syndrome, "a disorder that includes a beer belly, high blood pressure, poor cholesterol, and high blood sugar." To hell with winning World War II, if mass were the sole criteria, *we* are the greatest generation.

Unraveling the mystery of fat American asses isn't difficult: Secretary of the Department of Health and Human Services Tommy Thompson—no Calista Flockhart himself—pins the blame on "our modern environment," while the CDC in Atlanta warns that physical inactivity, "a major contributor to obesity," is skyrocketing. Perhaps another reason conservatives don't talk about obesity is because they're simply not comfortable with the word *environment* in any context. But our modern environment *is* making us fatter. We drive everywhere and eat while we drive; we work all day sitting on our asses and eat while we work; we sit on asses all night watching television and eat while we watch TV.

At the same time that our lives have become numbingly sedentary, the portions served up by the food and beverage industry have grown to ridiculous proportions. Why are muffins and bagels bigger than our heads? Who decided that movie theaters should serve Coke in drums you could drown a dog in? Just how many places can Domino's hide cheese on their pizzas anyway? Has anyone notified the CDC that Baby Ruth bars are bigger than baseball bats? Speaking of baseball, the Cracker Jack sold at ballparks now comes in breakfast-cereal-size boxes. There are 820 calories in those 7½-ounce boxes of Cracker Jack you can buy at ballparks today, compared to the old 1 ounce, 106-calorie boxes of Cracker Jack.

If I weren't such a fan of sin and self-indulgence (and bacon and chocolate cake), I would join Jenny Craig and Tommy Thompson in condemning American gluttony, wagging a self-righteous, skinny finger in the faces of my fat-assed fellow Americans. If I were a skinny cultural conservative, perhaps I could find a few somber lessons in a breakfast-cereal-size box of Cracker Jack. Where is our self-control? Our sense of proportion? Whatever happened to the virtue of moderation? But who am I to stand between American gluttons and their pleasures? If William J. Bennett, Jerry Falwell, and Robert Bork want to pursue happiness by stuffing themselves with carbs and saturated fats, well, that's their inalienable right. Seeing as how these men deny themselves so many other pleasures, from drugs to infidelities, I couldn't live with myself if I came—even rhetorically—between Robert Bork and his Krispy Kremes.

In a way, I admire Falwell and other conservatives for letting themselves get fat; it's something I wish I could allow myself to do. If I could let myself get fat, I wouldn't have to monitor the foods I put in my mouth or go to the gym anymore. Yes, fat kills people, but we all gotta go sometime, and someone who goes out eating at least goes out smiling, so when it comes to gluttony I wish I could be more like Falwell; I wish I could let myself eat and eat and eat. There are things I'll put in my mouth that Falwell would never put in his, Lord knows, and one look at Falwell tells me that he's putting things in his mouth that I *want* to put in mine and won't let myself. As a pro-sin and pro–self-indulgence American, I have to admire Falwell's gluttonous abandon—and for the purposes of this book, I'm going to try to emulate him.

To indulge myself in the sin of gluttony Falwell-style, I decided to surround myself with world-class, guilt-free gluttons, the kind of people who eat and eat and eat without guilt—the out, proud, and loud members of the National Association for the Advancement of Fat Acceptance (NAAFA). Founded in 1969, NAAFA is "a human rights organization dedicated to improving the quality of life for fat people." In order to make the world a better place for fat people, NAAFA's fifty chapters battle three "myths" about people who are fat: "If they really wanted to, they could lose weight." "It's not healthy to be fat." "Fat people are ugly."

On NAAFA's Web site I learned that they were holding a "celebration" over Memorial Day weekend in San Francisco, aka "Sodom by the Bay." Actually, NAAFA's convention wasn't really *in* San Francisco. Instead of meeting in a hotel downtown—close to San Francisco's restaurants, tourist attractions, theaters, clubs, and museums—NAAFA was meeting in a soulless concrete bunker about a mile from San Francisco International Airport. At NAAFA's weekend-long celebration, I hoped to commune with the guilt-free fatties who swell NAAFA's ranks. I love food, and my adult relationship with food is extremely unhealthy. Maybe eating with folks who don't obsess about the consequences would help me embrace the one and only sin that Falwell, Bennett, and Bork find so easy to swallow.

"It's mostly women here," the large woman sitting next to me said, smiling up at me, picking bits of paper from the bottom of an oily bran muffin. "Lots of women, no men," she sighed, before she turned and gave me a wink. "That's good for you, but bad for us."

Teresa introduced herself and then introduced me to her girl-friend, Shawn, who was sitting to her right peeling the bits of paper off the bottom her own oily bran muffin.

"So is this your first time at a NAAFA event?" asked Teresa, batting her eyes and popping a tiny piece of bran muffin into her mouth. I nodded.

Still picking away at her muffin, Teresa asks why I wasn't at last night's dance.

"Late flight," I lie.

My flight was late, as are all flights into San Francisco. I missed Friday night's sit-down dinner ("A Mexican feast!") on account of my delayed flight, but the dance was still going strong when I arrived at the hotel shortly after midnight. Thumpa-thumpa-thumpa dance "music" drifted down the hall from the hotel's ballroom as I waited for the elevator, room and mini-bar keys in hand. I intended to head up to my room, brush my teeth, change my shirt, and then head back down to the dance. But as I sat on the edge of the bed, flossing bits of airline food from between my teeth, a grim CNN anchor warned me that the home video I was about to see was very disturbing. A mass of people at a wedding reception were jumping up and down on a ballroom dance floor when all of a sudden the dancers seemed to dip in unison. The dance floor collapsed under their weight, and the dancers disappeared in a cloud of dust. When the dust cleared, there was a black hole where the dance floor used to be. People screamed, the tape ended, and the anchorwoman informed me that twenty-five people were known dead, and many, many more were buried under the rubble. Suddenly dancing with a lot of fat people in a hotel ballroom didn't seem like the best idea.

The next morning, I headed down to the hotel's ballroom for a buffet breakfast and a speech by Bonnie Bernell, author of *Bountiful Women: Large Women's Secrets for Living the Life They Desire*. I rode an elevator down to the lobby with three hugely fat women. Two appeared to weigh somewhere in the neighborhood of three hundred pounds—fat, yes, but reasonably robust looking—while the third must have weighed upwards of six hundred pounds. She didn't look healthy; she looked like a woman dissolving in a vat of oil. My perception may have been colored by the fact that this woman was too fat to walk. She sat in a motorized chair and chatted with her friends as we rode down the lobby.

The urge to do the math was irresistible.

The posted weight limit in the elevators at the San Francisco Airport Westin is 3,500 pounds. Exceed an elevator's posted weight limit, and its cable will snap, I assume, sending the elevator and everyone on it plunging down the elevator shaft. Why post a weight limit otherwise? Quickly doing the math in my head, I figured that seven—count 'em, seven—five-hundred-pound women would have to join me on the elevator before we exceeded the weight limit, snapped the cable, and plunged to our deaths. While there was no shortage of five-hundred-pound women at the NAAFA convention, I didn't need to worry about plunging to my death. The Westin's elevators were pretty small; you would need a shoehorn, a snowplow, and a fifty-gallon drum of vegetable oil to wedge seven five-hundred-pound people into one.

The hall outside of the ballroom was full of fat people—some reasonably fat (think Bennett), some distressingly fat (think Falwell)—and almost all of them were women (think Michael Medved). The gender imbalance struck me as odd, as there were plenty of photos of fat men on NAAFA's Web site, including famous fat men, like Winston Churchill, Orson Welles, John Candy, and Santa Claus.

Feeling rather conspicuous, I made my way to the registration table, where I picked up my information packet and meal tickets; then I headed to the ballroom. I was anxious to share my first meal with people who didn't feel guilty about eating, and looking forward to the first guilt-free Danish of my adult life. According to my information packet, NAAFA members were fat, happy, healthy, and attractive. NAAFA's FHHA membership rejects anti-fat bigotry, celebrates people of all sizes, and does battle with the evil airlines, a biased medical establishment, and the diet industry that, according to NAAFA, actually makes people fatter. (Not that there's anything wrong with being fat, of course. But if you don't want to get fat, NAAFA argues, then you shouldn't diet.) NAAFA's three-day convention would be a series of seminars broken up by meals—glorious, indulgent, delicious guilt-free meals, according to the brochure.

Some people may think that the battle for fat acceptance is over, with NAAFA the clear victor. In 1969, the year NAAFA was founded, only 25 percent of American adults were overweight or obese. The percentage of American adults who are overweight today is 61 percent and rising. Fifty-four percent of the 1.4 million Americans in the armed forces are overweight, according to a report released by the Pentagon in January of 2002, a 10 percent jump in just six years. A report in the *Journal of the American Medical Association* warned that "American children are getting fatter at an alarming rate." In 1986, researchers reported, 8 percent of black children were overweight, 10 percent of Hispanic children, and 8 percent of white children. By 1998, twenty-two percent of black children were overweight, twenty-two percent of Hispanic children, and twelve percent of white children. Those percentages are surely higher now. How many Americans will have to be clinically obese before NAAFA declares victory and passes out the Cinnabons?

The floor of the ballroom was intact, having withstood last night's dance. Saturday morning's breakfast lecture was in a small ballroom. Breakfast itself was laid out over three long tables: bagels and cream cheese, Danish, oily muffins, small boxes of sugary cereal, whole milk, sweetened yogurt. Best of all, there were warming trays full of buttery croissants stuffed with scrambled eggs and bacon. The buffet was open when I came into the room, but no one was in line—everyone was ignoring the food. I was hungry, though, having missed last night's Mexican feast, and headed straight for the buffet table. I loaded up a plate and found an empty seat at a nearby table.

When Teresa told me I was in luck—so many women, so few men—I smiled and nodded and said nothing. She was right. Lots of women, not many men. But I wasn't really sure why that was lucky for me—oh, hey, wait a minute. . . .

It can take me a moment or two to realize when someone is flirting with me. Gee, I thought to myself, this attractive woman with shoulder-length black hair who appeared to weigh about 250 pounds seems awfully interested in my flight. I mean, she was leaning towards me, nodding her head, and listening. . . . Hey, wait. . . . *She's putting the moves on me.* Even in places where I can reasonably expect to be flirted with (bars, clubs, confessionals), I'm pretty slow on the uptake. Being fat as a kid damaged my self-esteem and self-image. (I'm still fat in my head.) In the looks department, I place myself somewhere between (on a bad day) porn star Ron Jeremy and (on a good day) conservative commentator Tucker Carlson. I'm even slower to come to the realization that I'm being cruised when the person doing the cruising is someone I would never sleep with—like, say, a woman, any woman, big or small, fat or thin, living or dead. I hadn't anticipated getting hit on at the NAAFA convention, and I began to panic. Picking away at my bagel (oh, glorious carbs!), I silently prayed the speaker would begin and put an end to our conversation.

"Have you been to any BBW events up in Seattle?" Teresa asked. "I hear they have some really good BBW parties up there."

BBW?

"Big, beautiful women, silly," said Teresa, patting my forearm.

When I told Teresa that this was my first BBW event other than normal family functions, she feigned amazement.

"So what brings you to the convention?" Shawn interjected, leaning towards the table to get a better look.

"Oh, I don't know," I stammered. "I guess, um, I was just, you know, curious."

"You came all the way down here for your first event instead of going to one in the town where you live?" Teresa said, giving Shawn a nudge. "Don't you want to meet a BBW who lives a little closer to home? Someone you could actually date?"

I smiled and shrugged, unsure of what to say. While I knew I would be a very thin person at a very fat convention, I naively assumed I would blend in and I hadn't prepared a lie to justify my presence in case I didn't blend in. There would be a lot of people coming and going, I thought, so who would even notice skinny lil' me?

"So how long have you been an FA?" asked Teresa.

An effay?

"Fat Admirer," said Teresa. She laughed and turned to look at Shawn. "He's not very up on the lingo, is he?" Turning back to me, Teresa said, "Well, we're just going to have to teach you everything you need to know. Everything."

Teresa explained that some FAs like pear-shaped women, like herself, while others prefer apple-shaped women, like Shawn.

"So what's your preference?" Teresa asked, batting her eyes. "Apples? Or pears?" (Suddenly I was Tony Curtis in *Spartacus* being asked by Laurence Olivier if I preferred oysters or snails.) Teresa and Shawn were both looking at me, waiting for an answer. Apples or pears? Which one of them was going to get lucky this weekend?

"I'm not sure which I prefer," I replied miserably.

Now I've been hit on by women before, and while I would normally clear up the confusion immediately—"See here, miss, I am a faggot. . . ."—I felt obligated not to shoot Teresa down. I was at a fat *acceptance* convention, for Christ's sake, and I didn't want Teresa to think I was rejecting her because she was, you know, *fat*. So I kept right on smiling, nodding, offering polite, one-word responses to her questions, which only dug me in deeper. I felt like a hiker cornered by a bear who lies down on the ground and plays dead in hopes that the bear will go away and then suddenly remembers that he has a candy bar in his pocket.

"Are you going to the pool party tonight?" Teresa asked. She leaned forward. "There's a hot tub by the pool, and that's where the action is these weekends."

Holy Christ.

Playing dead wasn't working, so I did what I had to do. I confessed that my preference was for banana shapes.

"Of course, the only halfway decent-looking guy here is gay," Teresa said, throwing her hands up in mock despair. "And I've been sitting here making a fool of myself." She took what I thought would be devastating news—that I was unavailable—in ego-shattering stride.

"So are you here to meet big men?" asked Shawn.

"No!" I responded, a little too quick. "I mean, I have a boyfriend already."

"Is he big?" asked Teresa.

"No, he's skinny—not that it makes any difference to me." I was lying, and they could tell. I'm not attracted to fat guys (sorry, Jerry), something I've always felt guilty about. But I couldn't tell Teresa and Shawn that I wasn't attracted to fat guys; if there's one place on earth a fat person shouldn't have to listen to a skinny person talk about why he's not into fat people, it would have to be at the table next to the buffet at a fat acceptance convention. Not that I needed to explain; the damage was already done. My too-quick-too-loud "No!" made it clear to my new fat friends that I'm not only not attracted to fat people, but that I wouldn't want anyone to think I might be attracted to fat people either.

"So what on earth are you doing here?" asked Shawn.

There was that question again. I didn't want to tell them the truth—I came to dine with the gluttons—but I had to say something.

"Well, I wanted to check it out. Most of the people in my family are"—I shrugged—"big. Looking around this room, I feel like

I'm home for Thanksgiving. So I thought I'd come and see what the issues are."

As lies go, it was pretty lame, not that it really mattered. Teresa and Shawn didn't seem to be listening. Their eyes were darting around the room as they wrapped the remains of their muffins up in napkins.

"We are *so* getting daggers," said Teresa.

"Absolutely," Shawn agreed.

Teresa put her hand on my arm and leaned in close. We were girlfriends now, and Teresa spoke to me in a throaty mock-conspiratorial tone used by girlfriends all over the world, in contrast to the girlish voice she used when she was flirting with me. "You're the only halfway decent looking guy at this event, and of course everyone assumes you're an FA—"

"Teresa certainly did." Shawn laughed.

"—and we snagged you the second you got here. There's an unwritten rule at NAAFA that says we're supposed to let the FAs circulate and give everyone a chance."

There aren't enough FAs to go around, Teresa explained, which was why Teresa broke the ice by telling me I was in luck. A good-looking, single, presentable FA at a NAAFA convention can have his pick of the women. About 250 people were at the Westin for the NAAFA celebration, and 95 percent were women. The whole reason most women come to these events, Teresa explained, was to meet men.

"It's nice to see old friends and socialize," Teresa laughed, "but it's the sex that keeps us coming back."

There was nothing on the NAAFA Web site or in the brochures, I said, about the convention being a meat market. I thought we were all here to, like, advance the acceptance of fat and, you know, stuff like that.

"That's what the political fat people are here to do," Teresa said, "but most of us are just here to have fun."

Which is what I came for, I guess—only I was looking for a celebration of gluttony, not lust. I felt like I'd gone to a porn shoot only to find everyone sitting around fully clothed eating dough-nuts.

Looking around the ballroom full of women, Teresa let out a loud sigh. She said she was worried that her last NAAFA event was going to be a total bust.

Her last NAAFA event?

"Yes," Teresa said. "I'm just not fat enough for NAAFA any-more."

A rail-thin blonde—a physician and a NAAFA board mem-ber—stepped up to the podium at the front of the room before I could ask Teresa what she meant. How could she not be fat enough for the "size acceptance" movement? The thin woman at the podium invited all of us to attend a series of movement classes she would be teaching over the weekend, and implored the women in the room to incorporate more movement into their daily lives—not with weight loss as a goal, but only so that we could be healthy and fit whatever our size.

"Why don't we do some movement right now?" the thin woman asked.

The thin woman told us to inhale; we inhaled; the thin woman told us raise our arms up over our heads; we raised our arms up over our heads; the thin woman told us to exhale and bring our arms back down; we exhaled and brought our arms down. We re-peated this movement three more times—feel the burn!—and then she led us in a big round of applause for ourselves.

Teresa and Shawn slipped out of the ballroom while the thin woman introduced the morning speaker. They'd been to a million NAAFA events, she whispered as they gathered themselves up, and they knew all the speeches by heart. They asked for my room num-ber and told me that, gay or not, I was going to tonight's formal dinner and dance with them.

"Sleep with whoever you want to," Teresa said, "but you're danc-ing with us."

The speaker was a big woman dressed in an alarming shade of yellow, not a color fat women usually wear. Before she began her speech, the speaker asked us all to look around the room.

"Have you ever seen so many big, bright, beautiful, bountiful women?" the speaker asked.

I didn't look at the—what were they now, BBBBWs? Thanks to Teresa and Shawn, who had just finished explaining that the women of NAAFA all assumed I was there to fuck the fat chicks, I was afraid to make eye contact with anyone. I didn't want the BBBBWs to think I was undressing them with my eyes. Using my amazing powers of peripheral vision, however, I could see that I wasn't the only man in the room. There were a few others: the speaker's rail-thin husband, introduced to much applause, and two or three other skinny husbands sitting next to enormous wives. Two men—one hugely fat, one extremely short—sat at the next table over; they appeared to be a couple. While I may not have been the only man in the room, I did look like the only man who came stag.

The woman in yellow began to tell us what inspired her to write her book. She was from a long line of doctors and medical re-searchers, and it was something of a family tradition to donate your body to science when you died. "And when I tried to make the arrangements," she said, looking suddenly very serious, "they told me that they didn't want my body." Women began to hiss. "It turns out that if your body is thirty or forty pounds overweight, they don't want it." The hissing grew louder. "I was shocked and horri-fied. What started out as an honorable act on my part was turned into one more time to feel ashamed about my size."

That experience inspired her to do a collection of fat women's stories—good and bad, inspiring and infuriating—and the speaker asked if she could share some of the stories with us. One story in particular, about a woman whose doctor misdiagnosed a serious illness, got the women in the ballroom hissing again.

"Since all this doctor could see was a fat woman," she clucked, "and not a patient, he overlooked a very serious illness that had nothing to do with her weight."

More hissing, some boos.

"These people hate doctors," I scribbled in my notes—and so they would. Being fat is undeniably, indisputably, irrefutably Bad For You Big Time, and while the friends and family of NAAFA members know better than to say anything negative about being heavy, a physician who avoids the subject is guilty of negligence. Of course, it's equally negligent for a physician to ignore the health complaints of a fat person, or to tell a fat woman that he can't help her at all until she loses some weight (like the doctor in the speaker's book). Still, the medical establishment drives NAAFA nuts with statements like this one:

"While obese individuals need to reduce their caloric intake and increase their physical activity, many others must play a role to help these individuals," Dr. Jeffrey Koplan, the CDC's director, was quoted in a press release. "Health care providers must counsel their obese patients; workplaces must offer healthy food choices in their cafeterias and provide opportunities for employees to be physically active on-site; schools must offer more physical education that encourages lifelong physical activity; urban policy makers must provide more sidewalks, bike paths, and other alternatives to cars; and parents need to reduce their children's TV and computer time and encourage outdoor play. In general, restoring physical activity to our daily routines is critical."

There isn't a single statement in the above paragraph that NAAFA would sign off on. Telling people to reduce their caloric intake presumes that obese people overeat, which NAAFA disputes; health care providers shouldn't pester their obese patients to lose weight, since being fat isn't bad for you, according to NAAFA; fat people have a right to eat the foods they enjoy and thin employers and friends shouldn't be wavin' apples under their noses; telling people they can lose weight by getting out of their cars or "restoring physical activity to [their] daily routines," presumes that fat people aren't already active, and fat people are just as active as thin people, NAAFA argues. Just look at all the fat women at the convention today—here it wasn't even ten o'clock and they'd already raised their arms up over their heads! Three times!

Most of the stories in the speaker's book were about fat women who found love, and soon the ballroom was filled with *awws* instead of hisses. One woman profiled in her book actually met her soul mate while filling her shopping cart with half-price Marshmallow Peeps the day after Easter. It turned out that they both shared a passion for those mushy Easter candies, which come in toxic pink and a shade of yellow very similar to the color of the speaker's dress. The story was a popular one, apparently, as most of the women in the room seemed familiar with its details. Indeed, there were boxes of Peeps for sale in the lobby, the candies having been transformed into a kind of love talisman by the women of NAAFA.

"Flirt!" the speaker implored us as she wrapped up her speech. "Flirting is such a good thing to do! Don't assume rejection! The message fat women hear all the time is, 'Get thin, find love.' The message I want you to take away from our talk this morning is, 'Get confident, find love.' Live your life now, as you are, and live bountifully. Flirt!"

There I was, sitting in a ballroom full of fat women, a presumed FA, and the speaker was whipping the women of NAAFA into a flirting frenzy. Feeling like I had a bull's-eye on my ass, I thought it might be prudent to get a head start, so I slipped out of the ballroom when the thin board member came back up to the podium to thank the speaker for her inspired remarks.

On my way out of the ballroom, I snagged a Danish from the buffet table. There were dozens left. No one seemed to be eating.

I ate my Danish as I walked through the trade show in an adjacent ballroom, checking out the super-plus-size T-shirts, jeans, lingerie, and swimsuits. At one table I picked up some fat-activist political pamphlets: "Fat people are not unhealthy!" "Fat people do not eat too much!" "Fat is not unattractive!" Based on the condition of the buffet table after breakfast, I had to concede that fat people didn't seem to eat too much—not in public, at any rate. But the first two propositions—fat wasn't unhealthy, fat was attractive—still struck me as dubious. If you're fat and happy, then you should be willing to accept the increased health risks and live your life. Pleasurable pursuits often carry some risk. Downhill skiing carries some risk, drinking and drugs can be dangerous, sleeping around is emotionally and physically risky. An adult who pursues happiness in booze, drugs, sex, or food has to accept the higher risks; indeed, most sinners will tell you that the happiness they derive is worth assuming whatever risks come along with their pleasures, and reasonable sinners take steps to minimize their risks. But there are always risks, and there are sometimes consequences. Sinners can't really ask the Surgeon General to protect us from reality, and it's not bigotry to point out the increased health risks of being heavy or drunk or high or promiscuous.

I was lost in thought in the trade show when Teresa tapped me on the shoulder. I was happy to see her because I wanted to ask her about something she said at breakfast. What did she mean by not fat enough for NAAFA anymore? Teresa told me we would have to leave the hotel if I wanted to talk about being too thin for NAAFA. Whatever it was she had to tell me, it wasn't something she wanted other NAAFA members to overhear her discussing. We made plans to have lunch, outside the hotel.

"People in NAAFA were used to seeing me when I weighed four hundred pounds," Teresa explained over sushi in a Japanese restaurant a mile or so from the Westin. "Women who get too skinny are looked down on at NAAFA. And God help you if you go from four hundred pounds to a normal weight. They treat you like a traitor."

Born and raised in San Francisco, Teresa has two siblings, both heavy. While she had been fat since age five, her brother and sister didn't get fat until middle age. Intelligent and quick-witted, Teresa never went to college because she feared not being able to fit into chairs with attached desktops common in classrooms and lecture halls. Teresa went to work as a bank teller after high school; she still works at the same bank, but now she's a supervisor for the tele-banking department. She joined NAAFA in 1991 primarily to meet men who were attracted to fat women. Teresa was already some-thing of a BBW celeb at that point—she'd had been spotted by a producer for the *Donahue* daytime talk show dancing in a night-club in New York City called Goddesses that caters to BBWs and FAs, and appeared on the talk show with her then-boyfriend. In the mid-1990s, Teresa met a fat admirer at a NAAFA event, fell in love, got married, and let her NAAFA membership lapse. She weighed about three hundred pounds at that point.

"My husband was a big-time FA," Teresa said. "So he loved it when I started gaining weight." Her husband wasn't a "feeder," Teresa made clear. Feeders are men who get off on stuffing their wives or girlfriends with food, with the goal of making them as fat as possible. The wives and girlfriends of feeders are called gainers.

"So it wasn't a feeder-gainer thing. I was just naturally getting bigger, but he loved it."

Like a lot of FAs, Teresa's husband encouraged her to wear leg-gings and shirts that showed off her rolls of fat. During her mar-riage, Teresa grew from 300 pounds to 450 pounds. Teresa is five feet four inches tall. As she gained weight, Teresa began to have nightmares about immobility. Teresa watched some friends get so big (whether on their own or because they're married to feeders) that they gradually became disabled—some couldn't get out of bed anymore. She met a woman at a NAAFA event in 1991 who had been disowned by her family—her father was a film producer—because of her size. Through NAAFA, Teresa's friend met and mar-ried a feeder. Her friend weighed four hundred pounds at that point. The last time Teresa saw her friend at a chocolate-themed NAAFA party, she was so big that she couldn't get off the couch.

"Her husband had to do everything for her," said Teresa. "She could barely move." Teresa thinks her friend weighed about six hundred pounds at the time of the chocolate party. Recently, Teresa's gainer friend and her feeder husband made a videotape to celebrate their wedding anniversary. The tape documents her friend's growth over the years, and Teresa estimates that her friend now weighs more than eight hundred pounds.

"The tape is all over the Web. It's a turn-on for feeders," said Teresa. "She gets out of bed only two times a day to go to the toilet. She's enormous, and her skin has these huge bubbles all over it, pockets on pockets of fat. He's feeding her doughnuts, fried food, pizza." Teresa shakes her head. "I call it her death tape. Watching it was liking watching my friend being murdered before my eyes."

Teresa's marriage began to fall apart when her husband started putting on weight. "You want to know one of the dirty little secrets of NAAFA?" Teresa said. "There's a lot of talk about accepting people of different sizes and how beautiful fat is and fat people are. Well, most BBWs aren't attracted to fat men. I know I'm not. Most of us want nice, good-looking men. Thin men." Why? "For all the usual looks reasons. When I was really big, I would look at my body and feel disgusted. I don't want to feel that way when I look at my husband's body."

Over her husband's objections, Teresa went on the diet drug combination fen-phen in 1996. She lost 182 pounds in eight months. (Luckily, Teresa wasn't harmed by the drug combination, which was pulled from the market when it was discovered to have life-threatening side effects.) Teresa's husband told her he wasn't attracted to her anymore, and they agreed to divorce. Teresa wasn't upset. She wasn't attracted to her husband anymore either, as a result of his weight gain. A year after the divorce and off the fen-phen, Teresa was back up to four hundred pounds.

Shortly after her divorce, some of Teresa's oldest friends from NAAFA began dying. A thirty-one-year-old woman who weighed seven hundred pounds sat up in bed one day, took a breath, and slumped over dead. She couldn't be cremated in Sacramento because no funeral home had an oven that was big enough to accommodate her body. Another friend who weighed six hundred pounds slipped and fell in her apartment and broke her hip. It took eight firemen to pick her up and put her in an ambulance. Her heart stopped while she was on an X-ray table. Another six-hundred-pound friend died of a stroke.

"I was almost five hundred pounds at this point," Teresa said. "I knew it was going to happen to me. There was not a question in my head: I was so fat that I was going to die."

This was the point in her life when Teresa began to contemplate something that would forever brand her a traitor in the eyes of her friends from NAAFA.

"I underwent WLS. Better WLS and some small risk of dying from complications than knowing I would for sure drop dead from being fat."

WLS? Flipping through the NAAFA convention's schedule in my hotel room the night I arrived, I noticed a listing for a seminar titled, "Help! My Friend Is Getting WLS!" I couldn't figure out what WLS stood for. All the other seminar titles were upbeat and self-explanatory—"Fat Friendly Healthcare," "Combating Workplace Discrimination," "How to Get What You Want: Sexual Communication"—which made this mysterious WLS seminar all that much more intriguing. It would have to be something pretty awful if you needed help when your friends started getting it. Was it some sort of weight-related disease or syndrome? After all, people don't "get" good things; we "get" audited, we "get" cancer, we "get" cable. Whatever this WLS stuff is, I thought, it must be pretty awful.

Like a lot of fat people, Teresa has gone through life reading disapproval on people's faces. Over the course of her fat life, as she called it, she got pretty good at spotting people who were going to give her grief about her weight—people on airplanes who would see her coming down the aisle and make the face, people in grocery stores or restaurants who would make comments to her about the food in her cart or on her plate. Adept as she was at reading faces, Teresa could tell that I was lost.

"WLS stands for weight loss surgery," she explained, leaning across the table and whispering. "It's the reason I didn't eat very much at breakfast. My stomach is about as big as your thumb."

Teresa wasn't planning to attend the WLS seminar; she was afraid she would be attacked for having undergone the surgery. Shawn felt the same way—she wasn't going to spend two hours of her Memorial Day weekend holiday being attacked. For many NAAFA members, Shawn's decision to undergo WLS was a bigger betrayal than Teresa's. In the mid-1990s, Shawn had operated two of the first Web sites devoted to BBWs and FAs. But by November of 2000, the five-three, thirty-four-year-old computer programmer had grown to four hundred pounds, couldn't do her own laundry or clean her own apartment anymore, and had just broken up with her boyfriend, an FA who was encouraging her to get bigger. Worst of all, Shawn was a roller-coaster fanatic who couldn't ride roller coasters anymore due to her size.

"I was fine and active at three hundred and fifty pounds," said Shawn. "But your body can only take so much. When I got up to four hundred pounds, I was just existing. I wasn't living, and I was going to die in ten years. I decided I would rather live for ten years at a normal size and have some fun than sit in my apartment in misery for the same ten years and then die."

Seven months after undergoing WLS, Shawn was down to 275 pounds. Her goal is 200 to 225 pounds.

"That's still fat for someone my height," Shawn said. "I will always be big. I like being big. And I'll always be a part of the fat acceptance movement. But I don't think I can be part of NAAFA anymore."

Sitting on a couch in the lobby, Shawn told me she weighed just 250 pounds when she attended her first NAAFA event.

"People told me I wasn't big enough," Shawn remembered. " 'Oh, you're not a real BBW,' they'd say. Can you believe it? You're told all your life that you're too big, and then you join this club and all these people are telling you you're too *small*. So you start to eat and eat and pretty soon you're up to four hundred pounds. That's how I got so big. All my friends were in NAAFA, and you see all your friends getting bigger, and so you get bigger."

Shawn got hundreds of e-mails after she went public about having WLS. While some were from women and men curious about the surgery, most were negative, and the most vicious e-mails came from NAAFA members she thought of as friends.

"They said, 'You did it because you don't love yourself.' 'You butchered your body because you hate who you are.' I didn't do this because I hate myself. I did it because I love myself. I wanted a better life. I don't want to wind up in a wheelchair. I wanted to go skydiving. I wanted to bungee jump."

Shawn was sure I would hear only the negative about WLS at the seminar. "Don't let those women lie to you," Shawn warned me. "They're going to say you can be any weight you want and be happy and healthy. That's bullshit. When I would ask, 'What's too big?' they would say, 'You can't be too big. It's sizeist to talk about being "too big," ' I would say, 'What if you're so big you can't walk?' And they would say, 'You can use a wheelchair.' I thought to myself, This is ridiculous! I don't want to be a part of this crowd anymore!"

Shawn and Teresa both felt that many NAAFA members were threatened by WLS; some fat members didn't want their fat friends to have the option of being skinny. As for FAs, "It's their worst nightmare," Shawn said, laughing. "What are they going to do if we all get skinny?"

There are, however, some NAAFA members who remember earlier versions of WLS in the seventies and eighties—much riskier surgeries that wound up killing their friends. WLS today is vastly safer, and thousands of people have had the surgery, most famously the singer Carny Wilson.

ey're old school," said Shawn. "They've been in NAAFA ___ the beginning, and they remember when people had the intestinal bypass surgery and died. They don't want to admit that there's this new procedure and that it actually works."

Both Shawn and Teresa were quick to admit that WLS has side effects. Shawn doesn't absorb enough protein, and her muscle mass is low; Teresa has to get shots for vitamin B_{12} deficiency, and she takes supplements for other vitamins.

"You can't have WLS and walk away from it," said Shawn. "You have to constantly monitor your health and food intake."

But couldn't Shawn and Teresa have avoided becoming hugely fat if they'd simply monitored their health and food intake all along? Neither woman would have grown to more than four hundred pounds if they had paid as much attention to their diets before undergoing the surgery as they've been forced to after undergoing it.

"Oh, I love the people who say, 'Just stop eating,' " said Shawn, rolling her eyes at me and looking to Teresa for support. "I tried to do that for thirty-four years. I'd been on diets since I was ten. I was addicted to food. I admit it. I had a food addiction; I couldn't stop eating. WLS forced me to stop."

Three women were on the WLS panel: the moderator and two sisters, one who had the surgery and one who wouldn't have the surgery if you put an icing gun to her head. The sister who had had WLS was a nurse. The nurse was wearing jeans and a sweatshirt, very little makeup, and her hair was reddish brown. She looked pretty nervous and was sitting close to the door. The sister who hadn't had the surgery designs jewelry for big women. She had bright, blond hair, and wore a flowing, vividly colored dress, tinted glasses, and a few pieces of her own jewelry. I'd checked out some of her jewelry earlier in the day at the trade show. Apparently, designing jewelry for fat women, as opposed to thin women, mostly involves considerations of scale. A necklace that would look fun and chunky on a woman who weighed 125 pounds would get lost

on a woman who weighs 400 pounds. The pieces the jewelry designer makes for her clients are lovely, but only big women could
wear her stuff. On a four-hundred-pound woman, her pieces look
fun and chunky; a woman who weighs 125 pounds, on the other
hands, would look like she was wearing a solid gold manhole cover
on an anchor chain.

There were about twenty-five people at the WLS seminar, and
everyone was silent before the moderator began to speak. The
moderator was a fashionably dressed woman with a therapist's
calming voice and demeanor who implored us all to keep our
minds open. Then she handed out a fact sheet she had prepared
that ripped apart WLS. It was clear that the moderator—who was
big but not too heavy—had a closed mind when it came to WLS.
You could sense the tension when she invited the nurse, the sister
who had the surgery, to share her story. The nurse told us she had
the surgery after watching several patients undergo it, and wit-
nessing their improvement. Her side effects were minor, and her
feelings about her decision were positive. The surgery had changed
her life, she said. The only negative? She lost some of her "eating
friends," much like a reformed alcoholic might lose his drinking
buddies.

The moderator then invited the jewelry designer to share her
side of the story. She was shocked that her sister would even consider WLS. She loved her sister unconditionally, of course, and had
watched her lose weight, but her feelings about the surgery were
unchanged. She didn't want to lose weight, and she thought her
sister looked better when she was bigger. The moderator thanked
the nurse for her bravery, but not the jewelry designer. Since everyone at "Help! My Friend Is Getting WLS!" was presumed to be opposed to weight loss surgery it was only the nurse who was being
brave.

The moderator opened up the discussion for questions or comments, reminding us once again not to engage in personal attacks.
The nurse looked around the room, and I could see her bracing for

the condemnations that seemed certain to come. She sat up straight in her chair, squared her shoulders, and rolled her lips between her teeth. The moderator implored us to speak only to our own feelings and, once again, not to engage in personal attacks.

A big man with a red, sweaty face raised his hand—the only other man in the room besides me—and the moderator called on him. The man was perched on the edge of his chair, and was so agitated as he began to speak that he visibly shook. He was having the surgery, he announced. He had diabetes, joint problems, trouble walking, sleep apnea, he couldn't fit in an airline seat anymore, and could no longer tolerate the daily abuse—the slights, the stares, and the jokes he had to put up with at work. Whenever a tool went missing at the plant where he worked, someone would ask him if he had eaten it.

His ultimate reason for having the surgery, though, was the knowledge that he would soon be disabled by his weight. He couldn't stop himself from eating, and he would rather take his risks on the surgery than wind up housebound or in a wheelchair. He told everyone in the room who objected to WLS to open their eyes: the halls of the hotel were full of NAAFA members who were so fat they had to use canes to walk, and there were others who had given up on walking entirely, getting around in wheelchairs and motorized carts. People he knew from years ago, "people who might have been fat and fit once upon a time," were now fat and dying.

The moderator looked horrified, and after she managed to wrest the floor back from the fat man, she explained that people don't get fat because they eat too much. She told us about a recent weight-gain study that proved that some people are genetically programmed to store more fat than others. They put a large group of people, fat and thin, on identical, high-calorie diets. While some people gained as little as ten pounds during the months-long study, others gained thirty or more pounds. This proved, she said, that some people were genetically predisposed to gain weight. Fat people, she corrected the red-faced man, don't get fat because they eat too much. They get fat because their bodies are programmed to be heavy.

The moderator didn't address what seemed like the obvious lesson of the study: People who gain more weight eating the same amounts of food as other people should probably bear that in mind when they belly up to the buffet and eat less. Of course, it's not fair that one person can eat a pint of ice cream every day and remain thin while another person will get hugely obese. But as my fellow conservatives like to point out, America is about equal access, not equal outcomes. Every American may have equal access to ice cream, but there's no guarantee that the outcome of eating ice cream will be equal. And, hey, if there's no shame in being fat—if fat is fit, fun, and sexy—why does it matter so much to NAAFA why someone gets fat? Overeating? Genetic predisposition? Who cares? If fat is good for you, if it's fun and sexy, should it matter how someone gets big? It seemed to me like a rather curious, blame-shifting argument for a fat activist to make. The skinny people blame the fat people for overeating; the fat people blame their genes for overstoring. But if you don't believe there's any shame in being fat—or if you don't believe there should be—why spend time assigning blame? Why not just have another pint of Chocolate Chip Cookie Dough ice cream?

The moderator passed the floor to a very tall woman who weighed at least five hundred pounds. The woman objected to the red-faced man calling fat people who could only get around in wheelchairs or motorized carts as "disabled." They were, she sniffed, "differently mobile." Instead of getting the surgery, fat people should demand bigger airline seats, better treatments for weight-related health conditions, and fat-tolerant workplaces. The next woman to speak, a woman with a huge belly that hung down to her knees, held up her canes and tersely explained to the red-faced man that she never really enjoyed walking all that much, so not being able to get around on her own was no great loss. She lived to read, she said, and she couldn't care less if she could walk. The red-faced man snorted; the moderator silenced him with a look. The nurse who had undergone WLS was in the clear, as the red-faced man was drawing all the fire.

The floor then passed to an apple-shaped woman sitting next to me. She paused and took a deep breath after the moderator called on her. She had just undergone WLS, she said, and pleaded with her fellow fat women to respect her decision. All her friends were eating friends, she said, and she wound up with diabetes and such bad back pain that she couldn't sleep at night. She made up her mind to have the surgery when she had to send away for a special implement to wipe herself after defecating.

"It was a stick," she said. "A stick. I had to wipe myself with a *stick*."

A young woman with a blond bob spoke next. She had also undergone WLS, and said it was something she had to do for herself and her kids.

Three women sitting together began to speak all at once. They challenged the idea that being fat meant they or anyone else in the room was unhealthy. One woman (apple-shaped) said that she rides her bike everywhere she goes, hikes, and swims three times a week. Another woman (pear-shaped) said that it was only a myth that being fat was bad for you; fat people needed to eat right and move, but they didn't need to lose weight to be healthy. The third (gourd-shaped?) insisted that her eating wasn't out of control and insisted she didn't have any "eating friends," only friends she eats with. All three of the "fat and fit" women looked to be in their mid-twenties, and none appeared to weigh more than 250 pounds. They did look fit—especially compared with the woman with the canes who didn't care if she lost her ability to walk.

All of this was too much for the red-faced fat man, who began speaking without waiting for the moderator to call on him. He wagged a finger at the three fat-and-fit women. While they may not be experiencing any weight-related health problems now, they would sooner or later. They were like smokers who insist that smoking can't be all bad for you because they haven't come down with lung cancer yet. The three fat-and-fit women began to argue with the fat man, which prompted the moderator to wrap up "Help! My Friend Is Getting WLS!" before a brawl broke out. This wasn't what I came to San Francisco for! I wanted to spend the weekend with happy, content gluttons, a hotel filled with happy, content, fat people enjoying guilt-free meals. Instead I found myself trapped in a hotel full of fat people tearing each other apart.

I kept my word and escorted Teresa and Shawn to the formal dance on Saturday night. The walls had been opened up to create the largest version of the Westin's collapsible ballroom, and soon after we arrived the ballroom was full of fat women wearing the kinds of outfits fat women are rarely seen in—flashy sequined numbers, sleeveless gowns, and little black dresses held up by little black straps. There was a lot of exposed flesh and a lot of time and trouble had been taken with hair and makeup. Most fat women try to get through the day without being noticed; most don't want to attract any more attention to their already hyper-scrutinized bodies. But the Westin's ballroom was filled to bursting with big women in outfits that screamed *"Look at me!"*

There were very few men in the room when we arrived—there were actually fewer men in the ballroom at dinner than there had been at breakfast. But we passed a dozen or more men lurking in the hallways outside the ballroom on our way in.

"The FAs are out in force," Teresa said as we made our way to the ballroom. While a lot of FAs enjoy watching women eat, Teresa explained, most of the FAs who attend NAAFA dinner dances typically skip the dinner and buy a dance-only ticket.

Teresa and Shawn ate very little, just like they had at breakfast. Their small stomachs require them to eat five or six little meals over the course of the day, instead of three large meals. If they eat too much at once, they'll throw the food up. When dinner was over, the doors to the ballroom were flung open and FAs seeped in like a gas, spreading across the ballroom while me and the BBWs were finishing our desserts. Most of the FAs were older, some were dressed rather fussily, and every last one was at least as skinny as I was.

"The National Association to Advance Fat Acceptance believes that a preference for a fat partner is as valid as any other preference based on physical characteristics, such as a particular height, eye color, or hair color," reads NAAFA's official position paper on fat admirers. "Individuals who are attracted to a fat partner should be able to pursue, date, and make a commitment to a person of their size preference without fear of societal ridicule. Further, NAAFA believes that in a society where at least 55 percent of the population is considered fat, a preference for a fat partner is normal and should be encouraged rather than discouraged."

NAAFA's position paper on FAs urges these men to come out of the closet and organize their own movement. The FAs at the dance, lurking in the corners, didn't seem like "movement" types. When I approached an FA near the bar in the ballroom and asked him what he found attractive about fat women, he wasn't able to look me in the eye. Maybe he could tell I wasn't an FA, and he wasn't comfortable discussing his preference with me. After an awkward hesitation, he said, "Not until you run your hands over someone supersized can you appreciate how wonderful all that flesh feels." Then he slunk off.

The general consensus at our table was that most FAs are a little creepy; a lot of them are ashamed of their attraction to fat women, and they're not very good at concealing their feelings of shame. They come to NAAFA events (indeed, NAAFA encourages them to come), seduce fat women in hotel rooms, and then run home to skinny wives and girlfriends. When one particularly notorious FA was spotted in the room, a brassy blonde in metallic silver hot pants and a matching bra ran from table to table, warning her fat sisters about this particular FA's MO.

"He'll say, 'Oh, I love you, I want to marry you, I want you to meet my mother,' " she warns the women at my table, "and the moment you sleep with him, he's gone."

As we dished the FAs, I remembered something I read on NAAFA's Web site before I came to San Francisco. "At different times throughout history, the fat figure was looked upon as the ideal, desirable figure," according to NAAFA. "Today, the American cultural aesthetic of beauty ranges from the thin supermodel whose proportions are unrepresentative of the naturally occurring shape of the human female, to an emaciated, sunken-eyed look termed 'heroin chic.' "

Beauty ideals are not and have never been democratic; if majority rule applied to beauty ideals, then fat would definitely be in. The reason certain traits become beauty ideals is precisely because of their rarity or the difficulty the average person has in achieving them. When food was scarce, heavy people were beautiful; when most people worked in the sun all day, white skin was sexy. Now that food is plentiful—even the poor are obese—thin is beautiful; now that most people have to work inside all day, tan skin is sexy. The thin that's sexy isn't just your run-of-the-mill thin, but a thin that says, "I can look on all the food spread before me every day and ignore it, not indulge. I can control myself. I can starve myself." America's current beauty ideal isn't so much anti-fat as pro-youth and pro–self-denial, both increasingly rare traits in the United States as boomers age and their asses spread like Krispy Kreme franchises. Fat will be back in style when famines are.

But now it's time to dance.

I'm all for sin, and I'm pro-gluttony, but I'm not deluded. A sober celibate who eats very little and drinks next to nothing will probably outlive me—he'll outlive everybody who indulges in drugs, sex, food, and booze. (Unless he gets run over by a beer truck driven by an oversexed pothead, which would serve him right.) The value of a single life, however, isn't only measured in time; quantity of life is important, of course (who wants to die young?), but quality of life also matters. The sober celibate may live to be a hundred, but what good is a hundred years of life if you're miserable the entire time? Sober celibates aren't necessarily miserable, of course, but personally, I would be a miserable sober celibate. I thank God and Thomas Jefferson and the rest of the founding fathers that I'm free to enjoy my life and indulge myself and sin and pursue happiness in ways that carry some risks, even if the way I choose to live shaves a decade or two off my life.

All I ask of the world and my fellow citizens is to leave me alone; I don't ask, à la NAAFA, that everyone pretend my sins are risk-free. I went to the NAAFA's weekend celebration to spend time with big, fat, gluttonous, *content* Americans. What I found was an organization that couldn't admit that the pleasures of gluttony were worth the health risks of obesity—and I found very little public gluttony. The women who were having the surgery and becoming "too thin" for the size-acceptance movement, couldn't eat much at any one time; women who were content being fat didn't eat much in public either, as that might contradict NAAFA's fat-people-aren't-fat-from-eating-too-much dogma. No one at any of the buffets I attended cut loose.

But it was time that I did.

Like the nurse and the other woman at the WLS seminar, I have a special eating friend. Tim is a straight guy and in good shape, but he has fat-hoarding genes and he has to watch what he eats. He rides his bike everywhere, eats salads for lunch, and tries to have plain grilled chicken breasts for dinner a couple of times a week. I follow pretty much the same routine. But our resolve goes to hell when we eat together. We're like a man and woman who are desperately attracted to each other but, alas, married to other people. It's not a good idea for Tim and me to spend much time together.

The two of us have gone to restaurants and ordered three appetizers and three entrées. If we're out together and Tim doesn't order an appetizer, I'll order one for him. We can never pass up dessert when we eat together, something we're capable of doing when we're with other people. Once in a very expensive restaurant, we were having a hard time deciding which one of the five items on the dessert menu we would split. Tim got up to go to the bathroom, leaving me to choose. All five desserts were sitting on the table when Tim returned. Nothing remained of our desserts when we staggered out of the restaurant an hour later.

Our dining relationship is sick and self-destructive. We both refer to eating together as MAD, for "mutually assured destruction," a reference to the Cold War stalemate that kept the peace for half a century. Basically, if I'm going to get fat, so is Tim, and vice versa. I suspect there's some repressed erotic component to all this oral gratification. Tim's girlfriend, a doctor, weighs about ninety pounds and would forget to eat if Tim didn't remind her. Abbey takes no great pleasure in food and, unlike Tim and me, Abbey doesn't see the thrill in eating her way through the dessert menu in an expensive restaurant. Abbey eats, but without passion. My boyfriend, on the other hand, loves food, and eats constantly. But Terry is a six-foot-tall, 150-pound swimmer—he's basically 139 pounds of bone and muscle, 10 pounds of skin, and 1 pound of hair. Terry will never be fat, no matter how much he eats, so food has no dire consequences for him, no danger. For Terry, crème brûlée is not an act of glamorous, self-destructive transgression. It's just dessert.

With me, Tim can share a sinful passion that his girlfriend will never understand; with Tim, I can tempt a fate (obesity) that Terry never has to worry about. Since eating together feels so much like we're cheating on our partners, I had to say no when Terry tried to invite himself along on a date Tim and I made to eat at Claim Jumper, a West Coast restaurant chain famous for its huge portions. Tim and I planned to go MAD.

It was a chocolate cake that brought me to Claim Jumper. A seven-layer chocolate cake taller than it is wide, the Motherlode confronted us as soon as we entered the Claim Jumper. The cake squatted in a glass pastry case facing the door, looking for all the world like an upside-down trash can covered in chocolate frosting and studded with walnuts. The frighteningly phallic cake looked enormous and threatening in the pastry case, dwarfing the enormous pieces of cheesecake, six-inch square brownies, and grapefruit-size muffins arranged around it. Since the display case holding all these superpastries faces the restaurant's supersize doors, the Motherlode is the first thing every diner who enters a Claim Jumper sees.

Stunned by the sight of this chocolate cake—picture the mountain in *Close Encounters of the Third Kind* covered in chocolate frosting—it took me a moment to notice the teenager peering over the top of the pastry case. The hostess had to ask us for the number of people in our party three times before I finally heard her. She took our names and told us the wait would be about forty-five minutes. Then she handed us a pager and a square piece of cardboard with DANCE HALL GIRLS printed on it. Apparently, when our table is ready, she would beep us; if we failed to respond, she intended to humiliate us by shouting, "Dance Hall Girls, party of two, Dance Hall Girls."

There are twenty-nine Claim Jumper restaurants in California, Arizona, Colorado, Nevada, and Washington State. It doesn't much matter which Claim Jumper we're in, nor does it much matter what city or state we're in. All Claim Jumpers have the same Old West theme, the same slowly rotating fans and Tiffany-style lamps, the same tin ceilings and wood posts, and the same moose and buffalo heads staring down from the same faux river-rock walls. And like so many restaurants in the United States, the Claim Jumper we visited served food to white folks prepared for us by brown folks. What makes Claim Jumper unique, though, is not the Old West theme, but the portions. Everything at Claim Jumper is huge, from single orders of onion rings that can feed eight people, to their thirty-two-ounce serving of prime rib, to that monstrous chocolate cake in the display case. Each Claim Jumper location seats five hundred people, and all together the twenty-nine Claim Jumper restaurants take in about $200 million per year.

The Claim Jumper location I visited sits in the middle of nowhere, off a highway, not far from a mall—all Claim Jumpers are in the middle of nowhere, off highways, near malls. The only way to get to a Claim Jumper is by car; the only way to leave is by car. The food is trucked in, the waiters and cooks and hostesses park their cars in the far-off corners of the huge parking lots that surrounds the restaurants. We drove past a Tony Roma's Famous For Ribs, an Outback Steak House, a Chi-Chi's, two Houlihan's, and a Rainforest Cafe on our way to the Claim Jumper. Like those other mall restaurants, a Claim Jumper isn't really a place. It's an intersection. Cars filled with customers cross paths here with trucks filled with food.

While we're both gluttons, I have one distinct advantage over Tim when it comes to avoiding obesity: I don't smoke dope quite so often as Tim does. Marijuana makes gluttons out of normal people, so it's probably not a great idea for people who are already gluttons to smoke dope in a car parked outside a restaurant that serves foot-and-half-high pieces of chocolate cake. But the suburbs make Tim nervous, so after we put our names on the greasy waiting list, we went back out to the car, beeper in hand, and took the edge off. I hadn't planned to get high, but I took a hit. I figured that, like a runner doing wind sprints before a race, a little appetite-enhancing pot would help me get through the marathon of a meal we were about to embark on.

"Two hits should probably do us both," he whispered.

As I pointed out in the "Sloth" chapter, I don't smoke a lot of dope, and two hits can do me in. But I didn't want to make Tim feel self-conscious about how much dope he was smoking, so I took a second hit.

"You know, the car is a long way from the restaurant," Tim said, taking a third hit, "and we wouldn't want to come all the way back here in the middle of dinner. . . ."

The Dance Hall Girls wound up taking a third and a fourth hit before we stumbled out of the car and back to the Claim Jumper. Once inside, I was drawn back to the Motherlode, which I stared at with an intensity that unnerved the hostess; she shot me some dirty looks from behind the pastry case. I only managed to pull myself away from the pastry display case when I noticed that there were pieces of Motherlode cake on plates all along the counter surrounding the Claim Jumper's pizza oven. I floated over. The teenage white boys and Mexican men making pizza didn't seem to mind that I was leaning over their counter, staring at the slabs of chocolate cake.

"It's plastic," said one of the boys behind the counter, gesturing towards the cake. He had a mouthful of braces and was looking at me through narrowed eyes. Over the pizza boy's head a sign in Old West lettering read PIZZA & DESSERTS GRILL EST. 1849 RE-EST. 1977.

"Plastic?" I asked.

"Fake," he said. "That piece, the stuff in the pastry case. It's for display only, you can't eat it."

I rushed back to the pastry case. Of course! There was a single slice of Motherlode cake on a plate in the pastry case, but the towering cake itself was uncut—and the piece that was on the plate was perfectly uniform! The frosting's complexion was unblemished (no nicks from the slicing, no dents from being set on the plate), and the layers of brown frosting between layers of dark cake were perfectly even. What's more, all the pastries on display were fake! The massive slices of cheesecake weren't sweaty, like they would be in a cooler, there were no grease marks in the two or three empty spots on the trays of brownies and cookies; there were no crumbs anywhere near the muffins. Plastic pastries!

I grabbed Tim and pointed out the fake cake, the fake cookies, the fake brownies, the fake muffins, the fake cheesecakes . . . and suddenly the Buffalo heads and fake cakes and the surly hostesses and fat patrons and the pizza grill established in 1849 all seemed pretty hilarious. We were laughing so hard we doubled over. We tried to get ourselves under control, but no doubt we looked like two very high, very skinny guys who didn't really belong in a restaurant filled with large, sober, suburban gluttons. Heavy women in baggy T-shirts moved away from us, while grown men in baggy shorts and baseball hats looked around, trying to figure out what was so funny. I thought we were about to be tossed out when the hostess crooked a finger at us, calling us back up to . . . oh, no! NOT THE PASTRY CASE FULL OF FAKE CAKES!

Instead of throwing us out, the hostess quickly showed us to an enormous oversize booth. We'd been waiting for only twenty-five minutes, and our pager hadn't gone off, so I asked the hostess if she was seating us early to get us the hell out of the waiting area. She just smiled tightly, handed us menus, turned on a heel and marched back to . . . oh, no! THE PASTRY CASE FULL OF FAKE CAKES!

We were still laughing about the fake cakes when our waitress arrived and set two water glasses on our table—two enormous water glasses that, when we held them up and took a sip, made us look like toddlers waiting for Mom to bring us PB&Js. Soon we were laughing our asses off about—oh, no!—the huge water glasses! The water glasses at the Claim Jumper were not an accident, if you ask me, nor were they designed to spare Claim Jumper's waiters the agony of refilling our water glasses (that was our waitress's explanation). No, like the oversize plates the food is served on and the oversize stools at the bar for people too hungry to wait for a table, and the oversize booth we were escorted to by the furious hostess, the Claim Jumper's enormous water glasses are designed to make enormous Americans feel like they're not really that enormous. "Come on," the glasses say, "you're a tiny little kid. Have some onion rings, have a piece of cake. . . ."

After our waitress told us about the specials and left to get our drinks, we tried to focus on the menu: burgers, ribs, chicken, pizza. While the portions we'd seen waiters and waitresses carrying around the restaurant on platter-size plates were huge—more than living up to the hype—the prices on the menu were no higher than those at restaurants serving normal size portions of the exact same foods.

"Jesus, how do they make money doing this?" Tim asked, looking through the menu.

"Yeah, how do they do it?" I said.

Then a disturbing thought popped into our pot-addled heads—suddenly we knew how the Claim Jumper did it, how they sold huge portions at regular prices and turned a profit. Or, I should say, we *thought* we knew how they did it. Before I share this realization let me preface it with one fact about pot: Mild paranoia is a well-known side effect of smoking marijuana. So Tim and I were both feeling a little paranoid when we concluded that the only way Claim Jumper could sell twice as much food for the same amount of money as other restaurants was by . . . God Almighty . . . was by . . . buying the *cheapest, rankest, lowest-end* cuts of "meat" that they could possibly find. Claim Jumper's first concern when ordering food from wholesalers would have to be mass, Tim observed, quantity, not quality.

A spokesperson for Claim Jumper might insist that they can sell huge portions at low prices because they buy quality foods in bulk, and that may very well be the case. There wasn't a spokesperson for Claim Jumper in our booth with us, however, and so no one challenged our conclusion about the food. Our conclusion—whether it's true or not, whether Claim Jumper buys quality in bulk or buys crap in bulk—had an immediate impact on our order. Tim had originally planned to have the meat loaf, but we quickly ruled *that* item out. Meat loaf is ground beef, and there's no floor with ground beef. You can grind up lips, assholes, udders, pigeons, rats, and busboys, call it "ground beef," shape it into a loaf, and serve it without having to worry about the customers catching on.

So the burgers, nachos, potpies, and meat loaf were out.

We figured that we couldn't be too badly abused by the whole roast chicken. With a whole chicken, there's a floor. Claim Jumper would have to serve us something that, after preparation, looked like something that was once a live chicken. When it comes to a whole chicken, there's a point past which no restaurant chain can dare sink and still get away with calling the thing on your plate chicken. I ordered the whole roast chicken. Tim ordered barbecued baby-back ribs. Like chicken, ribs have to look like ribs. They might come from the scrawniest, most underfed, miserable pig that ever lived and died in an airless shed on an industrial farm, but they would have to be recognizable ribs, not udders and assholes and index fingers.

Unless . . .

After Marshmallow Peeps, the scariest processed food product currently available in the United States is McDonald's McRib Sandwich. Lift the top of the bun off a McRib Sandwich and the meat sitting on the bottom of the bun looks just like ribs, with familiar rectangular ridges where the rib bones cut through the meat. But there are no bones in a McRib Sandwich—no one is dumb enough to buy a sandwich with bones in it, not even people who eat at McDonald's. So why will we buy a sandwich with a processed patty made from shredded pig meat that has been sculpted to look like a tiny slab of ribs, bones and all? I suppose it was possible that the Claim Jumper's "whole" chicken or "slab of baby-back ribs" could be from shredded bits of the cheapest pigs and chickens, just like a McRib Sandwich. And even if my chicken arrived with what appeared to be bones in it, well, how could I be certain that what was on my plate wasn't processed chicken scraps mushed into a "whole" chicken shaped over a set of reusable fiberglass chicken bones?

While I contemplated these and other horrors, Tim asked our waitress to get us some onion rings. We were going MAD.

Everywhere we looked while we waited for our food, we could see uniformly fat men and women digging into meat loaf and ribs, Motherlodes and slabs of cheesecake—unlike the NAAFA convention, no one was holding back. This particular Claim Jumper wasn't full of people who wanted to be exonerated for being fat;

they came fat or they came to get fat. One of the women who spoke at NAAFA's WLS seminar described her out-of-control eating as slow-motion suicide. There was no one at Claim Jumper who appeared to be eating himself or herself to death—no one in a motorized cart, no one who weighed more than three hundred pounds—but there was something perverse and self-punishing about Claim Jumper. What self-destructive impulse drives people already struggling with their weight to go out of their way to eat in a restaurant where they're going to be overserved?

So besides that, Mama Cass, how was the food?

Huge. The bushel of onion rings our waitress brought to the table could have fed a dorm full of stoned college students, and while our beefsteak tomato salads were inedible—the huge slices of bright red tomato crunched like celery and tasted like Styrofoam—my whole chicken and Tim's barbecued ribs were, if not delicious, still not the worst things that ever happened to a couple of farm animals. The chicken was mysteriously moist, if completely without flavor, leading Tim to conclude that the bird had been dunked in a deep-fat fryer before it took a quick spin on the Claim Jumper's wood-fired rotisserie. Tim's ribs were flavorful, but the meat was not "falling off the bone," as the menu promised.

Readers of *Consumer Reports* magazine—no doubt awestruck by the enormous portions—ranked Claim Jumper as the fourth-best chain restaurant in the United States. If volume is the best measure of a restaurant's performance (and not taste and texture), then perhaps Claim Jumper is the fourth-best restaurant chain in the United States. Two old ladies in the old Woody Allen joke would certainly approve: Sitting in a restaurant, one complains that the food is terrible. "Yes," the second old lady responds, "and the portions are small." Those old ladies would love the Claim Jumper, where the food may be terrible food but the portions are *huge*.

Writing about gluttony, Saint Gregory warns us of the Five Fingers of the Devil's Hand: eating at inappropriate hours, "overdelicacy" in a person's choice of meat and drink, overindulgence, overly curious in experimentation with exotic food and drink, and greedy table manners. Americans have only three fingers of the Devil's Hand, as we overindulge, have awful table manners, and eat at all hours. We are not, however, particularly picky about *what* we will and will not eat; everything set before us at the Claim Jumper was garbage, and the place was packed.

But we didn't really come here for the chicken or the ribs or the onion rings. We came for the cake, the Motherlode, and though we were already full (our meals came with corn muffins as big as our heads that—surprise!—were just huge pieces of yellow cake), we nevertheless did our duty and ordered a piece of chocolate cake. À la mode.

We'd been at the Claim Jumper for two hours by the time we were ready for our cake; while the hostess was anxious to seat us, the kitchen didn't seem all that anxious to feed us. For two hours I'd been watching waiters set down Motherlodes in front of other diners, and each and every customer had the exact same reaction: Their eyes went wide, they laughed, and then looked up at the other people at their table, expressions of shock and delight playing on their faces.

When our waitress, Lisa, set our slab of Motherlode down on our table, Tim and I gave each other that same shocked and delighted look. Only then did I realize that I'd seen this look before, the look we just shared, the look I'd been seeing all night, over and over again, as slabs of Motherlode were set on tables. It was the look people give each other just before they jump out of airplanes wearing parachutes or off bridges with bungee cords wrapped around their ankles. It was a wide-eyed, nervous, I-can't-believe-we're-going-to-do-this look. Sitting in this intersection tarted up as a restaurant, ordering cake, we were all sharing the high we usually experience in moments of death-defying danger, however contrived the circumstances. On airplanes and bridges, the look asks, "What happens if my parachute doesn't open?" or, "What happens if the bungee cord breaks?" At the Claim Jumper, it asks, "What happens if I eat this whole piece of cake?" The answer to all three questions is the same: You will die. That's what makes jumping out of airplanes and off bridges so exciting—and it's what makes that piece of chocolate cake so exciting.

The whole point of this corporate gimmick of a chocolate cake is its death-defying size, not its taste—and it truly was an enormous piece of cake. Eating an entire piece of Motherlode in one go could kill any normal person and that, of course, is the point. The Claim Jumper chain has successfully repackaged dessert as an extreme sport, but instead of asking "How fast can I ride my bike down this mountain?" diners at the Claim Jumper ask themselves, "How much of this foot-and-a-half-long, eight-inch-wide piece of chocolate cake can I stuff in my mouth?"

The most exciting part of jumping out of an airplane is the moment before, that split-second when you make the final decision to jump, to physically propel yourself out of the aircraft and into thin air. Ask anyone who jumps. The descent is almost beside the point, a two-minute anticlimax as you float down to earth. It's that split-second, death-defying decision to jump that keeps you coming back. While the Claim Jumper does provide its customers with an almost perfect death-defying-dessert experience, please be warned: The experience is complete before you take a single bite. The death-defying rush comes when you decide whether or not to *order* a piece of that cake. We'd seen the Motherlode when we walked in, and we'd seen it on plates hitting tables all over the restaurant while we ate our dinner. Lisa even brought a homey-looking dessert tray filled with plastic replicas of all the Claim Jumper's desserts to our table before we ordered. We were already full from dinner. We looked at each other. Would we order dessert? Yes, we would! Let's do it! Let's go! Go! GO! And so . . . the rush. We did it! We jumped! We ordered a piece of that huge fucking cake! Dude!

Then Lisa had to go and ruin our high by bringing us a piece of cake. The Motherlode she set down on our table looked a lot like the fake cake in the pastry case, but with some slight imperfections: the frosting was nicked off one corner, the cake wasn't perfectly centered on the plate. With a piece of the cake finally sitting in front of us, I suddenly felt the same way I do when I find myself sitting in the front passenger seat of a huge gas-sucking SUV: I felt like a complete asshole.

The Motherlode is to chocolate cake what the Ford Expedition is to automobiles: a ridiculous exaggeration, a self-conscious, pushy, no-one-really-needs-something-that-big, show-offy parody of a piece of chocolate cake. We picked up our forks and took our first bites. Like two guys floating down to earth with parachutes strapped to our backs, we realized that the truly transcendent moment had come and gone and that the rest—the falling, the eating—was all anticlimax. As cheap chocolate cake goes (and I'm a fan), the Motherlode was a disappointment. Like everything else at Claim Jumper, the cake was greasy; each bite instantly turned into a sort of gritty paste in our mouths, and the only clue that the cake was supposed to be chocolate was its color.

My eating friend and I did our solemn duty, though. With the help of the pot we smoked in the car, we managed to polish off our Motherlode. Jerry, Robert, Rush, and William would've been proud of us.

Meet the Rich

Envy has shaped and continues to shape our political culture. That is probably why it is front-page news in the New York Times *that the United States displays greater inequality in wealth than other industrialized nations. The unstated assumption that makes this worthy of the front page is that there is something morally wrong, even shameful, in having greater wealth inequalities than other societies.* —Robert Bork

Men were kept from rootless hedonism, which is the end stage of unconfined individualism, by religion, morality, and law. To them I would add the necessity for hard work, usually physical work, and the fear of want. These constraints were progressively undermined by rising affluence. —Robert Bork

I wouldn't have to bring much with me to the pricey weight-loss spa outside Malibu. Whatever I wore on the daily hikes through the mountains would be washed at night by the maid and ready to wear the next day. The Ashram would also provide me with sweats, T-shirts, and bathrobes; many Ashram veterans, the voice message continued, arrive at the spa with just the clothes on their backs, their hiking shoes, and their toothbrushes.

Just a short drive from Cher's house, the Ashram has been helping affluent Americans drop unwanted pounds for more than twenty-five years. The spa's weight-loss program consists of a week's worth of forced marches up and down the mountains in the desert combined with a strict low-calorie diet. I'm not much of a hiker, I'm not affluent, and I didn't like the idea of some stranger taking control of my diet, but . . . I had packed on ten pounds dining with the ladies of NAAFA, stuffing myself at the buffets in Las Vegas, and eating at the German restaurant in the Julien Inn in Dubuque. In real life I could never afford to go to a place like the Ashram—the weeklong program costs $3,200, almost $500 bucks per day—but in book-deal life, well, how could I afford not to go?

Whenever someone points out that the rich have it better in the United States than the rest of us—better schools, better tax cuts, better spas—conservative pundits and politicians accuse him of engaging in "class warfare." Class warfare is a no-no in the United States because we're not supposed to have classes here, just taxpayers and citizens, all of us equal before the law. That's the way it's supposed to work. In reality, we've got classes, and a class war has been raging in the United States since Ronald Reagan was elected in 1980. Since 1980, the rich have gotten richer, and the working class has gotten screwed. Americans with full-time, minimum-wage jobs live below the poverty line; millions of Americans have little or no access to health care; and underfunded schools trap the children of poor parents in an unbreakable cycle of poverty.

While we're told there isn't money in the budget for, say, a national health-care program—which would do more to help working and lower-middle class American families than a thousand years' worth of Republican "pro-family" rhetoric—there never seems to be enough money in the budget for a program that would benefit the majority of American workers. There's always money, however, for a new corporate tax break, for another round of tax cuts for the wealthy. You've got to hand it to the Republicans—they've been wildly successful at convincing lower- and working-class Americans to vote against their own class interests (remember Reagan Democrats?), and they've somehow managed to convince working-class Americans that what's good for rich Americans is good for America, period, despite a mountain of evidence to the contrary.

Which brings me to envy and the Ashram.

According to Peraldus, a thirteenth-century Dominican friar, envy is the only sin that does not delight in itself. While lusty gluttons derive pleasure indulging themselves in sex and food respectively, the envious succeed only in making themselves miserable. Envy "creates sorrow out of joy," said Peraldus. I wasn't looking for sorrow at the Ashram, just envy, and a kind of envy that's taboo in the United States: class envy. Like the *New York Times,* I am distressed by the gap between the rich and poor in the United States. I don't have anything against rich people in general; like all people, I wouldn't mind being one of the rich people. Still, I'm often annoyed when the rich flaunt their wealth in a world of want. Using some of my publisher's money to buy a week at the Ashram would not only help me drop those NAAFA, Claim Jumper, and Vegas pounds, but it would also expose me to people who have more money than I do and to people who were in better shape than I was—and, really, aren't looks and money the two things Americans are most envious of in others?

Americans may heap praise on the virtuous, we may admire them, but very few of us envy them—that is, we don't want to *be* them. Based on a close reading of *People* magazine in the eighties and nineties, it's clear that Americans loved and admired Mother Teresa, who gave away all of her possessions and dedicated her life to serving the poor. Very few Americans if any at all envied her enough to emulate her. The people we envy, the people whose joys fill us with sorrow, are the rich, beautiful, famous, and fuckable. Mother Teresa, sadly, was only one of those four things.

At the Ashram, I hoped to observe the rich and the beautiful in a place where they don't have to interact with the poor and the ugly. Perhaps I would leave the Ashram with a slimmer, trimmer figure, fewer concerns about the gap between rich and poor, a new appreciation for tax cuts targeted at wealthy families, gated communities, and the wit and wisdom of Steve Forbes. That I would be able to write off my week's stay at the Ashram was the clincher: Seven days at a spa, hiking in the mountains, mixing with the swells, writing it all off—it's nice work if you can get it and, hey, I could get it for free.

Provided I could get into the Ashram.

The spa takes only thirteen paying guests per week, which means only 676 rich folks can get into the place in a year. When I first called the Ashram to make a reservation, I was told there wasn't much hope. They were booked solid for the next ten months. I wasn't even in at the Ashram yet, and I was already feeling envious. Other people—people with more money or better connections—already had reservations! Their joy, my sorrow. I was invited to put my name on the waiting list, but I was warned not to sit at home by the phone. Openings were rare, and the odds of getting in any time soon were slim. I hadn't been on the waiting list for more than a month when I got a call about a last-minute cancellation. If I could be at a hotel near the Los Angeles airport by noon the next day, Mary told me, the open slot was mine for $3,200. I booked a pricey, last-minute flight to Southern California, reassuring myself that my flight, like my week at the Ashram, was fully tax deductible.

I was in a rush to get my ass to the airport, so I took Mary's advice and brought very little, throwing just one pair of underwear and some gym clothes into a backpack. I paid full fare for my ticket, and the check-in clerk noticed and bumped me up to first class. I'd never flown first class before, and it was a fitting beginning to my journey. Not only was I headed to a place that most people can't afford (which makes 'em envious), I was sitting in first class, too! I was used to being treated like cattle on airplanes, flying exclusively in coach, and the level of service in first class was positively unnerving. I wasn't accustomed to being served by an aggressively servile steward, nor was I accustomed to being on the receiving end of the dirty looks grumpy people headed towards coach shoot people in first class. People flying coach envied my orange juice, they envied the real glass I was drinking it from, and, of course, they envied my wide leather seat. Envy may create sorrow out of joy, as Peraldus pointed out, but only for the person doing the envying. For the envied, envy is positively delightful. I know I'd never enjoyed a glass of orange juice so much in my life as I did on that flight to Los Angeles.

Once I got to L.A., I was reduced once again to cattle (my normal flying status), packed into a shuttle bus, and driven to a nearby hotel where incoming Ashramites rendezvous. Walking into the lobby, I spotted some of my fellow guests: handsome, well-preserved middle-aged women without much luggage. Everyone had the pensive expression of a kid on her way to camp, and each one was wearing incongruous-looking hiking boots. We would all be giving up control over our schedules, diets, and daily lives for the next seven days, and these moments in the lobby were our last chance to do whatever the hell we wanted. Most of the incoming Ashramites were having one last cup of coffee. Keenly aware that I wouldn't have access to my daily doses of refined sugar, I wolfed down a candy bar.

A big white van appeared in the hotel's driveway, and everyone made their way to the doors. THE ASHRAM was written on the side of the van in a groovy, Yellow Submarine–era font. A cute little "Love Is . . ."–style angel hovered over the name. The font and the angel betrayed the Ashram's early seventies' roots, but the van was brand-new. A tan young man with thick blond hair on his head and on his legs jumped out of the van. Randy stacked our bags in the back of the van as everyone took one last sip of their coffees and Cokes. There were nine of us; seven women and two men. Four other Ashramites were already at the spa, Randy told us, two women and another man, and the drive would take about forty-five minutes. The van was cramped, and no one spoke as we made our way out of Los Angeles.

We drove through L.A., in and out of canyons, along the Pacific Ocean, past Cher's house, and deep into the desert. When we were nearing Malibu, an older blond woman with a deep tan broke the ice by telling all of us about a wedding she'd been to recently. Apparently, the bride's family budgeted a hundred thousand dollars for flowers alone. My ride in first class suddenly seemed like ancient history as my class envy was kicked into gear. Soon two women sitting behind me started swapping stories about their horses. "I can always spot a horsewoman," the first horsewoman said to the second horsewoman.

We pulled up in front of the five-hundred-dollar-a-day Ashram, "the boot camp of spas," according to Randy, who was not only a driver but one of the Ashram's guides and yoga instructors. The boot camp of spas? For five hundred dollars a day I expected luxury—hell, I paid for luxury. The thirteen of us came to this spot in the desert to lose weight and reconnect with our spirits, sure, but before and after the daily hikes I expected private baths, thick towels, deep tubs, deluxe mattresses, and some swank window treatments. What I saw out the van's windows when we pulled up, however, didn't look promising. Randy parked the van in front of a completely unremarkable single-family home, sitting on a small hill at the end of a road near the bottom of a canyon. Aloe plants and cacti were scattered around, baking in the sun, while here and there paint peeled off statues of Saint Francis and Buddha. The house itself was covered with dusty white stucco and some dry vines.

The inside wasn't any better. A heavy Spanish-style door opened into a narrow vestibule; there were benches, cubby holes for our hiking shoes, and an ancient framed map of the mountains on the wall. The living room straight ahead was dominated by a low, semicircular couch/conversation pit upholstered in a purple-brown-green color that won't be cycling back into vogue any time soon. A low, heavy, dark-wood coffee table with a white marble insert sat in front of the couch, and a long dining room table was just a step or two away. The Ashram's tiny, L-shaped kitchen was just off the dining area, with crystals hanging on fishing lines strung up in the window over the sink. The living room had fake box-beam ceilings, several swag lamps, and gas flames lapping at fake logs in the fireplace. Hanging over the fireplace was a wood plaque: BE STILL AND KNOW THAT I AM GOD/ BE STILL AND KNOW THAT I AM/BE STILL AND KNOW/BE STILL/BE . . .

I was being charged five hundred dollars a day to hang out at my best friend's house in the suburbs, circa 1977.

The place had once been a single-family ranch house built in the early 1970s—think the Brady house. To accommodate thirteen paying-through-the-nose guests, rooms had been haphazardly added to the home. My bedroom was in a boxy, un–air-conditioned, two-bedroom addition on the side of the house that got late-afternoon sun. There was one bathroom in the addition, which I shared with four complete strangers. (For five hundred dollars a day, I didn't think I should have to use a can that someone else stank up.) The bright yellow bedspread on my bed matched the yellow curtains and yellow walls. A simple pine dresser was all that separated my bed from . . . *my roommate's bed.* I was paying five hundred dollars a day to share a bathroom and a bedroom with strangers at the Bradys' house.

Like other well-off conservative scolds, Robert Bork clearly recognizes the character-building benefits of other people's poverty. "Religion tends to be strongest when life is hard," he writes, "and the same may be said of morality and law." He's right, of course. A man who isn't sure where his next meal is coming from is likelier to be found on his knees in a church than he is in a restaurant. But if hardship and the fear of want render people and nations virtuous, it's hard to understand why Bork and other conservatives object so strongly to taxing the wealthy. If the government soaked the rich to finance a single-payer national health-care program it wouldn't make the working poor affluent, and therefore less virtuous. It would, however, make the affluent a little less affluent and, according to Bork's logic, a little *more* virtuous.

Even if money extracted from the wealthy in the form of taxes wasn't spent on social programs or anything else that might mini-mize the socially toxic impact that wealth inequality has in the United States, reducing the net income of the wealthy Americans is something we should do *for their own good.* In addition to making money available to provide for the common good (health care, meat inspectors, national defense), hiking the taxes of the affluent would make the rich less affluent and therefore—provided Bork is correct—more religious, moral, and mindful of the law. (Who knows? If Ken Lay had to shoulder a slightly more onerous tax bur-den, perhaps Enron wouldn't have been run so crookedly.) If the government should come between music lovers and rap, pot smokers and pot, adulterers and other people's spouses, well, why shouldn't the government come between the rich and their money? Even if envy is the motivating factor, as Bork believes, the end re-sult would still be a net increase in American virtue.

William J. Bennett is another big fan of other people's poverty, listing affluence among the many threats to the American family. Bennett's list of threats to the American family is long; it includes individualism, the Pill, women in the workforce, "legalized abor-tion" (illegal abortions aren't a threat to the family, just the women), "new rules governing male-female relations" (the new rules: men can't beat, rape, or murder their wives and girlfriends with im-punity; women aren't the property of fathers and husbands; having children is a woman's choice, not her obligation), popular culture, gay people who want to get married, gay people who don't want to get married, gay people who want to be parents, gay people who don't want to be parents, gay people who want to join the army, gay people who want fries with that, et cetera. If conservative scolds truly believe that affluence leads to rootless hedonism and threat-ens religion, morality, the law, and the American family, then where was Bennett when George W. Bush eliminated the inheritance tax? With the stroke of a pen, a Republican president condemned fu-ture generations of wealthy families to lives of rootless hedonism. The children of today's millionaires and billionaires (and their children, and their children's children) won't have to work a day in their dissipated lives thanks to George W. Bush. They'll know only affluence; they'll never fear want or have to engage in hard physical labor. The urban poor and the working class may envy the rich and aspire to rootless hedonism, but nothing enables an aspiring hedonist to become a world-class rootless hedonist like a large trust fund.

I was still recovering from the shock of having to share a room with a complete stranger in a five-hundred-dollar-per-night spa, to say nothing of sharing a bathroom with four people, when Randy began rounding us up. We'd been given some time to get settled, meet our roommates, and sit for an intake interview with the spa's director. Now it was time for our first day's hike. Some of the women who had been to the Ashram before asked why Randy was skipping the routine weigh-in before the first hike.

"We've been trying to get away from weighing people," Randy explained. "It's shallow. Our focus while we're here this week should be on our health and our energy and not on arbitrary, meaningless numbers."

There was a long silence.

The women looked at each other, then back at Randy; eyebrows were raised; women exhaled in not-so-silent protest. Sisterhood is powerful—the eyebrows and loud sighs weren't lost on Randy. He must have known that no one came to the Ashram for the deluxe accommodations; the ladies were here to lose weight. So was I. At the end of the week, we would all wanted to know just how much weight our three thousand dollars lost us, thank you very much. It wasn't just the women and the gay man who were fixated on the shallow stuff. My straight roommate, a fiftyish male movie-mogul type of very few words, wanted to be weighed, too. No doubt we would all compare our "before" and "after" weights at the end of the week, with the biggest loser being the most enviable Ashramite.

Randy was clearly disappointed in our shallow fixation on

weight, but he was also clearly outnumbered. One by one he called us into a shed behind the house. From the outside the shed looked like one of those assemble-it-yourself garden sheds for sale in the parking lot of Home Depot. On the inside, though, the shed was tricked out with a carpet, a double bed, a dresser, a lamp, and a scale. One Ashram staffer slept in the shed every night to prevent the guests from ordering pizzas or escaping into the mountains in search of coffee beans. The overnight staffer was also in charge of getting all of us up and out of bed at five A.M.

When it was my turn to be weighed, Randy called me out to the shed and asked me to strip—so the week wasn't without thrills. My arbitrary number turned out to be 185 pounds.

We may have looked like kids on our way to camp waiting to be picked up in Los Angeles, but now that we were at the Ashram, we began acting like kids at camp. As we headed out to the van, one woman announced that she had to sit in the front passenger seat because she was claustrophobic. With a nervous laugh—a nervous-because-it's-a-lie laugh—the woman, a music industry executive, started telling us about her lifelong phobia of enclosed spaces. It was simply impossible for her to sit in the back of the van, she said. She hoped we all understood. Another woman, an unemployed (if still wealthy) dot-commer, announced that *she* was plagued by motion sickness; the back of the van bounced around too much for her, so *she* needed to sit in the front passenger seat.

Neither could prove she suffered from the malady she claimed to have, and I assumed that both just wanted to ride shotgun all week long. I hung back, waiting to see how our group's first conflict would be resolved. Would they take turns riding shotgun? What about the rest of us? Could we vote them off the island? Then a second van pulled up, which I should've seen coming. Our entire group of thirteen guests and two trail guides wouldn't fit in one van. So it was settled: Ms. Claustrophobe hopped into the front of the first van; Ms. Motion Sickness hopped into the front of the second.

Now, it hadn't occurred to me to covet the front seat. I didn't really want the front seat—not, of course, until I couldn't have it. The women riding in the front seats seemed pretty pleased with themselves (joy), while I sat in the back of the van seething (sorrow). Hmph. How dare they lie and scheme their way into riding shotgun all week, I grumbled to myself, and I found it hard to concentrate on anything other than the injustice of it all. Now I wanted to ride shotgun. I *had* to ride shotgun. I *would* ride shotgun.

The nonseething members of our group got acquainted as we drove to the trailhead. We were nine women and three men; nine white people, two African Americans, and one Southeast Asian. One of the men was a German mogul who comes to the Ashram two weeks every year; my roommate was the well-known head of a big movie studio. One of the women was a singer with a couple of dance hits under her belt who needed to lose some weight before a big television appearance; the claustrophobic music-industry executive was the singer's best friend. There was a diplomat from the United Nations, a dot-com entrepreneur and motion-sickness victim lucky enough to cash out before the crash, an opinionated real-estate lawyer, a genetic engineer, a wealthy businesswoman about to marry into an insanely wealthy East Coast family, two housewives, and one impostor.

While I knew that long hikes were the main event at the Ashram—the secret to their rapid weight-loss program—I was unprepared for how grueling they turned out to be. Looking at mostly middle-aged women in the van on the way to the Ashram, I thought the hikes couldn't be that difficult. No one on the van looked like an athlete, nor did anyone appear to be obese. I asked the spa's codirector, a Swedish woman with a deep tan and a way of beaming at people that made her seem slightly mad, why it was that everyone was so fit. I had expected people to be heavier. The Ashram's program, she explained, is too grueling for people who are too out of shape.

"We're not known as the boot camp of spas for nothing," said

Olga. "You can't be a hundred pounds overweight and make it up the trails you'll be hiking, yeah?"

Olga was "assessing" me when we had this conversation, helping me outline my goals for the week. We were in her office on the second floor, sitting in brown wicker chairs. Olga made notes on what looked like a medical file while we spoke. They didn't get many men my age at the Ashram; the movie mogul was in his fifties and the German mogul was in his seventies. While two of the women in my group were younger than I (the singer and the claustrophobic music-industry executive), most of the other Americans were in their forties and fifties.

"You are young, yeah? You are fit. Why are you here?"

I couldn't tell the truth. ("I'm here to hang with the affluent and pudgy, Olga.") So I mumbled something vague about my metabolism.

Olga nodded, beaming. She wanted more.

Uh . . . and I was eating way too much sugar lately?

More nodding, more beaming.

Uh . . . and I was drinking way too much caffeine lately?

"Yes. I can see that," Olga said, sounding grave but still beaming.

The real reason I was at the Ashram, of course, was to hobnob with the enviable rich. Oh, I'd been around rich folks before, but I had never attempted to pass myself off as one. As a fellow guest at this five-hundred-dollar-a-day spa, I hoped the other guests might assume that I was rich like they were.

Olga looked deep into my eyes. She told me there was something wrong with my liver or my kidneys, I don't remember which, perhaps because I was so startled. We were in a quasi-medical setting, and it sounded like a diagnosis. My jaw dropped. Were the whites of my eyes yellow? How did she know there was something wrong with my internal organs? She wasn't looking at the whites of my eyes, Olga told me. She was looking at my irises.

"You need to drink a lot of water, yeah? We will detoxify you while you are here. No caffeine, no sugar, yeah?"

Yeah, I thought, except for the two bags of M&M's in my back-pack. I'd purchased them at the hotel in L.A. before the van came, you know, just in case. Maybe there's a black market at the Ashram; I could imagine that, late at night, the guests get together and swap contraband, candy, and caffeine tablets when most of the staff members were asleep.

"You will probably be sick one day while you are here, as your body rids itself of the toxins. That day only you should take it easy, yeah?"

Yeah.

"And look at you! You're so white!"

Olga grabbed my left hand and turned my arm over. She examined the underside of my forearm.

"My goodness! Look at you!" she said in mock horror as she traced a finger along one of my visibly blue veins.

"I live in Seattle." I shrugged. "Not much sun."

"You will be out in the sun while you are here," Olga said, beaming, beaming, beaming. "And you will take off your shirt when you hike. I want to send you home not so pale, yeah?"

Our first hike was the shortest of the seven we would go on, just under five miles, but it was straight uphill, and it was late af-ternoon, and it was hot. Here's what I learned about myself on that first hike: Not investing in a pair of hiking boots turned out to be a mistake; clothes appropriate for gossiping in an air-conditioned gym in Seattle aren't ideal for hiking up mountains in the desert. I was even less prepared for looking like a member of a cult. All thir-teen of us were hiking in a line along the trail when we passed three people on horseback riding in the opposite direction. (Two of the riders, a young man and a young woman, were impossibly beautiful; the third rider, an older man with a beard and a gut, was teaching them how to handle a horse. They appeared to be actors learning to ride for a film.) We Ashramites were all wearing some combination of high-end hiking gear and red-and-white Ashram

T-shirts and sweatpants. If the thirteen of us didn't look like a cult—nine women and three men dressed all alike, marching along in a line, taking orders from two guides with walkie-talkies—then we looked like a work-release detail from some New Age prison for white-collar criminals.

A hike routine was quickly established: Fast hikers pulled ahead early; slow hikers brought up the rear. My roommate, the movie mogul, was the fastest in our group, pulling ahead of the pack early on every day's hike. To keep track of the hikers, one Ashram guide would march at the front, marking turns in the trails with little piles of stones so that no one would get lost. (And people do get lost on these trails; while I was at the Ashram, a boy out hiking with his father got lost and barely survived spending three days and nights wandering around hills crawling with mountain lions, rattlesnakes, and wealthy middle-aged women in red sweatpants.) A second guide marched at the rear, to make sure no stragglers got left behind. There were supposedly ways to evacuate hikers who got injured, but the structure of the hikes made it very difficult for anyone to bail out, no matter how much pain we were in. The Ashram vans dropped all thirteen of us off at one end of a twelve- or fifteen-mile trail and picked us all up at the other end. If you went too slow or had to bail, you knew you would be holding the whole group up. So we all pushed on through the pain, up the mountains, and onto ridges that provided us with beautiful views of the Pacific Ocean. Oh, and Cher's house.

Another routine was established the first night at dinner: The women talked, and the men didn't say much. A group of women went from complete strangers to beloved girlfriends in less than twenty-four hours. Men can't do that—or we won't do that, or we don't know how to do that, or we're afraid someone might think we're gay if we did do that. But on the trails the very first day and at dinner on the very first night, the nine women in our group were opening up to each other about their divorces, second husbands, and stepchildren. Walking along the trail that first day, I caught parts of conversations about breast cancer, addiction, and the deaths of parents. By the end of dinner on the first night, the lawyer from New York invited everyone to Thanksgiving dinner at her place. The invitation was made to the whole group, but it was clear she meant only to invite her new girlfriends.

Oh, and that first dinner? After a five-mile hike, an hour of yoga, and a weight-lifting class? A tiny bowl of lentil soup and a single wheat-free cracker.

Later that night, feeling like an emotional cripple compared with the women in our group (and, yes, I was envious of their ability to be so open), I tried to bond with my strong, silent, movie-mogul roommate. I'm bad at small talk in general and guy talk in particular. Tonight would be no exception. In order to bond with my straight, white, older, married, power-hiking roommate, I chose to make bitchy, disparaging comments about the curtains and bedspreads: Didn't they look like stuff you might find at your aunt's house? I mean, wasn't it hilarious that the Ashram, at five hundred dollars a day, was so tacky and spartan?

The movie mogul looked up from his book, glanced up at the curtains. "I suppose so," he said, returning to his book.

I was surprised, I jabbered on, by just how dowdy absolutely everything about the Ashram was! I mean, swag lamps? Hello? No tubs in the bathroom? And that couch? Ugh. For five hundred dollars a night, I expected more in the way of creature comforts. The movie mogul, who was back at the Ashram for the fourth time, looked over at me and slid a bookmark into *The Leadership Engine: How Winning Companies Build Leaders at Every Level*.

"There are other places that have tried to copy what the Ashram does," Movie Mogul said, "but with deluxe rooms and private bathrooms and all that crap. You know what? It doesn't work. In those places people just want to sit around all day in their rooms. Part of what we're paying for is to get away from luxury we're surrounded by in our normal lives. There's no reason to stay in your room here. The point of this place is the activity, not the facility."

Then Movie Mogul said good night, turned out his light, and went to sleep.

Just my fucking luck, I thought to myself, sitting in my bed, pretending to read a three-year-old issue of *Cosmo* that I found in the bathroom. I decide to go hang out with the rich folks for a week and somehow manage to pick the place where the rich folks go to get away from luxury.

I tried to go to sleep, but the two women in the next room—Ms. New York Lawyer and Ms. Marrying Very Well—were bonding kind of noisily. Wedding plans were being hashed over, and I was privy to all the alarming details. Unable to sleep, I got up and explored the Ashram's living and dining room. I looked through the bookshelves in the living room for something to read, without luck. *Ramtha, The World's Great Religions, Bodymind, Baba Satya Sai* didn't interest me because I'm not a spiritual person. *Scentual Touch: A Personal Guide to Aromatherapy, The Brethren* by John Grisham, and stacks of old *Cosmopolitan* magazines didn't interest me because I'm not an idiot.

So I read the walls. In addition to the plaque over the fireplace, there were little framed affirmations all around the Ashram, admonitions like MANIFEST YOUR OWN REALITY and THE LIGHT LIVES WITHIN ME. Displaying affirmations has always struck me as somewhat idiotic; I mean, what if someone who isn't a very nice person comes into your living room? Would you want the next Hitler to read "All the things I want are good" on your living room wall?

I once visited the home of someone I took to be a level-headed cynic, much like myself, and was shocked to find framed affirmations on her walls. I couldn't go anywhere—not even the toilet—without her apartment reminding me that I was a good person, a valuable person, an interesting person, a beautiful person. There was even a little basket of affirmations by her front door, filled with laminated pieces of construction paper: PEOPLE LIKE ME!, I CAN MAKE IT HAPPEN!, SEIZE THE DAY!

When my friend saw me picking through her little wicker basket of affirmations, she folded her arms across her chest, cocked her hip, and said, "Go ahead, Dan, make fun of me." She was asking for it. So I pulled out an affirmation, said, "I'm Adolf Hitler," and then I read Hitler's affirmation: "I'm a good person, and I want good things."

"That's awful!" my friend said.

"I'm Pol Pot: 'I strive to spread love and understanding.' "

"I'm Richard Speck: 'I am respected and admired, and people want to be near me.' "

"I'm Trent Lott: 'My inner beauty is like a bright light.' "

By now my sensitive friend was, yes, *crying*.

I know, I know: I'm a terrible person. Which is precisely my point. The problem with setting out a basket of affirmations is that you're assuming each and every person who comes into your home or spa is a good person who wants good things. With all the respect due a basket of laminated affirmations, I beg to differ. Most people are bad, and if it pleases the court, I would like to introduce a world-history textbook into evidence. Pogroms, witch burnings, war, total war, religious war, the slaughter of Native Americans, the Holocaust, the Serbs, the indifference of Europeans and Americans to genocide in Rwanda, murderous Islamo-fascists—people pretty much suck. No thinking member of a species that has produced African slavery, the Armenian genocide, and *The Mirror Has Two Faces* should sit around smugly telling herself that everything she wants is good.

I got blisters on the first day's hike, but the second day's hike drew blood. After Randy woke us up that morning, I put on my hiking gym clothes from the day before. I'd tossed them in the wash the night before, but a single washing at the Ashram transformed my old pair of cotton briefs into a lethal weapon. Maybe it was the soap, maybe the water at the Ashram was particularly hard. Whatever it was, the ribbing along the seams of the legholes was so stiff after one washing at the Ashram that the second day's hike—a brutal fifteen-mile slog in one-hundred-degree heat—left my crotch bloody and raw.

I sensed that my underwear was a little stiff when I pulled them on in my darkened room at five in the morning. But the painful consequence of stiff underwear didn't make itself apparent until it was far too late to do anything. By the time I realized something was going terribly, terribly wrong in my underwear, I was halfway up a mountain in the desert. There was no way to turn back. It was just me, the sun, the trail, the rich folks, and my saber-toothed underwear. The starched ribbing in my underwear gradually chewed its way through the very uppermost part of my thighs, where leg meets crotch, slowly sawing through layer after layer of skin. When we finally made it back to the Ashram, I limped into one of the bathrooms, locked the door, and pulled down my shorts. I was a bloody mess.

And that was day two; we'd only hiked twenty of the eighty miles we would hike before our week at the Ashram was over. On day three, I was in agony. It was 105 degrees outside, and we were hiking straight up the face of a mountain. Since I couldn't wear the only pair of underwear I brought with me to the Ashram, I was freeballing it. Now, as anyone with a scrotum knows, a hot, sweaty scrotum expands; it spread, droops, and sags. So there I was on a mountain, surrounded by rich people, when my hot, sweaty, and very, very salty scrotum began sliding back and forth over my chafed, bloody, raw upper thighs. It hurt so bad my eyes were watering.

So I picked up my pace and hiked as far ahead of the group as I could. I may have been one of the youngest in our group, but I wasn't the fastest. That title went to the movie mogul, my fiftyish roommate, who led the pack almost every day. I couldn't catch up with movie mogul or pass him, but I could pace myself so that I was always between MM and the rest of the group. When I was fairly certain that I was alone and that I couldn't be seen by anyone ahead of me or behind me, I put my right hand down my shorts, cupped my enormous, salty scrotum in one hand, and lifted it up and away from my burning thighs. I hiked like that for most of the rest of the week: alone, balls in one hand, water bottle in the other. I didn't have to worry about looking like part of a cult or a work-release program anymore; I just looked like a pervert. It didn't help me get any closer to the rich folks, but it kept me from howling in pain with every step.

"**A**ch, you heard them the first night." The German mogul and I are on the last leg of Thursday's forced march, walking side by side down a long, steep decline. " 'Come to New York; come to my apartment for Thanksgiving.' These women have known each other, what? Six hours? And they are best of friends. Absurd."

The German mogul was a tall, good-looking man in his early sixties, which was a difficult age for Germans not too long ago. Until very recently, being a German senior citizen invited a lot of questions about your whereabouts in the 1930s and 1940s. Not anymore. A sixty-year-old German today wasn't yet born when Hitler came to power; the German mogul was just five when the war ended. I was wrapping my head around the concept of old, innocent Germans as we sweated our way through the longest of the week's hikes, a seventeen-mile ass-blaster. The German mogul—GM for short—was on the second week of his annual fourteen-day stay, so he had hiked this trail last Thursday. He'd been hiking this trail twice a year every year for fourteen years.

Me and GM hadn't spent much time together before Thursday's hike. I was usually out in front of him during the hikes, holding on to my balls, praying no movie stars on horseback would spot me, worrying that I'd wasted a lot of my publisher's money coming to the wrong place. The Ashram wasn't filled with rich people enjoying their envy-inducing wealth, but with rich people spending five hundred dollars a day to live like poor people—starvation rations, forced marches, uniforms. I wasn't getting much insight into the lifestyles of the rich and famous at the Ashram. GM and MM, my roommate, kept to themselves, and my attempts to join in the women's conversations weren't all that successful. I was beginning to think that everyone suspected, rightly, that I just didn't belong— not as a guest, anyway. Or, shit, maybe they'd seen me marching along the trails with my hands in my shorts.

I was on a long, unauthorized break during Thursday's hike when I saw GM coming down the trail, so I let go of my balls and joined him. He was by far the wealthiest person in our group, so I figured I'd hike a ways with him. I'd overheard one of the other Ashram veterans, the real-estate lawyer, telling the other women that GM owned newspapers and a publishing house and, in- evitably, horses. "He's worth," she said, lowering her voice two oc- taves but speaking just as loudly, "an awful lot of money." I've always enjoyed Germans, rich or poor—heck, even German senior citizens—so I endured the misery of my sweaty balls moving back and forth between my bloody thighs to spend some time with GM. In this case, there was the added incentive of learning something about the absurdly affluent—namely, why someone with the money to go anywhere and do anything would go to the Ashram to be starved and marched through the desert.

This time I played it cool, refraining from making any airy-fairy comments about the curtains and bedspreads back at the Ashram. I told GM that I lived in Germany for two years, and soon we started talking about WWI, WWII, the Cold War, the wall, and German reunification. GM met JFK, and as a young man advised LBJ during the Vietnam War. ("My advice? I told him to get da hell out.") He was friendly with the Reagans. We walked; we talked.

"Why pay for this?" I asked GM as we rounded a bend in the trail. "You've been walking these trails for years; you must know them by heart. Why not come get a cheap motel room for a week and walk them alone. You'd save, like, twenty-five hundred dollars."

"Wouldn't work. I'd be sitting in my room making phone calls and watching cable TV, and if I ever did get out on the trails, I'd quit before I was halfway up. It's the psychology of the place that keeps you walking."

The psychology?

"Yes. You keep walking when your feet and legs are aching because everyone else is walking. You keep walking because you don't feel like you have a choice. The others are walking, so you are walking. You cannot quit."

I wasn't going to argue with a German about the psychology of a forced march—not even a guiltless German. We walked on in silence for a few minutes.

"If we were women," he suddenly said, "this is probably the point where one of us would say, 'You will come and stay with me, yes?' It is something I will never understand about women. How do the nine know each other a day or a week and decide, oh, we are best friends now?"

I can read between the lines, especially when they're drawn right in front of me in thick, black strokes: No invitation to spend the holidays at GM's country place (a castle outside Munich, as I later learned) would be forthcoming. An hour talking on the trail together barely qualified us as acquaintances, much less friends. We were sensible, stoic, unfeeling men, after all, not mushy, effusive women. Unlike "the nine," as GM called the women in our group, we discussed only what we had in common: our opinions about German history (his were somewhat more informed than my own), our opinions about forced marches (ditto), and our time together at the Ashram. We didn't discuss our lives, wives, kids, hopes, dreams, diseases, or traumas.

Long, painful hikes through the desert weren't the only way the rich people at the Ashram lost weight. We were starved, too. We were fed three times a day, like any other prisoners, but we weren't fed much: one egg for breakfast, a tiny salad and two pieces of vegetarian sushi for lunch, a bowl of soup for dinner. We were taking in a lot fewer calories than we were burning out on the trails in the morning—to say nothing of the calories we were burning in the yoga sessions (in a geodesic redwood dome), pool exercises (in the teeny, tiny pool), and weight training classes (in a gym with a sloped floor and rusty equipment) that filled our afternoons. On the trails, people stopped sharing stories about breast cancer and divorce and started sharing stories about restaurants and snack foods.

The rich folks seemed to take the deprivation in stride—deprivation was, after all, what they were paying for. Their normal lives were filled with too much: too much food, too much free time, too much money, too much freedom from want, too much luxury. Here at the Ashram, they were paying good money to experience too little: too little food, too little control, too little comfort, too little luxury. Our days were filled with hardship, deprivation, and hard physical labor. It's impossible to overstate the misery of hiking a long, steep trail in the desert. You look ahead and see the trail disappear around a bend. You push on, hoping that just around the bend the trail will level off or—please, God—the blessed descent will begin. You force your legs to pick up your feet, you round the corner, and . . . up the trails goes, until the trail rounds another bend, and you round that one and still the trail goes up.

We were powerless to do anything about our predicament—a point driven home one day on the beach. One of the seven hikes took us from the Atlantic side of the Santa Monica Mountains all the way to the Pacific Ocean. The hike was a killer, so the distance between the pack leaders—Movie Mogul, German Mogul, Motion Sickness, and me—and the stragglers was considerable, so Randy loaded those of us who finished the hike early into a van and drove us to a beach, where we could lie in the sand and while the rest of the group finished the hike. (I got to ride shotgun—*yes!*) The four of us were wearing Ashram T-shirts and sweats and carrying water bottles. We looked like, again, the members of some strange cult when Randy dropped us off on a crowded beach. Halfway through our week at the Ashram, we were all starving, all the time. All along the beach vendors were selling hot dogs, ice cream, and soft drinks . . . and there we were, a wealthy German, a wealthy movie producer, a wealthy tech businesswoman, and me, without a cent between us. Our clothes, ID, credit cards, and cash were all back at the Ashram.

It had been a decade since I was broke and hungry and exhausted and powerless to do anything about it. The joke was on me: I had gone to the Ashram to envy the rich up close and personal only to discover that the rich go to the Ashram to live like the poor. For a mere five hundred dollars a day (which is more than the annual per-capita income of 33 percent of the people on the planet), the Ashram's guests are bossed around, fed starvation rations, marched through the mountains, and coerced into various yoga positions. GM, MM, and The Nine came to the Ashram to enjoy what may be the only perk of poverty: It's slimming, darling.

There is power and status in freely giving up your power and status for a set period of time. Pretending to be poor and powerless has always been an option for the rich and powerful. Marie Antoinette dressed up like a milkmaid and sat on a silver stool in a twee little farmhouse she had built on the grounds of Versailles. According to the Roman historian Suetonius, the Emperor Nero would disguise himself as a common citizen and carouse in Rome's slums and taverns; the Emperor Commodus liked to fight in the Coliseum as a gladiator (his opponents were given swords made of lead). At the end of the day, though, Marie Antoinette left the farm and returned to being Queen of France. While the rich can afford to live like the poor for a day or a week, only the rich can experience how the other half lives. The wealthy can go slumming, but it's not so easy for the poor to go mansioning.

The thirteen of us at the Ashram were guilty of a kind of conspicuous nonconsumption—there was certainly something hedonistic about our week at the Ashram. We were paying five hundred dollars a day for a shared room, starvation rations, and forced marches through the desert in one-hundred-degree heat—all so we could lose a little weight. (I lost ten pounds, coming in second place; only the woman about to get married lost more than I did.) Even hardship is a commodity in America, a product that is packaged and sold to the wealthy. Want to get away from luxury? Treat yourself to a week at the Ashram. Hardship is in such short supply in our rich, comfortable country that the ability to purchase a little poverty has become a thoroughly modern status symbol. Everyone at the Ashram that week was a spiritual descendant of Marie Antoinette, I guess, but I unfortunately didn't get to tag along when everyone joyfully returned to their palaces—much to my sorrow.

PRIDE

Jake and Kevin and the Queen of Sin

Nothing's more offensive than flaunting sexuality in public, and the most offensive spectacles of all are Gay Pride events. Bearded, paunchy guys prancing around in bras and high heels do not impress the straight majority as an act of political liberation. Dykes on Bikes? Take a hike! Can't you "express yourself" without throwing it in our faces! —Bill O'Reilly, *The No Spin Zone*

But the liberty to pursue happiness means that each of us pursues whatever it is he may desire. We are to move away from the restraints in pursuit of we know not what. Such a person leads a precarious existence. —Robert Bork, *Slouching Towards Gomorrah*

Kevin and Jake pursue happiness in Los Angeles.

Kevin is in his thirties and so is Jake. Kevin makes a lot of money and so does Jake. Kevin looks much younger than his actual age and so does Jake. Kevin has a gym-built body and so does Jake. Kevin is deeply tanned and so is Jake. Kevin is clean-cut . . . and so it goes.

Kevin and Jake are one of those enviable ubercouples upscale gay magazines will occasionally profile. ("Meet the guys who have everything—including each other!") Together three years, Kevin and Jake had just moved into a new home when I invited myself over for the weekend. The previous owners of their home, an older straight couple, did a lot of damage to the fifty-year-old house before selling it to Kevin and Jake. It was late June when I came to visit, and this pair of all-American homos were dividing their summer between the beach and Home Depot.

While they showed me around the house, Kevin delighted in describing the design sins of the home's former owners: window treatments, flower beds, and wallpaper choices so offensive that he shuddered when he described them. Kevin and Jake had undone most of these sins by the time I visited; windows were bare, flower beds mostly empty, wallpaper stripped away. After the tour, Kevin handed me a small photo album. "The before pictures," he said with mock gravity. The pictures were appalling; while I personally don't care how many times bell-bottoms and skin-tight T-shirts cycle in and out of fashion, may God protect us from the return of cork walls, shimmery wallpaper, and swag lamps. (Still, before-and-after pictures of a house you're redecorating seems like a peculiar form of boasting; it's a way of saying, "Look at how much better my taste is than the taste of the people who used to live here." In Kevin and Jake's case, considering the age of their home's previous owners—and the design-challenged era in which they lived and decorated—better taste isn't much to boast about.)

Kevin and Jake are one of those only-in-L.A. gay couples: ridiculously successful, absurdly handsome, deeply tanned, sexually adventurous, and, uh, *very well accessorized.* During the tour of the house, Kevin showed me a spare bedroom that the men were turning into a "playroom." What's a playroom, Mr. Bork? Well, picture a home entertainment center devoted to energetic, athletic sex rather than lethargic, sedentary TV-viewing. Most playrooms have padded floors (the better to kneel on), no windows or blacked-out windows, mood lighting, shelves filled with sex toys, and—for the main event—a black-leather sling supported by chains that hang from hooks in the ceiling. Kevin and Jake did some house-sitting for a gay friend who had a playroom, and they had such a great time that they ran out and bought a sling. Since they didn't want their friends to spot—or tease them about—telltale hooks in the ceiling of their bedroom, they decided to build a playroom of their own.

Spending the day with guys like Kevin and Jake always makes me wish I were richer, handier, and better looking. Good-looking, rich, fit gay men fill me with envy, and in this particular case, I had a definite touch of sling-envy. Compared with these guys, my boyfriend and I are lazy, average, boring—in and out of bed. Like Kevin and Jake, we live in a house we bought from an older couple. Unlike Kevin and Jake, we haven't done anything about the appalling window treatments, flower beds, or wallpaper left behind by the previous owners. We don't have to haul out a photo album to make visitors shudder at the previous owner's horrifying wallpaper selections; all we have to do is just open the doors and turn on the lights. And while we own a sling (it was a gift, Mom, I swear), we've never actually used it. Our sling sits in a box in our basement, gathering dust. While my boyfriend enjoyed his one ride in a sling (in an kinky, upscale boutique hotel in Amsterdam that I was writing up for a design magazine), he doesn't see himself as the kind of guy who has a sling in his house, much less a playroom in his basement. There are hooks in the ceiling of our bedroom but, alas, only to support the swag lamps installed by our home's previous owners.

As I watched Kevin and Jake hammer a new window frame into place, I tried not to feel too bad about my walls, windows, floors, and the sling rotting in a box in my basement. Kevin and Jake have to be trendy and edgy; they live in Los Angeles, after all. Kevin owns an extremely successful, high-end home lighting fixture and design business. (Madonna and Janet Jackson are clients.) Jake is a big-deal exec at a movie studio. As an up-and-coming gay power couple in status-conscious Los Angeles, Kevin and Jake's home has to scream success. They have to tend to their abs and cultivate a sexual edge; with so many good-looking, available men in Los Angeles, gay men who have boyfriends either keep the home fires blazing or lose their lovers to someone younger, hotter, and hipper.

Thankfully, my boyfriend and I don't live with the same pressures. Jesus Christ himself is likelier to drop by our house unannounced than Madonna; and Seattle falls somewhere between Dubuque and Buffalo Grove on the sexual energy scale.

When I told a friend that I was looking for a hip gay couple who were planning to attend the gay pride parade in Los Angeles, he gave me Kevin and Jake's phone number. I called, and they invited me to come down and spend the weekend at their place. It was a hot Saturday afternoon in late June when I arrived, the day before the pride parade, and Kevin and Jake were working on the patio behind their sprawling, one-story, wood-frame house when my cab pulled up. I was offered something to drink ("Beer?") and something to smoke ("Pot?"), and I accepted a beer. Then I sat scribbling away in my notebook as Kevin and Jake strolled around shirtless, digging up some plants, watering others, and answering my questions. While the men walk and talk and look and dress alike, Kevin, originally from the Midwest, was more talkative, more willing to entertain my questions than his boyfriend, Jake, who is originally from the East Coast. I had only one basic question for Kevin and Jake, however, one I asked them over and over again for the next two days: Why on earth were they going to the pride parade?

"The pride parade is about seeing your friends and having fun," Kevin said, hosing down some strange plant. "And it's fun to laugh at the freaks."

Every June, American cities with large gay populations host pride parades to commemorate the Stonewall Riots in New York City in 1969.

The Stonewall Riots in a nutshell: Once upon a time, on a humid night in June, the New York City Police Department conducted a routine vice raid on a routinely sleazy little gay bar called the Stonewall Inn. Instead of meekly filing into paddy wagons, some sweaty, angry queens decided to resist. Judy Garland's funeral had taken place earlier that day, and the queens just weren't having it. With Judy gone, what else did they have to lose? A crowd gathered as the cops tried to drag the kicking, screaming queens out of the Stonewall. Someone in the crowd began pelting the cops with pennies. Ten minutes later a dozen of New York City's finest were barricaded inside the gay bar they had come to raid while an angry mob hurled stones, bricks, bottles, and parking meters through the bar's one small window. Someone tried to set the bar on fire with the cops trapped inside. Thus began the Stonewall Riots, which went on for three nights and heralded the emergence of a more militant, confrontational gay rights movement.

The Stonewall Riots are often made to sound like the big bang of gay politics—the beginning of gay time—which isn't entirely accurate; a handful of gay activists had staged small protests before the riots, to little effect. Even if Stonewall wasn't the beginning of gay politics, it did change everything. Pre-Stonewall, meek gay groups issued pleas. Post-Stonewall, noisy gay groups made demands. Pre-Stonewall, gay men in ties and lesbians in skirts picketed politely, at considerable risk to their private and professional lives. Post-Stonewall, gay men in short-shorts and lesbians in painters' pants marched constantly and rioted occasionally, at ever-less risk to their private and professional lives. Ironically, archive footage of the few pre-Stonewall gay rights protests are in black-and-white, like Dorothy's Kansas in *The Wizard of Oz*. Post-Stonewall footage of gay rights marches are in blazing color, like the Land of Oz itself.

Early gay pride marches had two missions: First, let the straights know the gays weren't going to hide anymore; and, second, let closeted gay people know that it was safe to come out. (Of course, it wasn't safe; it still isn't entirely safe. The *certain* misery of being closeted, however, is so far outweighed by the *potential* for happiness outside the closet that most gays and lesbians are willing to risk it.) Pre-Stonewall, gays and lesbians were made to feel ashamed of themselves; post-Stonewall, gays and lesbians were instructed to be proud. Like the women's movement ("Equal Rights Now!") and the African-American civil-rights movement ("Black Power!"), the gay movement chose a slogan that laid aggressive claim to the very thing the wider culture had denied us. Women didn't have equal rights when they took their slogan, and blacks had not much in the way of power. Likewise, few gays and lesbians took pride in themselves back in 1969.

For a group of people condemned as sinners—and some are understandably still sensitive to the charge, as it's still made—it's ironic that gays and lesbians should select a sin as our rallying cry. And not just any sin, but the sin Pope Gregory the Great unironically called, "the queen of them all." But it made sense at the time: the whole world conspired to make gay people feel ashamed of themselves. It worked. Straight people viewed homosexuality as disgraceful and disgusting, and so did most gays and lesbians. Shame was the poison that kept gays closeted and prompted us to off ourselves at slightly higher rates. Clearly, strong medicine was called for, and pride was the obvious antidote. Being gay was nothing to be ashamed of, gay activists insisted. Being an openly gay, reasonably healthy, functioning adult was something that a person should be proud of! After all, any homo who survived a hostile family, homophobic employers, corrupt police departments, and hateful churches had accomplished something significant. So pride parades: Gay is bad, they said. Gay is good, we replied.

Pride was tremendously meaningful and important and radical and revolutionary—thirty years ago. Back then, very few gays and lesbians were out of the closet, and the central metaphors of the pride parade—we have nothing to be ashamed of!—resonated with vast numbers of gays and lesbians still too scared to tell their parents what kind of bars they liked to hang out in. As an antidote, pride was effective: Every year, at each successive pride parade, more and more gays and lesbians showed up. We became less closeted and less fearful, which made it increasingly difficult for our families, employers, and elected officials to pretend we didn't exist or talk us into offing ourselves.

The funny thing about antidotes, though, is that they're usually toxic themselves. If you've been bitten by a poisonous snake, you're supposed to take the antidote, yes, but you're not supposed to *keep* taking the antidote, day in, day out, for the rest of your life. Looking around gay neighborhoods (or looking in gay magazines, newspapers, and inside gay heads) thirty years after the antidote arrived, it's clear that gays and lesbians are in renewed danger of being poisoned—only the poison threatening us now isn't shame. It's pride.

The message at gay pride parades in the United States hasn't evolved; it's still, Gay is good! There are two problems with this: First, it's misleading. Gay isn't good or bad, it's just gay. (Yes, yes— Michelangelo was gay. But so was Jeffrey Dahmer.) Second, what relevance does a "gay is good" message have to the vast majority of American gay men and lesbians who, like Kevin and Jake, don't believe that there's anything in the least bit shameful about their homosexuality? What relevance do pride parades have to hip, secure, handsome gay men like Kevin and Jake? What was in it for them? Why were they going? Why did they still need the antidote? Weren't they cured? Or do they go to the pride parade to remind themselves how far they've come, like a former cancer patient who, despite having been completely cured, reminds himself he isn't sick anymore by dropping by the hospital once a year for a little chemotherapy?

Kevin and Jake assured me that, no, they didn't feel any vestigial shame or guilt and, no, they weren't any the worse for wear on those years when they missed the pride parade.

So why do they go?

The fourth time I asked, Kevin stopped what he was doing and looked right at me. I'm uneasy around extremely good-looking gay men; I like to look at good-looking gay men, of course, but I find it intimidating to be regarded by them. It always makes me feel like I need to go and do some sit-ups or iron my underwear or pluck my eyebrows or something. So I felt suddenly self-conscious when

Kevin looked at me like he couldn't quite bring me into focus. (Maybe it was the pot and not the question?) He turned away, shrugged, and sat down on a lawn chair. I asked again. Surely there are better ways for him to have fun? With his equally beautiful boyfriend? On a sunny Sunday afternoon? In a house with a sling? Why go to the pride parade?

"It's important for gay youth," Kevin finally said, speaking to me very slowly. Perhaps he wanted me to take down every word. Perhaps he had concluded I was retarded.

"Gay kids in their teens and early twenties come to the pride parade," Kevin continued, "and so do other people who are just coming out. It helps them to see lots of different people there. It gives them hope." Attending the parade is social work? "Yes, it has a component of that. Young people and people who are just coming out need to see that gay people really are every color of the rainbow. Hot and hideous; young and old; smooth and hairy."

We're just doin' it for the kids.

That's the party line these days—every party's line. Right, left, and center, politicians run for office to make the world a better place for our children and our children's children and our children's children's children's children. The unwinnable war on drugs must continue so that we don't send kids the wrong message about drugs; energy companies drill for oil in ecologically sensitive areas so that our children can live in a world with power; environmentalists fight energy companies so that our children can live in a world with caribou. One Seattle TV news show has the absurd motto, "For Kids' Sake." Nothing is permissible in the United States these days unless it somehow lifts up our children, who, in case you haven't been paying attention, are our future. (So how come millions of American children live in poverty, lack health insurance, and don't have enough to eat? Never mind.)

Sadly, gay people are not immune to kid-mongering. Ellen DeGeneres didn't come out of the closet to resuscitate a dying sitcom;

no, she came out to help gay youth. Olympian Greg Louganis didn't come out after his diving career was over to sell some books; no, he came out to give gay teenagers hope. Recently Chuck Panozzo, the bass player in the long-forgotten 1970s rock group Styx, came out of the closet. To get attention? To get laid? Sick of the closet? No, Panozzo came out, he said, "to make this a better world for the next generation." Gay porn stars tell the fawning interviewers at porn magazines that they're not making porn for the money or the thrills or the smack. No, no, no. They're making porn to give gay youth hope. (Do not despair, O Gay Youth! There's a place for you! A place where men shave their ass-cracks! Pierce their nipples! Gang bang!)

When I tell Kevin that I'm not convinced that gay pride—the concept, the rhetoric, the parade—does much good for gay youth, he smiles at my cynicism. When I tell him that I think the current understanding of gay pride—Gay is good!—actually does more harm than good, he frowns at my heresy. One of the dogmas of modern gay life is that pride is always good for us, like vitamin C. And like vitamin C, massive doses can supposedly cure anything. HIV infections rising? Spend public health money to boost gay men's self-esteem and feelings of gay pride. (Never mind the studies that show that the more self-esteem a gay man has, the likelier he is to take sexual risks.) Not convinced that hate crimes laws and employment protections for homos are good ideas? Clearly you suffer from a worrisome case of gay-pride deficiency. Think gay men over fifty look ridiculous with their bare asses hanging out of leather chaps? Take these gay pride supplements, and you'll feel differently! The gay man who doesn't take pride in all things gay—without question, without thought—has long been accused of self-hatred. These days they're also accused of Demonstrating Insufficient Concern for Gay Youth. Gay pride isn't a slogan anymore or a rallying cry. It's dogma. Gay pride has become a sort of gay civic religion.

A well-accessorized religion.

No one has ever gone broke underestimating the insecurities of the gay and lesbian consumer. In every city large enough to have a pride parade, there's a store dedicated to selling "pride merchandise" year-round. Gay people who don't get their fill of gay-is-good at their annual pride parades can fill their apartments with bric-a-brack that reinforces the gay-is-good message any day of the year. Rainbow stickers for our cars, rainbow flags for our front porches and balconies, rainbow drinking glasses for our tables, rainbow Christmas-tree lights for the holidays, rainbow windsocks for . . . for our wind, I guess. Ye Olde Gay Pride Shoppe near my house sells rainbow-striped dog collars for men and women into bondage and S&M.

It gets worse. A gay mail-order company that advertises in porn magazines sells a line of pride merchandise. Right under the Make Your Own Dildo Kit ($69.95) and the latest fuck-and-suck video, there's a small box with a selection of pride merchandise. Feeling something less than prideful? You can order up a Pride Nuts Necklace ("Don your nuts as an everyday accessory and know that you're doing your part for gay visibility!" $7.95), Pride Chrome Chain Anklet ("It's elegantly masculine, and it will be noticed by all the right guys!" $7.95), Pride Teddy Bear ("Wuz Fuzzy Wuzzy Gay? Wuz he? . . . The perfect gift for your favorite Gay Teddy Bear Collector!" $29.95), Pride Pet Bowl ("Let your dog chow down with Pride!" $19.95), and Pride CD ("Take pride in hosting your very own circuit party!" $19.95). For those who want to feel proud inside and out, there's—I hope you're sitting down, Mr. Bennett—the Pride Plug, "a fulfilling anal plug in the classic sensual shape," a steal at $17.95 (large) or $14.95 (small). Buyers are admonished to "wear your Pride Plug proudly!"

First of all, you don't "wear" a butt plug. You insert it. And how, I wonder, do the makers of Pride Plugs avoid selling their "fulfilling" plugs to people who might wear them with feelings of shame or despair? Perhaps they don't ship to Utah. Or Vatican City. And what's to stop jaded homos in Chicago or Los Angeles from wearing their Pride Plugs with feelings of indifference?

All this pride pimping would be funny, I suppose, if it weren't helping to create a gay culture equal parts intellectual vapidity and moral obtuseness. These days, the hurdles to coming out are so much lower than they used to be (in general—individual circumstances vary), and yet the insistence that we take pride in being gay grows stronger and louder with each passing year. Being accepted by your family and comfortably out at work are the rules now, not the exceptions. (A gay man I met who works at a viciously anti-gay right-wing magazine—he works in design, not editorial, he's quick to point out—brings his boyfriend to company dinners.) Since gays and lesbians no longer have to struggle against *outrageous* levels of parental hostility, *extreme* social pressure, or *toxic* levels of homophobia, emerging as a relatively healthy gay person simply isn't the accomplishment it used to be. That means, of course, that we have *less* to take pride in now than we used to. So perhaps it's time to ratchet down the self-congratulatory "gay pride" rhetoric, retire the windsocks, and insert those butt plugs for pleasure, not pride.[1]

Since the pride gays and lesbians are instructed to feel can't attach itself to the struggle to overcome the ever-smaller obstacles to being openly gay, it simply attaches itself to being gay, period. In thirty years we've gone from, "You're gay, and you should be proud

---

1. A brief footnote about butt plugs: A butt plug is a perfectly pleasant little sex toy with a perfectly dreadful image. Thanks to the name, many straight people and naive young gay people assume that butt plugs are used by men who've lost control of their bowels as a consequence of too much anal sex. People hear "plug" and think "cork." Nothing could be further from the truth. A butt plug is merely an anal insertion toy with a wide body, a narrow neck, and a flared base. (Picture a small Lava lamp.) While a dildo will quickly fall out of someone's butt if it isn't held in place, a butt plug is held in place by the anal sphincters themselves, which grip the narrow neck of the butt plug, while the flared base prevents it from disappearing into the anus. The body of the butt plug fills the rectum, where it presses against the prostate. During orgasm, as the anal sphincters contract and release, the butt plug is moved against and stimulates the prostate, which greatly intensifies orgasm.

Popular among gay men, butt plugs are also an ideal sex toy for straight men curious about anal stimulation. Unlike dildos, butt plugs do not resemble penises, and therefore do not necessarily provoke gay panic. A straight male who is secure enough in his sexuality to insert a butt plug before engaging in vigorous vaginal intercourse with his girlfriend or his wife will be treated to a mind-blowing orgasm. FYI.

of yourself for surviving the bullshit, overcoming the obstacles, and emerging as a reasonably healthy adult," to "You're gay! Be proud! Buy a butt plug!" Anything that can be construed as an expression of gayness—wearing anklets, using sex toys, dragging someone around on a leash—is something to take pride in.

Don't get me wrong. There's nothing wrong with anklets, butt plugs, and leashes. (Though there is something deeply distressing about grown men who collect teddy bears.) I've worn two of the three things on that list. If using a butt plug gives someone pleasure, well, he should be encouraged to pursue that pleasure. It's his inalienable right, after all. Butt plug consumers harm no one and keep those butt-plug factories humming, which is good for our economy. But buying a butt plug or putting on an anklet that lets "all the right guys" know you're gay isn't something that should fill anyone with pride. Butt plugs, anklets, and dog collars may be a good time, but they're not accomplishments.

By far the biggest problem with "gay is good" is that so many gay people—especially those fetishized gay youth—fall for it. I don't remember much about my first pride parade: I was eighteen years old, living in Chicago, and arrived at the pride parade drunker than I'd ever been in my life. There was lots of booze flowing at the pre-parade party I attended, and I was too young to know my limits. (I'm from a family of heavy drinkers and at eighteen assumed I must have the high–alcohol tolerance gene. Imagine how crushed I was to learn that two beers can do me in.) Clearly, I exceeded my limits that Sunday afternoon; I think I threw up in some bushes along the route.

As embarrassing as my behavior was that day, I'm most embarrassed to report that I fell for it—and fell hard. The usual gay pride rhetoric was spilling forth from the stage at the post-parade rally: gay is good; gay people are your brothers and sisters; each and every member of the gay community cares about each and every other member of the gay community; it's all about love and caring and respect. I had made it safely out of the closet and somehow managed to make it out of high school without getting pounded to a pulp. Still, it wasn't until I made it to my first pride parade that I finally felt safe. I was in a huge crowd of gay people! My brothers and sisters! Michelangelo! Oscar Wilde! Gertrude Stein! No one could hurt me anymore! Not with all my gay brothers looking out for me! I bought some gay T-shirts and pierced my gay ears and put on some gay buttons. All in all it was a beautiful, moving day in June. I was proud.

Come October, I was being stalked by one violent ex-boyfriend, pressured into sex by an older gay man I mistook for a friend, and taking antibiotics to clear up a sexually transmitted disease given to me by my recent ex-boyfriend's soon-to-be ex-boyfriend. The scales fell from my eyes. Gay people—myself included—weren't necessarily good. The realization that no one was looking out for me, that I would have to be as on my guard in the "gay community" as I had been in high school, crushed me. And while the homophobic jocks in school could only beat me up, gay men who took advantage of my youth and inexperience could break my heart.

Gay men weren't good—and they weren't my brothers, like I heard at the pride parade. I should have known. I mean, I have two brothers, actual biological siblings, and neither one had ever given me a hickey, an STD, or a rope burn. Why was I told to regard other gay men as my "brothers"? We certainly don't tell young straight girls to think of older straight men are their *brothers*. We tell them to be careful around straight men who take an interest in them, as their motives probably aren't entirely pure. So why, as a teenager, was I being told that older gay men were my brothers? Why are gay teenagers still being told this appalling lie? Because telling young gay people the truth—lots of gay men are manipulative, horny abusers, just like lots of straight men—might give some people the impression that some gay men do things they should be ashamed of, not proud of.

What gay youth need to be told is what I learned that bruising summer: It doesn't matter *that* a person is gay, it matters *how* a person is gay. It's a pretty simple distinction and, from an adult vantage point, a fairly obvious one. But I've never heard anyone make this distinction during a speech at a gay pride parade—which someone really should do if pride parades are for gay youth. All you hear at gay pride parades—and all you read in the dull gay magazines (which is to say, all you read in *all* gay magazines)—is gay is good, gay community, gay brothers and sisters. "Gay is good" is just as big a lie as "Gay is bad," one that's almost as destructive, a lie that would be self-evident if it were not for the gay pride idiocracy. John Wayne Gacy was gay; Jeffrey Dahmer was gay; Andrew Cunanan was gay. There are gay men out there giving other gay men HIV on purpose; lesbian murderers sit on death row; some gay men kick their dogs and beat their lovers and wear anklets. Once a gay kid comes out, the people most likely to fuck him over or harm him or take advantage of him are other gay men, not big, bad straight bigots.

I learned all of this the hard way. I didn't learn it reading gay magazines or attending gay pride parades or at the feet of HIV/AIDS prevention educators (who seem most concerned with maximizing the amount of sex a gay man has rather than minimizing his risk of contracting HIV). Going to gay pride parades when I was a kid didn't help me. Gay pride hurt me.

Kevin and Jake were going to an all-night rave the night before the parade. I wanted to sleep. Despite the fact that they'd known me less than six hours, Kevin and Jake left me alone in their new house; the gay-is-good assumption was working to my advantage in this instance. The same assumption that got me into so much trouble as a young adult led Kevin and Jake to give me the benefit of the doubt. Since I was gay and I knew someone they knew, and the person we knew in common was also gay, Kevin and Jake assumed I wouldn't rent a truck and empty the house or rummage through their porn collection while they were out dancing. And I probably wouldn't have rummaged through their porn tapes if they hadn't been stacked right on top of the VCR.

The next day—pride day!—we drove to the home of Kevin's business partner, Tim, who lived close to the start of the parade route. The plan was for all of Tim's friends to park at his house, have a few drinks, and then walk (walk! in L.A.!) the seven or so blocks to Santa Monica Boulevard. An extremely attractive, short, athletic blond with an impossibly beautiful body, Tim was running around shirtless when we arrived. Tim was highly strung and a little effeminate—character traits that derailed his acting career. On the drive over, Kevin told me that Tim just spent thirty thousand dollars having all of his teeth capped by Britney Spears's dentist.

"Say something nice about his teeth," Kevin instructed me.

Tim was running around the house when we arrived, donning and doffing T-shirts in an effort to put together the perfect pride parade look. With the exception of the T-shirts scattered all over the living room, his house was immaculate (*Architectural Digest* was shooting it the next day), with examples of Kevin's and Tim's stylish and outrageously expensive light fixtures, floor lamps, and wall sconces dominating every room. The place was also packed with people when we arrived. Tim's friends were mostly men, each one tanner and more muscular than the next, with the exception of the one fat-and-funny faggot cracking jokes from the couch and a butch/glam lesbian couple more at home with gay men than with other lesbians. As far as I could tell, there was no one in the house who needed a dose of gay-is-good affirmation; everyone seemed hip, secure, and successful. No one at Tim's house looked to be racked with feelings of shame—least of all Tim.

"It's not about the floats," Tim told me when I asked him why he was going to the parade. Tim ordered me to follow him upstairs so we could talk while he continued his search for the perfect T-shirt. "The parade is about love. Love, dammit! Write that in your little notebook, mister. And it's about laughing at the freaks."

Again with the freaks. How, I asked Tim, could the parade be about love *and* laughing at the freaks? How does one reconcile those impulses?

"Well," said Tim, "I guess freaks get to laugh at us, too. We all laugh at each other, and that makes it fair."

"But the parade is really for people who are just coming out," a tan, toothy man standing in the door interjected. "It's really for all the gay kids."

Again with the gay kids!

I was going to ask Tan Man to elaborate, but he seemed pretty enthralled by Tim's T-shirt show. He might be Tim's boyfriend, I thought, and if he wasn't, he was going to be soon. Tim settled on a pair of baggy cargo shorts, a white half T-shirt that showed off his flat stomach, and big, blue-tinted sunglasses. I complimented the lamps next to his bed before we headed back downstairs.

"Do you like it?" Tim said. "It's one of my designs. Four thousand dollars for the pair. Janet Jackson bought eight pairs last week."

I was still in shock (two-thousand-dollar lamps?!) ten minutes later when we marched out of Tim's house and headed towards Santa Monica Boulevard.

"We're our own parade," Tim announced.

At an intersection blocks from Tim's house, our little group encountered a sweaty, miserable straight guy trying to push a stalled truck down the street and steer at the same time. Without being asked, five tan fags from our parade ran up and started pushing the miserable straight guy's truck. The straight guy hopped into the cab. After being pushed by fags for more than a block, he was able to start his truck and drive off, waving his thanks to all the beautiful tan fags who helped him out.

"It's all about love," Tim said, pointing at my notebook. "You write that down, mister. Love. Love and lamps. That's what it's all about."

The Celebrity Grand Marshal at the L.A. gay pride parade was a horse-faced comedienne who played a supporting role on a long-canceled, completely unremarkable sitcom. Her show ran in the shadow of Seinfeld for a few years, and now the comedienne divides her time between celebrity installments of *The Weakest Link* and the taxing business of marshaling gay-pride parades. To be fair, the comedienne was the best thing on her show but, nevertheless, I had a hard time figuring out what qualified her to be the grand marshal. Her sense of humor? Her red hair? Her presumed support for gay rights? (*Presumed* because I've never heard her say a word about gay equality.) Seeing as she was the *celebrity* grand marshal, did that mean there were other, equally grand, noncelebrity marshals waving from other convertibles somewhere else along the parade route?

Anyone who has been to a gay-pride parade or sat in their church basement and watched an antigay group's video of a pride parade knows exactly what was parading up and down Santa Monica Boulevard. All the usual suspects were there: a few beer trucks, some dykes on bikes, a few drag queens melting in the sun, a few half-assed floats, a few political groups, a few religious groups, and a few Christians holding up signs with Matthew Shephard's image and FAG MATT BURNS IN HELL! written on them. The gay Latino groups went all out, putting together elaborate floats and costumes—which was a treat for me; I've always had a weakness for the Aztec warriors pictured in murals in Mexican restaurants.

This being L.A., there were also hundreds of guys marching around in their underwear—including a car full of beautiful boys sponsored by a West Hollywood bar famous for filling its dance floor with six-foot-high mounds of soap suds, attracting crowds of beautiful, nearly naked men who dance (and, uh, more) under the cover of soap suds. The beautiful boys who work at the bar were carrying buckets of sudsy water and sponges. When they saw someone attractive in the crowd, they ran up and soaked the hottie with suds. When Tim, Kevin, Jake, and their good-looking friends saw the float coming, they moved to the back of the sidewalk to avoid being assaulted.

One guy on the soap suds brigade stood out. He was an older man in a lime-green thong and nothing else. (It's entirely possible he was "wearing" a pride butt plug, too.) It was really all about his dick, of course, which appeared to be a foot long. I found him appalling—and not because I have a problem with nudity. Or foot-long dicks. No, I have a problem with *thongs*. I would rather the guy were marching nude. Somehow it didn't fill my heart with pride to see Thong Man marching along, cigarette stuck in his mouth, his lime-green dick being batted back and forth by his thighs.

Curious how Thong Man's big cock was playing with the kids— you know, the gay youth Kevin and Jake and Tim were here to fill with hope—I began looking around for some gay youth. Oddly enough, I couldn't find any. There were a hundred thousand people at the parade, give or take a few thousand, so there had to be gay youth somewhere. But I couldn't find one.

Unlike the antigay groups who videotape pride parades in an effort to scare checks out of grannies, I wasn't bothered by Thong Man's overt sexual display. Nor was I bothered by this year's crop of sleazy gay T-shirts for sale at Don't Panic, West Hollywood's Ye Olde Gay Pride Shoppe: I JUST DID YOUR BOYFRIEND; SLEEPS WELL WITH OTHERS; PORN STAR IN TRAINING; INSTANT SLUT—JUST ADD ALCOHOL; FLAVOR OF THE WEEK; and my personal favorite, IF I WANT TO HEAR WHAT YOU HAVE TO SAY, I'LL TAKE MY COCK OUT OF YOUR MOUTH. Some might view Thong Man or filthy T-shirts—which were selling like hotcakes, of course—as a sad comment on gay men. We're too focused on sex, and the gay pride parade is too sexual.

To my mind, the overtly sexual displays at gay pride parades are much less offensive than the idiotic gay-is-good rhetoric. Being gay is about sex; sex is, after all, the thing that separates gay people from straight people. Who we desire and who we fall in love with sets us apart, makes us feel different, and that difference has social and political dimensions. So overt displays of sex—the good (Aztec Warrior), the bad (Soap Sud Assaults), and the ugly (Thong Man)—have a place in a gay pride parade, in much the same way that overt displays of Irishness—beer and shamrocks and beer and whiskey and beer—have a place in Saint Patrick's Day parades.

In fact, gay pride parades and the Saint Patrick's Day parades have more in common than Bill O'Reilly might like to admit.

Saint Patrick's Day parades were not always the respectable white-ethnic love fests they are today. When Irish Catholic immigrants first began coming to the United States in the 1830s to dig canals, and then kept coming in the 1840s to escape the famine, these early Irish Catholic immigrants were despised and discriminated against by "native" Americans—a term that used to mean WASPs born in the United States. Irish Catholics were thought to be inherently un-American, as they owed fealty to a foreign prince, the pope, and couldn't be trusted. The Irish were America's first urban social problem, as they crowded the slums and married free blacks.

The original Saint Patrick's Day celebrations in New York City and Boston in the early to mid-1800s were not the Everyone-Is-Irish-on-Saint-Patrick's-Day sentimental shamrocks-and-green-beer festivals of today. ("For one thing, the Irish drank whiskey," says my brother Bill. "Beer was a German thing." Luckily for my family, we're a quarter German.) Celebrating the feast of Saint Patrick—a Roman Catholic religious holiday—by parading around the city and proclaiming, essentially, "We're here, we're Irish, get used to it," was a slap in the face of the Nativist/Protestant majority. Mainstream Americans circa 1850 considered the Saint Patrick's Day parade a deeply offensive spectacle. Early Saint Patrick's Day parades were often attacked by anti-Irish mobs.

"Saint Patrick's Day parades were an assertion of identity by a category of people that many Americans wished would go away," says Bill, who teaches American Literature at Northwestern University outside of Chicago. "The fact that Saint Pat's now celebrates a stereotypical Irishness (drink, sentimental songs, drink, sentimental poetry, drink, brawling, sentimental making up after fisticuffs, drink) instead of an aggressive form of identity politics perhaps indicates that someday gay pride parades will be just as watered down. Who knows? Maybe one day everyone will be gay on gay pride day, just as we're all Irish on Saint Patrick's Day."

If my brother is correct—and he's never given me cause to doubt him—we may one day see Bill O'Reilly prancing down Fifth Avenue in a bra and high heels, wearing a KISS ME, I'M GAY button on his rainbow-striped bowler hat. It's almost too horrible to contemplate.

Kevin and Jake, Tim and Tan Man, and the rest of their friends gathered at the gates to the Pride Festival, a separate event that you needed a ticket to get into. We found a patch of shade under a tree and sat on the ground. Someone ran off to buy tickets to the festival; Jake strolled over to a Mexican man selling bottles of water out of a beer cooler on the corner.

Kevin and his friends intended to spend the rest of the day dancing in one of three tents set up on the festival site. Big name DJs would be spinning, and now that Kevin and his friends had done their good deed for the day—they'd gone to the parade, stuffed the kids with hope—it was time to pursue some grown-up happiness: Kevin pulled a little plastic packet out of his pocket and distributed ecstasy tablets to all his friends. His treat, he told us.

I'm not big on DJs or dancing or tents . . . but I do enjoy recreational drugs. Or I *did* enjoy them, I should say. Um, gee. Okay, time to come clean about all the other drugs I've used. Frankly, I've tried 'em all. Thankfully, I don't have an addictive personality (really, Laura, I don't), and when I've safely and responsibly used and enjoyed drugs like ecstasy, coke, acid, mushrooms, and GHB, my first impulse was never to rush out and do it again right away. Instead, I've always thought to myself, "Hey, that was fun. Maybe I'll do that drug again in a year or two." I don't understand people who find a drug they like and then use it on a daily or weekly basis; if you use a particular drug constantly, the effects are less dramatic and pleasurable.

When I became a parent, of course, I gave up strong recreational drugs, limiting myself to alcohol and pot on those moments when I need to indulge that old-as-humanity drive to alter my consciousness. Even then, I drink or use pot only when the kid is in one place and I'm in another. I didn't swear off hard drugs because I was worried about popping my kid into a microwave oven, and I gave them up long before George W. Bush merged the War on Terrorism with the War on Drugs. I gave them up—everything but pot, and only that on exceedingly rare occasions—because being the parent of a small child means never having the luxury of being totally wasted or thoroughly indisposed or completely useless or hungover. So no more ecstasy or 'shrooms or acid or GHB for me.

Of course, seeing as my kid was in one state and I was in another, I made an exception and graciously accepted a hit of ecstasy from Kevin. Moderation in all things, that's my motto, and I believe it applies to moderation itself.

We weren't the only ones at the pride festival on ecstasy. After we handed our tickets to the volunteers at the gate and made our way past the security checkpoints, we passed through yet another line of volunteers: young, pretty straight women handing out little slips of pink paper. PARTY SMART! the flyers read. IT'S SUNNY AND IT'S HOT AND SOME CLUB DRUGS CAN CAUSE YOU TO BECOME DEHYDRATED. SO BE SURE TO DRINK LOTS OF WATER! These slips of paper were handed to everyone who entered the festival, a huge public park that had been fenced off for the day, a park filled with food vendors, information tables, dance tents, and people selling gay pride merchandise (butt plugs, anklets, teddy bears), and tens of thousands of homosexuals. Warning everyone who entered the festival about drug-related dehydration seemed to me an admission on the part of the gay pride festival organizers that more people at the festival were on drugs than not.

Anyone who expects this to turn into an after-school special is going to be disappointed. In most films, books, and on television, the introduction of hard drugs into the plotline usually foreshadows some sad or tragic event. Let me end the suspense right now: No one in our little group overdosed or freaked out or died. We had fun, stayed hydrated, and made it home in one piece. The moral of this story? Recreational drugs, used in moderation, can be wonderful. Ecstasy is particularly wonderful; you fall in love with the world on ecstasy and find yourself telling people things you might have a hard time expressing if you weren't "rolling on E," as the kids like to say. For instance, ecstasy helped me tell Tim how much I liked his teeth.

"So are you having fun?" Kevin asked, throwing an arm around my shoulder. Yes, I was having fun, I admitted. In fact, I was having a blast. I was having fun laughing at the freaks, ogling the good-looking guys, and admiring Tim's, um, teeth. The sun was fun; the heat was fun. Hell, even the thongs were fun. But where were the kids?

"The kids?"

Yeah, the kids, the gay youth. The whole point of the pride parade, he told me, was reaching out to gay youth, giving 'em hope, letting 'em know we're hot and hideous, young and old, smooth and hairy. I pointed out that the youngest people at the parade and the festival seemed to be in their mid-twenties. And there weren't that many of them. The average age looked to be thirty-three. Kevin smiled and shrugged.

"Oh, yeah, gay kids . . . ," said Kevin. "Well, it's about fun, too. Fun and kids, and if the kids don't come, well, we still get to have fun. The first time I went to the parade I was, like, nineteen years old and already out," he continued. "You have to be out already to come to something like this. What it did, though, what's important about it, is that it made me feel more comfortable with being gay. It made me more confident."

"Oh, stop it, you two," said Jake, shirtless, sweaty, and fresh from the dance tent. "Blah blah blah. Enough with the gay youth already. Pride parades are like slings. Tell people you've got a sling, and they're clutching their pearls. 'Oh, my God, you've got a sling!'

But fucking in a sling is fun. Same with the pride parade. Tell people you're going and they can't believe you would even want to. But
once they get their asses to the parade they have a great fucking
time. And having fun is important—it's the whole point."

The whole point?

"Sure," Jake says. "When we were young, everyone said that the
gays were unhappy and no one likes us and that our lives would
be miserable. What better way to disprove all of that crap than having fun? With thousands of other 'miserable' gay people? In public? The party is the purpose of all of this. Pleasure is the whole
point."

Jake was right: Pleasure was the whole point. There we all were,
pursuing happiness, being responsible (making sure we kept hydrated), good citizens (helping that straight man push his truck),
happy, happy high people. It wasn't about pride booster shots,
keeping shame at bay, political liberation, or helping youth. We
were there to have fun. But why did it take all day and a hit of ecstasy before any of us could admit it?

It's odd that people who have to reject conventional concepts
of morality to justify their own existence can be so conventional
when it comes to justifying their own pleasures. But the average
fag won't tell a writer or a reporter that he's going to the pride parade to watch boys or hang out with his friends or take drugs and
dance. No, he's going to give gay youth hope. Somehow I can't
imagine the few gay teenagers who at the Los Angeles pride parade or festival derived much in the way of hope watching Kevin
and Jake get high and dance with their shirts off. I can't imagine
that the man in the lime-green thong did much to lift their spirits,
any more than one man I saw dragging his much younger
boyfriend around on a leash (black leather, not rainbow-striped).
No one at L.A.'s gay pride parade was committing the sin of pride,
as it turned out, just the sin of a good time. Isn't it funny that it
took all day, illegal drugs, the heat of the sun, and two hours on

the dance floor for everyone to drop the pretense and admit that the parade was about fun and pleasure and their particular pursuit of happiness?

Gay pride parades are bacchanals—ass-kicking, ass-licking parties—and perhaps it's time for gay people to admit it. We feel obligated, though, to wrap the pride parade up in goody-goody rationalizations, such as "We're here to help gay youth," or "We're fighting for political liberation!" Gays aren't the only Americans who feel obligated to rationalize their pleasures in this manner; pleasure-hating Puritanism runs deep in the United States. (When it came time to carve up the continent, Canada got the French, and the United States got the Puritans and their descendants. I don't know about you, but I'd rather we got the French.) Even hedonists in America have a hard time viewing simple pleasure as a legitimate pursuit: marijuana-legalization activists want to ease the suffering of people with glaucoma; swinging couples approach nonswinger couples because the lifestyle is a great way to enhance a marriage; casinos create new tax revenues that states can turn around and spend on schools.

One might expect that gay people, of all people, would be able to recognize the legitimacy of a good time for the sake of a good time. After all, coming out of the closet is about the pursuit of the most basic human happiness: sexual fulfillment. We come out to get laid and, with luck, find love. (A gay person can get laid without ever coming out of the closet, of course. Catholic priests have been doing it for centuries. But such closeted sex is miserable, furtive, paranoia-inducing, and emotionally unsatisfying.) Coming out is about pursuing happiness even at the risk of losing the love of your biological family and never getting to experience the joy of no-fault divorce proceedings. So why can't gay parades be a celebration of pleasure? And fun? And the pursuit of happiness? And honest?

Perhaps it's time for gay parades to come out of the closet. Gay people should admit that the pride parade is about pleasure, period. There's even a model for this new, honest, gays-just-want-to-have-fun parade. What is Mardi Gras in New Orleans but a huge, outrageous heterosexual pride parade? No one pretends Mardi Gras is anything but a party; Mardi Gras is streets packed with straight people in outrageous costumes abusing drugs and alcohol and shoving their sexuality in all of our faces. If gays and lesbians could stop tarting up a good time in the drag of good intentions, our annual parade wouldn't be an occasion for heterosexuals to grump at us about dykes on bikes, men in drag, and boys on leashes. If we dropped pride and politics from it and let the parade be a parade, people like Bill O'Reilly wouldn't be able to bitch about it. Right now, gay people tell Bill O'Reilly and the rest of the straights that the parade is about political liberation and gay youth and gay marriage and civil rights and equality under the law. But when O'Reilly turns on the TV, all he sees are men walking in lime-green thongs, men in drag, and dykes on bikes. Of course O'Reilly's offended—he's been lied to. Remember, it's not the sex that bothers O'Reilly, it's the lying about the sex.

So let's stop lying about it. Gay pride parades aren't about liberation anymore. We're liberated already. I know, I know—we haven't achieved full equality yet, but that's not stopping us from living our lives openly, honestly, and pursuing happiness like maniacs. Since being openly gay is about striving to live a happy, fulfilled, sexually complete life (with some integrity), fun and pleasure are a natural part of the parade. So let's be honest. Gay people should stop telling reporters and TV newscasters that the parade is about gay youth or gay marriage or gay rights or a protesting gay equality and then show up at the parade in lime-green thongs, take ecstasy, dance, make out, hook up, and take some more ecstasy. So long as we do that, the religious right will be there with their video cameras, ready to expose our hypocrisy. "They said it was a parade about gay rights and look at this video! *These men are dancing with their shirts off!*"

When you suggest this to most gay people—drop the politics

from the parade, drop "pride," drop "gay is good"—they insist that the parade can't change. After all, what about the gay kids? What about the newly out? What about gays and lesbians struggling with shame? Those people still need messages of pride, we're told. (Never mind that very few closeted kids and newly out folks actually attend pride parades.) But kids and the newly out would be just as well served, if not better served, by a parade stripped of both pride and politics. What most newly out gay people take away from their first pride parade—the thing that helps alleviate their shame—isn't anything they hear during the rallies or any of the flyers they're handed. What's important, what moves them, and what matters most, young gay people say, is not what they were told about being gay but what they *saw*: Gay people, all different kinds, all of them out and happy to be gay and having fun. That's the most transformative part of a pride parade for the young and the newly out, and that part would grow stronger in an honest gay parade, one that dropped the inch-deep claims about political liberation. Again, everything that gay pride parades supposedly accomplish now for young gay people could be accomplished by a parade that didn't have an easily exposed lie at its core.

For as long as we attempt to pass our Mardi Gras off as social work, the homophobes with their video cameras will go on exposing the gulf between our goody-goody rationalizations and what actually goes on at pride parades. So let's stop making excuses, let's drop the rationalizations. The gay parade is a good time, and that's enough. We shouldn't have to make excuses for our good time any more than straight people should have to make excuses for Mardi Gras. Mardi Gras is Mardi Gras. It's booze and drugs and sex and costumes, it's packs of young men shouting "Show us your tits!" at young women, and it's packs of young women shouting "Show us your dick!" at young men. It's a good time, period.

There are straight people who don't enjoy Mardi Gras. It's hard to imagine our current First Lady, for instance, showing her tits to her husband, much less a crowd of men throwing plastic beads. No one claims that Mardi Gras represents the political aspirations of all straight Americans, and no one who made such an absurd claim would be taken seriously. But straight Americans are told by gay Americans that the gay pride parade represents the political aspirations of all gay people everywhere, and straight people, in their ignorance, take the claim seriously. So long as there's a disconnect between what we're telling them the pride parade is about and what the pride parade is actually about, people like Bill O'Reilly are going to be offended.

"**B**ut the liberty to pursue happiness means that each of us pursues whatever it is he may desire," Robert Bork grouses in *Slouching Towards Gomorrah*. Note the *but* at the beginning of that sentence. The liberty to pursue happiness and the things that we desire is not, in Bork's opinion, a good thing. It requires a *but,* it's problematic. "We are to move away from restraints in pursuit of we know not what," writes Bork. "Such a person leads a precarious existence."

Kevin and Jake pursue happiness with an athleticism that I admire but couldn't keep up with. But there's nothing precarious about Kevin and Jake's existence. They've moved away from restraint in pursuit of they know precisely what: sex, love, pleasure. Kevin and Jake know what they want, they know what makes them happy, and they go for it. They certainly were ethical sinners: they shared with their friends, they were courteous to strangers, and they offered me, a stranger with a notebook, their hospitality. In no way were they reckless about indulging themselves. Knowing that drugs were on the day's agenda, Kevin and Jake loaded up on orange juice in the morning; when they got home late Sunday night, they downed protein shakes, took vitamins, and rested up. Recreational drugs are hard on the system, it's true, just as bacon and bourbon and bungee jumping are. If something that's hard on the system makes you happy, well, then you have to take special care of your system before and after you indulge. But from the outside looking in, Bork can't see the care or the restraint in Kevin's and Jake's use and abuse of drugs, sex, and each other. He only sees two self-indulgent men in hot pursuit of things that wouldn't make Bork himself happy.

"There is no reason whatever why a community should not decide that there are moral and aesthetic pollutions it wishes to prohibit," writes Bork, who would doubtless prohibit Los Angeles's gay pride parade, with its thongs and overt sexual themes. Indeed, Bork supports the enforcement of antigay sodomy laws. (These laws were upheld by the Supreme Court in 1986 but, Bork complains, by an insufficiently wide margin!) Bork is all about the political indulgence of the puritanical impulse: Your pleasures aren't my pleasures, therefore your pleasures are "moral pollutions." I don't approve of the places your pursuit of happiness takes you, so there ought to be a law that prevents you from going there. . . .

Bork is free to disapprove and judge and condemn and write and go on TV and rant and rave. Anyone who thinks pride parades and green thongs and ecstasy are awful is free to talk gay men out of them. Unlike some lefties, I'm not bothered by persuasion. If anti-choice activists want to spend their money on "Choose Life" billboards, if that's how they wanna pursue happiness, well, more power to 'em. And if anti-gay activists want to talk gay people out of being gay, well, they're free to take out ads in newspapers encouraging gay people to go straight. Not that the ads they do take out are aimed at gay people. Politically motivated Jesus-made-me-straight ads are an attempt to convince straight people that the issue of gay rights would go away if gay people just weren't so stubborn.

(Still it's odd that so many Christians can't seem to grasp the Golden Rule—"Do unto others as you would have them do unto you. . . ."—especially when it comes to sex. For example, I'm relatively certain that William Bennett doesn't want me dictating the content of his sex life. There are activities I enjoy that I doubt very much Bennett would enjoy. And guess what? I'm happy to let William Bennett pursue his sexual pleasures in peace and quiet. Why can't William Bennett do the same unto me? What about the right to be left alone? It's never occurred to me burst into the bedroom of a conservative Christian couple engaged in loving, missionary-position, procreative sexual intercourse and try and talk them into sodomizing each other. ["No, no, no. Fuck her in the *ass*!"] I would never do that unto someone. So how come so many fundamentalist Christians out there are trying to talk me out of my boyfriend's ass and into procreative, missionary-position sex with some miserable ex-lesbian? Why are they doing that unto me?)

Bork and his fellow scolds shouldn't attempt to prohibit my pleasures—or Kevin's or Jake's or Tim's or yours, dear reader, or each other's. First, because it isn't right and, second, because prohibiting pleasures simply isn't doable. Take me to the driest county in the most conservative state, and in two hours this determined hedonist will find you all the drugs, whores, and booze you'll need to pass an eventful weekend. But the biggest problem in prohibiting moral and aesthetic pollutions is, of course, figuring out who gets to decide what qualifies. One man's moral and aesthetic pollution may be central to another man's pursuit of happiness. And when and where that happens, well, the delicate sensibilities of the majority have to yield to the desires of the individual. For while I would never wear a lime-green thong in public myself, I will defend to the death Thong Man's right to do so.

I got separated from Kevin and Jake and Tim in the crowd. There was only so long I could stand around watching people dance, even Tim. So still rolling on ecstasy, I wandered out of the festival grounds and onto Santa Monica Boulevard. It was ninety degrees in the sun, and since I couldn't just stand around on street corners grinning like a lunatic, I decided to walk the six miles back to Kevin and Jake's house.

The premise of this book obligates me to celebrate the sin of pride, and the people I met while committing it. I failed in this effort, I suppose, since I don't have anything all that nice to say about the rhetoric gay people kick around every year at the end of June. While I can't stand mush-brained pride rhetoric, rainbow merchandise, and while I abhor the harm this rhetoric does to gay people and the confusion it sows among straights, what I can celebrate is the simple having of fun. The parade is, as Kevin and Jake insist, a good time. All the harm throwing the word *pride* does the gay community could be eliminated if we would drop the term, just as the African Americans dropped "black power," and feminists dropped "hear me roar." If you are a powerful black person, you don't have to defensively insist you have power; all you have to do is exercise it. Same goes for gay pride. If you're gay and you're not ashamed of it, you don't need pride. If you're gay and you are ashamed, you're a liar when you claim to be proud.

On the long walk back to Kevin and Jake's house, I passed the Tom Kat Theater, L.A.'s gay porn palace.

I paid my ten dollars and slipped into the Tom Kat Theater. Not wanting to risk sitting down on any recently deposited DNA samples, I stood at the back. Porn has never been my thing (there are places the sun isn't *supposed* to shine), nor is anonymous sex with strange men in dark theaters. (I have a hard time sharing a can of Coke with my boyfriend much less kissing someone whose mouth has been god-knows-where). But while the Tom Kat's brand of happiness wasn't one I would personally pursue, I was nevertheless thrilled that it was open and available to sinners who did find this brand of happiness—however icky, depressing, and desperate it might seem to me—in the theater's seats, bathrooms, and aisles.

Still rolling on ecstasy, I smiled at the aesthetic pollution on the screen and at the moral pollution creeping around the theater. The bottoms of my shoes were stuck to the floor as I watched one gay-for-pay straight porn star fuck another gay-for-pay straight porn star in the ass. The porn film I was watching? It was a new gay porn flick, the first installment in a series. *The Seven Deadly Sins: Pride.*

ANGER

My Piece, My Unit

I simply cannot stand by and watch a right guaranteed by the Constitution of the United States come under attack from those who either can't understand it [or] don't like the sound of it. —Charlton Heston

I'm holding a gun.

I've never held a gun before, and it's making my heart race. My instructor, Paul, is trying to give me some pointers about the proper way to handle a .22-caliber, clip-loaded handgun, but I can't hear him over the pounding in my chest. Handguns scare the shit out of me.

My dad was a Chicago cop who, like a lot of cops, hated handguns with the kind of passion that comes from being shot at every once in a while. When the subject of gun control came up at a neighborhood barbecue or family party, my dad wearily pointed out to anyone who was anti-gun control that handguns were designed to do one thing and one thing only: kill people. If a guy wants to hunt, he gets a hunting rifle; if a guy wants to protect his home and family, he gets a shotgun. If a guy wants to rob people on the subway or knock over convenience stores or kill a human being in cold blood, he gets a handgun.

My dad owned a handgun, of course: his service revolver, which he kept in a locked filing cabinet. I can't remember ever seeing him with his gun; he never showed it off to us, and he never encouraged us to play with toy guns, although he couldn't really stop us from making guns out of sticks, fingers, and PB&J sandwiches. My dad's attitude towards guns instilled a deep-seated fear of all guns in me as a child, and now, as an adult, about the only thing that scares me more than handguns are the nutcases who fetishize them. So I was a little nervous when I walked into the Bullet Trap, an indoor shooting range and a gun shop in Plano, Texas.

Plano is the ugliest place I visited while working on this book. Hell, Plano is the ugliest place I've ever been to, and I've been to a *lot* of ugly places, from mud-brick villages in southern Egypt, to crumbling Stalinist apartment blocks on the edges of Moscow, to Gary, Indiana. Unlike Egypt and Moscow, Plano can't plead poverty; Plano is a wealthy suburb of Dallas, where the houses are made of brick and built big. Builders have given their housing developments names like King's Court, Steeple Chase, Willow Bend, and Old Shepard Place. Judging by the names of these pseudo-neighborhoods, you would think Texas was crammed full of legal and illegal aliens from the British Isles, and not Central and South America.

Plano doesn't appear to be much of a Gomorrah—not at first glance. The anglophile/anglodenial housing developments are linked to each other by six-lane roads and an almost endless string of upscale strip malls. The too-numerous-to-count, big-box chain restaurants—the multiple Chi-Chi's, Bennigan's, and Tony Roma's—might make gluttony appear to be Plano's only major sin, but Plano has its very own club for married swingers, and nearby Dallas has at least a half a dozen. On a down note, Plano's youngsters have a serious drug problem; in the late 1990s, an epidemic of heroin abuse claimed the lives of dozens of teenagers from well-to-do families in Plano. (This is a tragedy, of course, but it's not argument for continuing the war on drugs. The war on drugs didn't keep heroin out of Plano, and if a war couldn't keep heroin out of a place like Plano, it's hard to imagine what, short of carpet-bombing, would.)

The Bullet Trap was in a long, low, industrial building behind a Whataburger, a fast-food chain indigenous to Texas. The gun range couldn't be seen from the road, and I wound up getting lost. I had to stop in a convenience store that sold soda, junk food, beer, rolling papers, dream catchers, and more than a hundred different kinds of lethal-looking knives (!) to ask for directions. From the outside, the Bullet Trap looked as if it could've been a dentist's office once or a print shop or a you-store-it warehouse. The inside of the Bullet Trap resembled a large rec room in a hobbyist's basement. There weren't any windows, the place smelled musty, the carpets were industrial, the walls were paneled, and guns were displayed in glass-topped counters. There were guns I'd heard of—Colt, Smith & Wesson, Glock—and guns I hadn't—Rugers, Taurus, Walther, Keltel, Beretta, Kimber, Sig.

The place was filled with men: big men, he-men, gun-lovin' men, men who probably would shoot me if they could read what was on my mind. Looking at the guns in the cases and on the walls at the Bullet Trap—guns for sale, guns for rent—I was thinking, Christ, I wish I lived in a country that didn't allow its citizens to own guns, any guns, handguns or rifles or shotguns. I hate guns.

Anger is the desire for vengeance, according to Saint Augustine, but that doesn't mean anger is necessarily bad. Saint Augustine recognized that there were times when anger was called for, moments when the thirst for vengeance is tempered by a justifiable righteous indignation. At those times, anger could be a force of good in the world.

American gun owners regard themselves as a force for good in the world—but they've always seemed like an angry bunch of yahoos to me, constantly fuming about black helicopters, "jackbooted thugs" who work for the federal government, and all the damn liberals and their damn laws mandating the use of trigger locks and the safe storage of guns, both moves that would save the lives of hundreds of children every year (and not the children of liberals). Owning a gun in America is one way for conservative white males to demonstrate their anger at crime, liberalism, feminism, and modernity.

Law-abiding gun owners, according to the National Rifle Association, aren't angry; they're merely realistic. This is a dangerous world we live in, and they need their guns to protect themselves, their families, and other law-abiding citizens from all the damn criminals (and the damn liberals who coddle them). Whenever some lunatic pulls out a gun in a school or a business and starts blowing people away, the National Rifle Association helpfully suggests that the problem isn't too many guns in the United States but too *few* guns. If only the murdered teachers, students, or coworkers of the deranged shooter or shooters had themselves been armed, they could've returned fire and saved lives. Guns aren't the cause of gun violence, the NRA insists, but the solution to gun violence. The more guns, the more better.

Never mind that a school cafeteria filled with hundreds of students blasting away at each other would result in more deaths; never mind that the presence of a gun in a home triples the risk of a homicide taking place in that home; never mind that the presence of a gun in the home increases the risk of suicide by five times; never mind that Japan, which strictly limits gun ownership, had just 28 gun deaths in 1999, compared with 26,800 in the United States; never mind that England's murder rate is one-sixth that of the United States, as *New York Times* op-ed writer Nicholas D. Kristof points out; never mind that firearms were used in approximately seven out of every ten murders committed in the nation in 1999.

And never mind the fact that the United States is already swimming in guns. There are 200 million privately owned guns in the United States, 65 million of which are handguns. If the presence of guns prevents violence, the United States should have the lowest levels of violence in the industrialized world, not the highest.

Never mind all that.

If the NRA, its members, and the conservative politicians they buy and sell ever admit that handguns make the United States an infinitely more dangerous place than, say, Canada, we still can't ban even handguns for two very important reasons.

First, if handguns are banned, only criminals will have handguns. "Gun control laws raise the cost of obtaining a firearm," Bork writes in *Slouching Towards Gomorrah*. "This is a cost that the criminal will willingly pay because a gun is essential to the business he is in." Banning handguns ultimately won't work, Bork insists, "[because] illicit markets adapt to overcome difficulties." Bork's argument against gun control could easily be applied to drugs: Since illicit markets adapt to whatever law enforcement measures are taken, it makes no sense to ban illicit drugs. Likewise, banning rap music, pornography, and sodomy—all things Bork would like to ban—won't work because illicit markets will sprout up to meet demand. Bork is a hypocrite, applying one argument to the proven evil of handguns, while using another for the dubious "evils" of rap, porn, sodomy, and so forth. What's more, Bork's argument against banning handguns falls apart when you consider the evidence. Judging by the comparatively low murder rates in Great Britain, Canada, Japan, and New Zealand, it seems that criminals do indeed have a difficult time coming by handguns.

Things get more problematic for gun-loving drug warriors when you consider the economic costs of gun violence. "A study of all direct and indirect costs of gun violence," according to Handgun Control Inc., "including medical, lost wages, and security costs estimates that gun violence costs the nation $100 billion a year." Conservatives point to the same figure—$100 billion in economic losses—when they argue for continuing the war on drugs. If the cost of drug use makes an open-and-shut case against legalization, how come the identical cost of gun violence isn't an open-and-shut case for a ban on handguns?

The other big argument against banning handguns is, um, let me see. . . . I had it right here a second ago. Christ, what was it again? Let me do a quick search on Google. Oh, right, the Second Amendment to the U.S. Constitution.

"A well-regulated militia, being necessary to the security of a free State, the right of the people to keep and bear Arms, shall not be infringed."

The Second Amendment presents a huge problem for people like me—that is, for big fans of our nation's founding documents— particularly that pursuit of happiness stuff in the Declaration of Independence. Owning guns clearly makes some very angry Americans very, very happy, and I'm not interested in coming between a heavily armed person and his definition of happiness. Also, unlike fundamentalist Christians, my conscience doesn't afford me the luxury of picking and choosing which bits of favorite centuries-old documents I'm going to take literally. If I want the full-meal-deal on the Declaration of Independence and the First Amendment, I feel somewhat obligated to sign off on the full-meal-deal on the Second Amendment. After all, it does say the right of the people to keep and bear arms shall not be infringed, which seems pretty straightforward.

But is it?

To his credit, Robert Bork acknowledges that the Second Amendment doesn't necessarily grant the average citizen the right to keep and bear arms. He characterizes the amendment as "ambiguous." "The first part of the Amendment supports proponents of gun control by seeming to make possession of firearms contingent upon being a member of a state-regulated militia," Bork writes in *Slouching Towards Gomorrah*. "The next part is cited by opponents of gun control as a guarantee of the individual's right to possess such weapons, since he can always be called to militia service. The Supreme Court has consistently ruled that there is no individual right to own a firearm. The Second Amendment was designed to allow states to defend themselves against a possibly tyrannical national government. Now that the federal government has stealth bombers and nuclear weapons, it is hard to imagine what people would need to keep in the garage to serve that purpose."

The First Amendment, on the other hand, is much less ambiguous than the Second (which has never stopped Bork and other conservatives from attempting to punch holes in it): "Congress shall make no law respecting an establishment of religion, or prohibiting the free exercise thereof; or abridging the freedom of speech, or of the press; or the right of the people peaceably to assemble, and to petition the Government for a redress of grievances."

The First Amendment has a fan base, as does the Second Amendment, and it's a shame that there isn't more overlap between the two groups. Much mistrust and mutual contempt separates the fans of the First and Second Amendments. As a First Amendment fan, I can't resist pointing out that the First Amendment does come *first,* but in the hopes of bringing Firsts and Seconds closer together, I'd like to clear up a couple of misconceptions. First off, First Amendment fans tend to live in crowded urban areas, and we're afraid of getting shot. Second Amendment fans tend to live in less populated areas, and they're afraid that people from urban areas are going to come and take their guns away. On behalf of all First Amendment fans everywhere, I'd like to tell Second Amendment fans that we're not coming to take your guns because—hello!—*we're afraid of getting shot* and you people have guns. If we came and tried to take your guns away, you would shoot us—I've seen Charlton Heston say exactly that on CNN a half a dozen times. So, really, we're not coming for your guns.

If it's not too much trouble, Firsts would love Seconds to find ways to make it harder for your guns to fall into the hands of the people who shoot at us on the subway or, for that matter, we'd like you to keep your kids from blowing their own heads off with your guns. To that end, we're for gun training, registration, licensing, trigger locks, gun safes, smart guns that fire only when they're being held by their owners, banning cop-killer bullets, and banning handguns and other concealable weapons. See? We don't want to take your guns. We just want to make the world a safer place.

(Why do Firsts care so much about protecting the children of Seconds? Because most Firsts are liberals, and liberals are very concerned about other people, especially children. That's why liberals are all over trigger locks and safe storage laws. I mean, come on— most of the people out there pressing for mandatory trigger locks and safe storage don't have guns in their homes. Their kids aren't around guns, and so it's not their kids who're getting their heads blown off in garages and basements. Maybe their concerns are misplaced; kids who grow up around guns are likelier to be right-leaning gun nuts when they grow up. If gun foes want to turn the tide against guns, maybe they shouldn't work so hard to save gunowners' children. Just a thought.)

It seems to me that Firsts and Seconds could compromise. This may get a little confusing but try to follow along: Seconds want the most liberal reading of the Second Amendment, while Firsts want the most liberal reading of the First; most Seconds favor a conservative reading of the First Amendment, and most Firsts favor a conservative reading of the Second. There's room for a deal here. If Firsts agree to sign off on a liberal reading of the Second Amendment (the right to keep and bear arms shall not be infringed), and Seconds sign off on the most liberal interpretation of the First Amendment (complete separation of church and state, total freedom of speech), perhaps we could end most of the culture war. Gun nuts don't have to worry about People for the American Way coming for their guns anymore, and First Amendment fans can write, print, publish, film, videotape, and chat on-line about anything we care to.

Is it a deal?

It was a Saturday afternoon when I first walked into the Bullet Trap, the place was pretty crowded, and the man behind the counter laughed when I asked if I could get a shooting lesson. The Bullet Trap doesn't give lessons on the weekends, he said, because they're way too busy. He told me to come back on Monday. I wasn't going to be in Plano on Monday, I pleaded, and then I made the mistake of telling the truth: I made a special trip to Plano to learn how to shoot; I was writing something about guns; I had to fly home the next day. Couldn't they squeeze me in?

The man behind the counter gave me a long, hard look. Then he asked me where I was from. It didn't occur to me that "where are you from" could be a trick question. When I told him I was from Seattle, he snorted and rolled his eyes.

"That's a pretty liberal place, Seattle. Did someone send you down to Texas to write something negative about guns?" he said, leaning over the counter.

No, no, no. I assured the armed, menacing man behind the counter that I wasn't writing something negative about guns—to the contrary! I was in beautiful Plano, Texas, because I wanted to write something positive about guns. There might have been a gun range I could have gone to in Seattle, I explained, but I didn't want to learn to shoot from someone who had gone soft living in Seattle, a guy who felt he had to apologize for shooting a gun. I wanted to learn to shoot from a guy who had never once doubted his right to keep and bear arms—and I wanted to learn to shoot in Texas because Texas and guns go together like rigor and mortis. Among the gun nut states, Texas is the gun nuttiest.

Yes, sir, I was in Plano because I wanted to write something positive about guns, something upbeat. Glowing, even.

The man behind the counter—his name was Dave—called his boss over, an even larger, more menacing man. (Now, none of these guys were menacing in reality, but they were all armed.)

"This fella is from Seattle," he explained to his boss, "he's in Plano special to learn to shoot, *and* he's going to write something about it."

The Bullet Trap's boss asked me if I was planning on writing something positive or negative, and I explained again that it was my intention to write something complimentary, something that would show gun owners in the best possible light. Christ, I thought to myself, for a bunch of rough, tough, armed-to-the-teeth types, the men who worked at the Bullet Trap seemed awfully nervous about the power of the printed word. What were they so afraid of? If Lee Harvey Oswald, James Earl Ray, Sirhan Sirhan, John Hinckley, Mark David Chapman, the school shootings in Pearl, West Paducah, Jonesboro, Springfield, Littleton, and Santee, and the ten children shot and killed in the United States *every day* aren't enough to convince the federal government to do something about the 200 million guns in this country, shit, then nothing I could write was going to get the Second Amendment repealed.

Fearing that my trip to Plano was going to be for nothing, I played my trump card. Write something negative about guns? Me? Goodness, no!

"My dad was a cop," I said, "I grew up in a house with a gun. I'm not afraid of guns. Really, I'm not here to write some big guns-go-bang exposé."

I didn't tell the men at the Bullet Trap that my dad was pro–gun control, of course, or that I thought the 65 million handguns in the United States was a social and economic disaster, or that I admired countries that banned the possession of firearms by average citizens. I guess I misled them. Despite misleading the men at the Bullet Trap about my own personal feelings about guns, I wasn't entirely misleading them about my intentions. I think guns are a sin—and I think it's clear that Jesus would be on my side on this issue—but I was working the pro-sin/pro-sinner angle, and I would find something nice about guns if it killed me.

Hearing that my dad was a cop, and that I grew up in a house with a gun, opened doors for me at the Bullet Trap. Cop for a dad, house with a gun: I may not have looked like a gun owner—jeans too baggy, hair too short, gut undetectable—but I was one of them. The boss okayed a special Sunday afternoon class. I was told to come back at 2 P.M. tomorrow.

Just as an aside to gun nuts who might be reading this.

Gun nuts talk and talk about needing guns to protect the rights and freedoms that all Americans enjoy, but when the rights and freedoms of Americans are under siege, gun nuts are nowhere to be found. I don't recall seeing any NRA members, for example, ever protesting an assault on the free speech rights of Americans by the feds—or the federal government's successful efforts to undermine our constitutional protections against government surveillance and unreasonable searches, their attempts to regulate speech on the Internet, limit abortion rights, and ban any public expression that's in any way sexually explicit. Where were all the freedom-loving gun nuts when the director of the Contemporary Arts Center in Cincinnati was arrested and (unsuccessfully) prosecuted for displaying Robert Mapplethorpe's photos?

So while gun owners are always saying that owning guns is about defending freedom, the only freedom gun owners seem interested in defending with their guns is the freedom to defend their freedom to own guns. For a freedom fan such as myself, this seems a little limited. All that firepower—200 million guns—dedicated to defending just one freedom? Charlton Heston, the actor and president of the NRA, says he "cannot stand by and watch a right guaranteed by the Constitution of the United States come under attack," and yet I don't recall seeing Charlton Heston on television complaining about John Ashcroft's recent assaults on, say, attorney-client privilege. If gun nuts want to convince non–gun nuts of the value of an armed citizenry, perhaps they should use their guns to defend *all* of our freedoms, not just your freedom to own guns.

According to Doug Honig of the American Civil Liberties Union, some gun groups have started to come around; upset by Ruby Ridge and Waco, some gun groups have engaged in polite protests against proposals to increase federal police powers. To me it seems like a case of too little too late—and why so polite? I mean, I thought the point of gun ownership was getting to use guns to defend our freedoms. If gun owners found all the rights Americans are guaranteed by our Constitution worthy of defending to the death, perhaps non–gun owners would be more sympathetic to the rights of gun owners.

It's just a thought.

When I showed up on Sunday, I was introduced to Paul, the man who would teach me to shoot.

Paul was my age, with a helmet of thick, blond hair. Like everyone else at the Bullet Trap, he was wearing a button-down, collared denim shirt tucked into a pair of black jeans. He had a slight drawl, and before he would let me pick out or handle a gun, Paul took me through his Four Big Rules for Safety.

"First, all guns are loaded," Paul said, "that's the first of four big rules. Some people say, 'Treat all guns as if they're loaded,' but that introduces some doubt in your mind. By telling yourself to think a gun *might* be loaded, you're also telling yourself that the gun might *not* be loaded. You're introducing subconscious doubt. You don't want to have that doubt. Say no to doubt. Tell yourself, 'All guns are always loaded,' and you'll always treat a gun as if it's loaded.

"The second Big Rule: Keep your finger off the trigger until your sights are on a target and you're ready to shoot.

"Third, never allow the muzzle to point at anything you're not willing to destroy. Some people think that if they point the gun down and toward themselves," Paul said, pointing the gun down and towards his crotch, "they're being safe. But if that gun goes off, you've gone and destroyed something you might not want destroyed.

"Finally, four: Know your target and know what's beyond it. If you miss your target, its a tactical disaster and it's socially irresponsible. If you're going to shoot at it, hit it. If you can't hit it, don't shoot at all."

Paul handed me some additional safety rules to read.

"These are the rules of the range," Paul said. "Read them, and I'll be right back."

The list was long, and the type was small. When I got to number 17, I read this: "At this time, please inform the Range Officer that is helping you that 'Barney is a great kids' show.' This will let him know that you are reading these rules." I was done reading the list when Paul came back, and he asked me if I had anything to say to him.

"Barney is a great kids' show," I said.

"Good boy," said Paul.

I told Paul I wanted to shoot a variety of handguns, and he recommended that I start with a .22-caliber pistol.

"It's easier to get used to shooting a .22, since there's less recoil. They're accurate up close, less accurate at longer ranges."

Some of the .22s in the case Paul walks me over to are so tiny they look more like PEZ dispensers than like guns. Most of the guns made for women are .22s, and some of the guns in the case have pink and light blue handles. "You can get 'em in lots of different colors," Paul said. "That way she can have a different color gun for every day of the week, if she likes."

I pick out one of the larger .22s, a black gun with a long shaft.

"That's an excellent gun, a fine gun," Paul said, removing it from the case and setting it down on the counter between us. "It's a real nice piece." He took the clip out, made sure it was unloaded, snapped it back in place, and handed me the gun. That's when my heart began to race. I'd never held a real gun before, but I immediately and instinctively placed my finger on the trigger.

"Take your finger off the trigger," Paul said. "You only put your finger on the trigger when it's time to shoot."

Paul showed me how to hold the gun: right hand on the handle, left hand wrapped around the right hand, trigger finger flat against the barrel until it was time to shoot.

"With your right hand, you push the gun forward, with your left hand, you pull it back," Paul said. "That steadies the gun, holds it level. And you never point a gun at anyone, ever."

Paul was on one side of the counter, and I was on the other, facing him, which meant that I was pointing the gun in his general direction, if not right at him. I couldn't turn and point it into the shop, which was filled with people, so I kept pointing the gun to one side of Paul. The only problem was that Paul wasn't the only person behind the counter helping customers, and every once in a while one of Paul's coworkers passed behind him, which resulted in me pointing a gun at his coworkers over and over again.

Paul set a small box of ammunition for the .22 on the counter and showed me how to load the clip. The bullets for a .22 gun are so small and so thin that they looked tiny and harmless. It was hard to believe that these little piece of metal would shoot out of the gun I was holding with such force they could blow lethal holes in another human being.

I was lost in homicidal thought when a big guy standing to my right, a man who had been observing my first gun lesson, began to chuckle.

"That's a nice piece," the man said, gesturing towards my gun. "But it's not a man's gun. Check out my unit." The man pulled a large, long .45 out of his carrying case, and held it up for me and Paul to admire.

"That's a fine unit," Paul said, admiring the stranger's gun, "a fine piece."

Piece, unit, piece, unit—there may be times when a cigar is just a cigar, but looking at the gun in my hand, with its thick shaft, comparing units with the man to my right like a couple of drunks at a urinal, I doubted that there was ever a time when a gun was *just* a gun. It's not an original observation, I'll admit, but after being in a room filled with men admiring guns, it's one I feel somehow obligated to make. There were women at the shooting range; some were shooting, but most were standing by and watching their husbands, boyfriends, and sons shoot. A large, plate-glass window separated the sales counter from the shooting range, and I watched a woman shoot while Paul talked with the man next to me about his piece. It was like watching a woman box or play football; there's no reason a woman shouldn't box or play football or shoot if that's what she wants to do, but it's almost impossible to shake the feeling that she's doin' something that is essentially masculine. A man is four times more likely to own a gun than a woman is, according to the Violence Policy Center, which may explain why men are six times more likely to get shot. Guns are big, loud, scary, and phallic, and men are free to pull out their pieces, admire them, swap stories about them, and blow them off in public—all the sorts of things men aren't allowed to do with their actual pieces.

Paul hands me a big pair of airport-style earmuffs, a pair of safety goggles, and a box of ammo. It's time to do some shooting. Paul puts the gun in a little gun cozy, a kind of large, semicircular fabric carrying case that zips up one side. The gun just fits inside, snuggly, and it looks like a quesadilla or a calzone with a gun filling. Paul points me towards the door that leads to the shooting range, tells me he'll meet me at lane number one. A sign on the door to the range says, NO ONE PAST THIS POINT WITHOUT SAFETY GEAR <u>ON</u>.

The shooting range looks something like a bowling alley; people stand in small clumps around their lanes and observe their friends and family blasting away, taking out paper targets instead of pins. There are little kids everywhere, mostly boys, including an eight-year-old kid standing right next to me, shooting a .45. It's a little nerve-racking.

I'm trying to remain calm, but the kid's .45 is going off right next to me and it is *loud*. To pass the time, I begin to load my gun, just like Paul showed me in the salesroom, and then it hits me— what an insane business! Paul took my ID when he gave me the gun, but fake IDs are easy to come by. Now I'm standing in a busy small business with a loaded gun. Crazy. A business where you hand loaded guns to your customers! The Bullet Trap is packed, the cash registers must be filled to overflowing, and any yahoo off the street who comes in with a state ID can ask for a gun, a box of ammo. What's to stop someone from walking in, renting a gun, and then sticking it in the face of the person who rented it to him and demanding all the money? How often does the Bullet Trap get robbed?

Not often, according to Paul, and a quick check with the Plano Police Department backs him up. "They've never been robbed, so far as I know," a Plano police officer told me. "The place is filled with people with guns, people who aren't afraid to use 'em. Robbing that place would be as good as committing suicide."

It wouldn't be right to go to Texas and learn to shoot without mentioning the former governor of Texas, George W. Bush.

During the 2000 election campaign, an NRA vice president, Kayne Robinson, told an audience of NRA members that "If we win, we'll have a president . . . where we work out of their office."

Bush promised to restore "honor and dignity" to the Oval Office during the 2000 elections, which was understood to be Clinton-bashing code for, "I won't be getting any blow jobs from interns in the Oval Office." The White House wasn't Clinton's house, Bush said over and over again, "it's the people's house." One way Bush has held himself to his no-blow-jobs pledge is by crowding his office with energy executives and NRA officials.

Bush's record in Texas was alarmingly pro-gun. He signed an NRA-backed Concealed Gun Bill in 1995, ending a 125-year ban on concealed weapons in that state. Then in 1997, he signed a bill that allowed Texans to take their concealed weapons into churches, hospitals, amusement parks, and old-folks homes. Bush also opposed mandatory child-safety trigger locks on guns—until his longtime support for all things NRA got him in trouble during the 2000 campaign, at which point he launched a voluntary trigger-lock program in Texas.

Ironically, for all George W. Bush's pandering to the NRA, we do have effective handgun control in the United States. It's wherever George W. Bush happens to be. This is hypocritical, to say the least. If George W. Bush believes that concealed weapons made Texas a safer place, if he believes that people should be able to carry weapons into God's house, shouldn't we be allowed to carry weapons into the people's house?

Again, the answer to gun violence, according to Bush's pals in the NRA, is more guns. If more guns make America a safer place, why shouldn't Bush set an example? If the answer to workplace violence is more guns, call off the Secret Service, get rid of the metal detectors, and let tourists—aka the people—carry their handguns on tours of the White House. If George W. Bush is worried about getting shot, let him carry a concealed weapon.

"You don't want to 'squeeze' the trigger," Paul tells me, as I stand pointing the gun at the paper target. "Squeezing is something with your whole hand, and if you do that, you'll move the gun. All you want to do is bring your finger back. Press the tip of your finger down on the trigger, moving only your finger."

Listening to Paul, all I'm thinking about is moving my finger, and I somehow forget that moving my finger is going to make the gun go—

Bang!

My .22 isn't nearly so loud as the .45 being fired by the kid standing next to me, but it's loud enough, and the .22 shell from the bullet I've just fired pops out of the top of the gun and hits me square in the middle of my goggles. Before Paul taught me how to squeeze the trigger, he told me not to focus on the target, but on the sights on the end of my gun. If I lined up the notch at the handle end of my gun with the tiny stump on the barrel end, and if I kept the target in sight, I would hit it. If I shifted back and forth between the target and the sight, the gun would shift back and forth, and my shot would be off.

My shot wasn't off. The very first bullet I fired hit a bull's-eye, blasting a small, round hole in the target just above the *X*. My next shot hit the same spot, and my next, and my next. I fire off seven rounds, all of them bull's-eyes except for one.

Holy shit. I'm a good shot—Paul tells me so, clapping me on the back.

"You're a natural shot," he said.

Natural isn't something I get called a lot in Texas.

I reload my .22 and take out the X in a fresh target. Paul points out a tiny clump of text: OFFICIAL 25-YARD TARGET. I proceed to put four bullets through four words that I can't read from where I'm standing. Then Paul points out the words BULLET TRAP INC. at the bottom of the target, and tells me to shoot at the B. I put three bullets through the B.

"You really are a natural!" Paul exclaims, asking me if I'm lying about never having shot a gun before in my life. I tell him that I'm not lying, and he tells me that I really should take up the sport. "You're good, you're a good shot. It's a gift."

Paul's compliments go to my head faster than a shot of Jägermeister. I'm good! I can shoot! Paul and I walk back out to the salesroom; I want to try a slightly larger gun, something with a little more kick. We pick out a .38 and head back into the shooting range. The gun is a revolver, and it's more of an effort to squeeze the trigger, since the trigger makes the barrel turn, and my first shot misses the target completely. But soon I'm back inside the target, taking out Xs, Bs, and OFFICIAL 25-YARD TARGET.

The only person more flabbergasted than Paul was me. While I was waiting for Paul in the shooting range, loading my .22 and watching the kid next to me fire his .45, I prayed I wouldn't embarrass myself. That was the most I could hope for. "Please God," I silently prayed, "let me hit the target a couple of times. I don't need to hit a bull's-eye, I just don't want to shoot a box of ammo and have everyone around me see that I didn't put one hole in the paper target."

I reloaded the .38, dropping the spent shells onto the floor. I took out another X, another B, another OFFICIAL 25-YARD TARGET. I was blown away. I felt like Charlton Heston would if he discovered one day that he gives a really mean blow job. I mean, who knew? Who could have predicted? How could it be? And how ironic! I was one of the picked-last-for-everything kids in school, way too wimpy for the rough-and-tumble boy sports of kickball or baseball or basketball. If only I had known then what I discovered on my trip to Plano. I was actually pretty good at the most masculine sport on earth: blowing things the fuck away, man!

There's nothing quite like that rush of discovering something you're good at, something you didn't know you could do, much less do well, until the very first time you tried it. We make most of these discoveries as adolescents, and I'd forgotten what a rush it is. When you discover a skill you didn't know you had, a voice in your head says, "You must keep doing this. You will get attention and praise if you keep doing this," and since everything is ultimately about sex, an even louder voice in your head says, "Keep doing this. This might get you laid."

My lesson was drawing to a close, but there was one last gun I wanted to try out: a .45. If that little kid standing next to me could handle a .45, so could I. Compared with the .22, the .45 Paul picked out for me was a big, silver monster—the Long Dong Silver of guns—and the ammo was just as impressive: big, thick, shiny, copper-colored slugs. I was tired of taking out *X*s, *B*s, and OFFICIAL 25-YARD TARGET, so I asked Paul to bring me one of the specialized targets. He brought back a surly-looking gangster, a blue outline of a human with a bull's-eye over the heart, and a large picture of Osama bin Laden. I picked bin Laden.

Some of my lefty friends were shocked that I decided to shoot at a picture of bin Laden; it seemed like such a thuggish, red-necked, proud-to-be-an-American thing to do.

"Too bad they don't have any targets with pictures of John Ashcroft on them," said one lefty friend when I got home.

I don't understand lefties who hate Att. Gen. John Ashcroft with more passion than they hate Osama bin Laden. Sure, John Ashcroft wants to tap our phones, hold people indefinitely, undermine attorney-client privilege, and sing in public; yeah, he accused people who raise concerns about the dumb ol' U.S. Constitution of "aiding terrorism," and he covered up the naked breast of a statue in the lobby of the Justice Department. Yeah, all of that sucks. John Ashcroft, what a dope.

Compared with Osama bin Laden, however, John Ashcroft is basically Barbara Walters—bad, yes, but endurable. What's more, any damage Ashcroft does during his tenure can, with some effort, be undone. The deaths of the Americans murdered by Osama bin Laden can't be undone, and the World Trade Center will not be rebuilt. And, shit, if Ashcroft taps my phone, he'll have to listen to me talking about things that will give him screaming nightmares. Any straight man who can't stand the sight of a bare-breasted woman in his workplace just doesn't have the constitution to listen to the gory details of *my* sex life.

Yet John Ashcroft wants to undermine American freedoms (hey, gun nuts: this is your big chance!), and that fills me with an angry desire to take vengeance—at the ballot box in 2004, when I hope my vote helps to turn his boss, George W. Bush, out of office. But Osama bin Laden killed thousands of Americans and that fills me with a thirst for vengeance that is tempered by some of that good ol' justifiable righteous indignation. If Osama bin Laden were in charge, he would slit my throat; my God, I'm an atheist, a hedonist, and a faggot. I shave my beard, I work with women, and I prefer to take my virgins here on earth, thank you very much. There are things that Ashcroft and I will never agree about—drugs, sex, indefinite detention—but there are a few things we do agree about. For instance, I don't like naked women any more than he appears to.

But bin Laden? We have nothing in common, he hates everything about me, and he wants me dead. I have no issues with dropping a bunker-busting bomb in his lap. So I don't feel the least bit guilty about blasting away at an Osama bin Laden target. But, hey, guilt's not one of the seven deadly sins, anyway. Anger is, and it was anger (and guns) that brought me to Texas, and what better way to blow off some steam than to blow off bin Laden's paper head?

So how did I go up against the evildoer? I fired seven bullets from my .45, but there are only four holes in Osama's forehead— but that's because three are single-bullet holes and one hole is slightly larger, since I put four bullets in the exact same spot. My shooting instructor tells me that the ability to put more than one bullet in the exact same place means I'm a consistent shot.

"Anyone who can put multiple bullets in the same place again and again has a gift," Paul said. "With some practice, you could learn to be a real marksman."

If I wanted to take up shooting as a sport, what would I have to do next?

"If you're serious about shooting," Paul told me, "you have to practice enough to get the fundamentals down." He suggested that I attend a shooting camp, where big, burly instructors would stand around in clumps and yell at me while I shot at paper targets. "It's a little different than having me there helping you out. These put some stress on you. It's a good way to see what you're capable of in a real-life defensive situation."

Hmm . . . a real-life defensive situation. For most members of the NRA, that would be a confrontation with a drug dealer or a rapist or an armed intruder or a damn liberal. I don't think I'll be going to any shooting camps or enjoying any simulated real-life defensive situations any time soon. As much as I enjoyed shooting in Plano, I'm not angry enough to become a part of the NRA. I liked shooting for the same reasons I liked to bowl: I'm kinda good at it. But just as I never got serious about the "sport" of bowling, I can't imagine I would get serious about the sport of "handgunning," as Paul called it.

I am, however, planning on doing some more recreational shooting at a range near my home—that would be Wade's Eastside Gun Shop, site of two recent suicides. As much as it pains me to admit it, spending a few hours shooting in Plano filled me with happiness. While I can't imagine ever owning a gun, and while I would never be so foolish as to keep a gun in my house, I am planning on doing some more shooting. Guns are fun, and, hey, I'm a good shot.

But I haven't gone over to the dark side. Like Jimmy Swaggart and pornography, I now count the seductive pleasures of handguns among the many reasons I'd like to see them banned. Swaggart knew that porn was too much fun to be legal; now I know that shooting is way too much fun to be legal. This may seem hypocritical, considering my position on recreational drugs, but recreational drug use is largely a victimless crime (links to terrorists notwithstanding), and would be completely victimless if they were legal—until guns are banned, I intend to indulge. Like Oscar Wilde, I can resist everything except temptation, and guns are too, too tempting.

Welcome to Gomorrah

I really believe that the pagans, and the abortionists, and the feminists, and the gays and the lesbians who are actively trying to make that an alternative lifestyle, the ACLU, People for the American Way—all of them who have tried to secularize America—I point the finger in their face and say "you helped this happen." —Jerry Falwell

The American people have got to go about their business. —George W. Bush

Running all over the country committing all seven of the seven deadly sins can take a lot out of a guy. Sloth is restorative and restful, and the "Sloth" chapter is nestled neatly in the middle of the book, but I was too busy working on this book to indulge myself in the brand of sloth I most prefer. Writing about pot-induced mental vacations for the last year didn't leave me much time to take any, so all the eating, gambling, parading, convening, and forced marches that I had to endure in the writing of this book were not leavened by any sloth. Celebrating sin in America is exhausting, and while I met some of the nicest people sinning in America—from Teresa and Shawn to David and Bridget to Kevin and Jake—I was worn out. Keeping up with the adulterers, gamblers, gluttons, rich folks, and gun nuts who make this country great was hard work.

Nevertheless, I planned all along to close this book with one last, sin-packed, blowout, wasted weekend; one more bash before I returned to my normal, non-book-deal life. I would get a hotel room and go off on a two-day sin binge, bravely attempting to commit all seven of the seven deadly sins in under forty-eight hours—at my publisher's expense, naturally. All the cities I visited while working on this book were charming American Gomorrahs. Looking at a map of the United States, I no longer see a continent-spanning nation but an archipelago of Gomorrahs, a chain of islands filled with American sinners. For the last chapter of this book, I decided to head to the Gomorrah of Gomorrahs, the one place where a man can commit all the seven deadly sins without breaking a sweat. After all, how could I write a book about sin in America and not spend some time in New York City?

I always planned to end this book in New York City, but I couldn't have known back in December 2000 that the very airline and hotel reservations I was making would allow me to commit one of the seven deadly sins. You see, by the time I got on a plane and headed to New York City, I was filled with anger—pure, white-hot rage.

Late in 2000, I planned a trip to New York City, making hotel and plane reservations for the weekend of October 5 to 7, 2001. Less than a month before I was supposed to get on a plane for New York City, Islamo-fascists—well, you know the whole ugly business: the Pentagon, the field in Pennsylvania, the World Trade Center. The American airline industry shut down for four days, and Americans were distinctly reluctant to get back on airplanes when they started flying again. New York City's $25 billion-per-year tourism industry, which employs 282,000 New Yorkers, was devastated. Hotels were empty, restaurants were going bankrupt, Broadway shows were closing. Newspapers all over the country were filled with stories about the thousands of waiters, bellhops, receptionists, and maids being laid off. Asked by Larry King on CNN what the people of New York City needed most from the rest of the country, U.S. Senator Charles Schumer said, "Come back and be tourists." Rudy Giuliani invited all Americans to visit and be part of "the New York miracle."

Getting back to normal, going about our business, returning to our regular patterns of consumption and travel—it wasn't just about making New York City whole. Pursuing happiness, credit cards in hand, was our patriotic duty. The *Washington Times,* an archconservative daily owned by the Unification Church (aka the Moonies), literally ordered its readers to "spend in the spirit of patriotism."

"Consumer spending accounts for something like 70 percent of economic activity," the *Washington Times* pointed out. "Consumers, get your credit cards ready. Your country calls." In November, the *State,* a conservative daily paper in Columbia, South Carolina, also ordered its readers to return to normal, which by then everyone knew to be code for, "Don't think too much about the war; pursue happiness instead!" Under the headline NORMAL ACTIVITY DEFIES TER-RORISTS, the editors wrote that if Americans didn't "return to normal . . . then the terrorists' objectives of bringing America down will be more successful than anyone could have forseen." What caught the attention of the editors at the *State*? A drop in the number of people golfing at a Myrtle Beach resort.

Even the president of the United States got into the act, encouraging Americans to show their anger towards and defiance of the terrorists by returning to our normal lives as quickly as possible—especially if our normal lives involved getting on airplanes. President Bush starred in a series of travel industry commercials that encouraged Americans to defy the terrorists by going on a cruise. Suddenly to American conservatives it didn't matter if Americans were buying rap CDs, booking passage on a gay cruise, or flying off to Las Vegas in search of degraded distractions, so long as we were spending.

I have nothing snide to say about any of this. I'm a patriot. On September 11, I didn't blame America; I blamed bin Laden. And while I may love this country for different reasons from the scolds and virtuecrats, I do love this country. I love the separation of church and state, for starters; I love the First Amendment; I love that "pursuit of happiness" stuff in the Declaration of Independence—and I've always loved New York City. REST OF COUNTRY TEMPORARILY FEELS DEEP AFFECTION FOR NEW YORK, ran the post-attack headline in *The Onion,* the brilliant satirical newsweekly. It didn't take three thousand deaths to make me love New York City. My affection for New York has been lifelong.

Since I've always been a big fan of pleasurable pursuits—I was hard at work on this book long before the terrorist attacks—and of New York City, George W. Bush didn't need to tell me twice: I was ready to consume, fly, and go back to my normal, sinful routines. Like anyone with a brain, I was angered by the attacks on September 11, and my anger was quickly tempered by righteous indignation. We had to act, and the ensuing war was just and remains just. While I didn't vote for George W. Bush, and I have no plans ever to vote for him or any of his relatives (I'm considering a move to Florida just so I could vote against Jeb), and while I want the Democrats to oppose Bush's domestic agenda tooth and nail, *nevertheless* I think the ol' cokehead has done a bang-up job with the war. If I could help W. defeat the terrorists by channeling my anger into a trip to New York City, I was ready, willing, and able to spend my publisher's money.

In the days before my long-scheduled trip to New York, the anthrax scares hit the city. No matter, I was going. I confirmed my airline reservations, hotel reservations, and hit up a well-connected friend for tickets to a mega-hit Broadway show. I went to New York City not only to fight terror but also to help save the jobs of all those waiters, bellhops, maids, receptionists, cooks, busboys, and stewardesses I'd been reading about in the papers. There was another group of New York City service providers I wanted to show my support for, hardworking men and women whose livelihoods were impacted by the attacks of September 11. We didn't hear much about this group, despite all these big-hearted men and women do to make New Yorkers, tourists, and business travelers happy. I wanted to go to New York to show my support for the city's whores.

The sexually liberated student putting herself through college working as an escort has become something of a cliché. The old prostitute stereotype—a drug addiction, tenth-grade education, track marks, bad skin, a dozen STDs, an abusive boyfriend—has been replaced by this newer, more user-friendly stereotype. Patronizing a prostitute seems a little less opportunistic if your money is helping to put someone through school, which will ultimately get her out of the business altogether. So I was a little disappointed to find that Emily, the New York City escort I rented my first night in town, was not a film student at Columbia or getting her master's in social work at New York University. She was, Emily said, "just a ho."

"I find that putting-myself-through-college line tedious," said Tracy Quan, author of the novel *Diary of a Manhattan Call Girl*, and a member of Prostitutes of New York (PONY), an advocacy group that is seeking to decriminalize prostitution. "Most of the pros I've known were not going to college," said Quan. "Most of the pros are materialistic, very attractive girls who liked to shop. Girls putting themselves through Columbia don't make very good prostitutes. They're usually badly groomed, they don't know how to dress, they don't really like what they're doing. The people who are really good at this are the ones who decide to make it their career."

Emily was definitely making it her career. A college dropout from New Mexico, Emily got into the business after she followed her rock-star-wannabe boyfriend to New York City. Her boyfriend's band broke up shortly after they arrived in New York in 1997, and she refused to return to New Mexico with him. Emily had fallen in love with the city and couldn't imagine living anywhere else ever again. When he went back to New Mexico, she stayed behind in New York, and within a few months she was working full-time as an escort.

"It was the only way I could afford the rent on the studio apartment we used to share," Emily told me over cocktails in the crowded bar of a crowded hipster hotel. "Once he moved, I had to make a lot of money or get a roommate, and I didn't want a roommate."

Emily didn't work for an agency, she didn't have a pimp, she wasn't a streetwalker, and she didn't work in a brothel. Instead, Emily paid a friend to maintain a Web site for her, which is where I found her. In my hotel room, the day I arrived in New York, I plugged in my laptop computer and logged on to my Internet service provider. Then I typed "Manhattan," "Female," and "Escort" into a search engine. I had somewhere in the neighborhood of fifteen thousand Web sites to choose from, and I spent some time surfing around before I found Emily's Web site. Her site had a few pictures, some tasteful nude shots, and a cell-phone number. I liked Emily's pictures: she didn't have big hair, wasn't wearing a ton of makeup, and didn't look like someone escorting out of desperation or against her will. There was also a disclaimer: "What my clients buy is my time," it said. "If anything happens during our time together, we're just two consenting adults with a professional relationship who happened to hit it off. It happens in offices and at workplaces all over the country every day."

Emily was expensive, however. She charged five hundred dollars an hour with a three-hour minimum. Why so expensive?

"I'm beautiful and charming and fun," her bio read. "You probably pay at least that much to talk to your lawyer. And you're lawyer isn't nearly as beautiful. Or fun . . ."

I called Emily, expecting to leave a message on an answering machine, so I was a bit flustered when Emily answered the phone. For some reason I was worried that Emily might not see me if she realized I wasn't interested in her for the same reasons her other clients were. I didn't want to have sex with Emily; I really did just want to buy her time. I was looking for an escort, not a euphemism.

"Is it okay if we just go out and have dinner, see a show? And nothing else happens?" I asked.

"We don't have to do anything you don't want to, Dan," she said in a soothing voice. "Is this your first time using a service like this?"

"Yes," I said.

"You should know that the time we spend together is your special time," Emily said. "I'm there for you. Things can go just as slow or just as fast as you want them to. Nothing has to happen." She asked for my first and last name and the name of my hotel; then she hung up and called me back at my hotel to make sure I was really a guest. That's when she reminded me that her time cost five hundred dollars an hour. She would also be happy to make dinner reservations at a nice place near my hotel, if I didn't have a place picked out already. I told her to go ahead and make a reservation.

"I'll meet you in the bar in the lobby of your hotel at six," she said. "Does that sound good?"

That sounded fine.

"If we meet and I'm not quite what you wanted," she said in an I've-said-this-a-thousand-times tone of voice, "you don't have to pay me. Cab fare back home would be nice, but it's not necessary." If I wasn't into her, I should say so within ten minutes, and she would leave, and there would be no hard feelings on her end. If I made her uncomfortable, or my personal hygiene was poor, she would say so within ten minutes, and she asked that there be no hard feelings on my end. If I wanted her to join me for dinner, I would need to hand her an envelope with $1,500 dollars in it for the first three hours. If I didn't have cash, she could take a credit card but would have to do it now, over the phone, and the charge would have to be approved before she came to the hotel. If things didn't work out, all but fifty dollars of the charge would be removed from my Visa bill.

Before we got off the phone, Emily asked what I would be wearing. I was confused. Did it matter what *I* was wearing? I'd seen her picture, so I knew what she looked like. I'd be able to spot her in the bar—

"I only ask because you said you want to go out to dinner and a show," Emily explained. "If you're in jeans and a sweatshirt and I show up looking like I'm on my way to the Golden Globes, we're going to make a pretty conspicuous couple. And if you're in a suit, you don't want me showing up looking like I'm ready to go clubbing."

I told Emily that I would be wearing what I've been wearing all of my life—jeans, a T-shirt, tennis shoes, and a jeans jacket.

"I'll dress down," she said. "See you in the lobby bar at six."

I almost fainted when Emily walked into the lobby two hours later.

The hotel's bar was, surprisingly enough, overrun with businessmen and hipsters, and I decided to wait for Emily in the lobby instead. I was sitting in a ridiculous oversize chair just outside the bar when she came through the doors. She was a stunningly beautiful woman—the pictures on her Web site didn't do her justice—with nary a track mark in sight. Emily's legs were longer than the Oscars. She was wearing jeans and a tasteful little top held up by spaghetti straps, and carrying a metallic silver jeans jacket. The jacket sounds trashy on the page, but in person it was just the right amount of flash. She looked like Cameron Diaz on her way to a club, which is to say, Emily was a total fucking knockout—a steal at five hundred dollars an hour.

I didn't wait for the ten minutes to pass; I handed her the envelope with fifteen one-hundred-dollar bills in it, which she tucked into the pocket of her jeans jacket, which I had to compliment her on.

Talk about your New York miracles—I'd been in town for less than four hours, and a beautiful woman had just been delivered to my hotel. If I were straight, this would have been the night of my life.

"Let's get a drink," Emily said, strolling into the bar.

I didn't go to New York City simply to sin and to defy Osama bin Laden and his Islamo-fascist pals. I was also in New York because Jerry Falwell pisses me off.

Falwell's comments after the terrorist attacks made me angry, and I wasn't alone; Falwell caught hell for his remarks, even from good ol' Diane Sawyer on *Good Morning America.* On some level, though, I was secretly thrilled by Falwell's remarks. By attempting to pin the blame for the attacks of September 11 on the American Civil Liberties Union, abortion-rights groups, pagans, gay men and lesbians, and federal judges, Falwell not only exposed himself for what he was (hateful, divisive, mean-spirited), but he also exposed Christian fundamentalism for what it is (hateful, divisive, mean-spirited). Thanks to Falwell, millions of Americans realized that Christian fundamentalists hate all the same things about the United States that the Islamic fundamentalists hate: liberated women, sexual freedom, secular culture, fundamental human rights. After Falwell opened his fat trap on the *700 Club,* people in the political center had to admit that the Falwells and Robertsons were, as John McCain dubbed them during the Republican primaries in 2000, "agents of intolerance." (McCain was slammed by the media for that bit of straight talk.)

After September 11, reasonable Americans could no longer pretend that all men of faith were harmless do-gooders. The nineteen hijackers were men of faith, and in their own twisted minds, they meant well—they thought they were doing God's work, just as Falwell thinks he's doing God's work. Osama bin Laden, if he's still alive somewhere, is a man of faith. John Walker, aka the American Taliban, is a man of faith.

Maddeningly, right-wing pundits have attempted to paint Walker, a religious conservative, as a hot-tubbing Marin County, California, liberal. "We need to execute people like John Walker in order to physically intimidate liberals, by making them realize that they can be killed, too. Otherwise they will turn out to be outright traitors." That comment by psychoconservative writer, commentator, and supposed "babe" Ann Coulter was greeted with cheers at the Conservative Political Action Conference in Washington, D.C., in February of 2002.

Fascist isn't a word that I toss around lightly—I can't stand lefties who cry fascist every time a Republican or a police officer enters the room—but that's the only word that accurately describes Coulter's politics. What's revealing about her comments and the comments of so many other right-wing pundits is their burning desire to convince us that Walker is some sort of liberal. Excuse me, but Walker didn't embrace the Marin County's live-and-let-live liberalism. Walker rejected Marin County's liberal ethos in favor of an intolerant, ranting, raving "faith." What's more, Walker and his co-religionists hate all the same things Falwell hates: liberated women, secular culture, homosexuals, religious freedom.

In the case of both Walker and Falwell—and in the case of September 11—faith wasn't the solution to the problem, faith was and is the problem. "If we believe absurdities," Voltaire said, "we will commit atrocities." On September 11, Islamo-fascists, heads stuffed with absurdities, committed the most appalling atrocities. It was religious fanaticism that brought down the World Trade Center, not secularism, and a murderous intolerance inflamed by hate-mongering clerics. Falwell did a real public service by reminding Americans immediately after the attacks that the Islamic world doesn't have a monopoly on religious hatred and fanaticism, nor does the Islamic world have a monopoly on hateful clerics.

It isn't just religious fanaticism that drives young Islamic males to become suicide bombers. It's also sex—or the want of it.

"In the sight of Allah, the ones who died are the lucky ones," a Pakistani Muslim told the *New York Times* in reference to the September 11 terrorists. "They have gone to paradise now, with all the pleasures they have been promised in the Koran. Now they will have girls, and wine, and music, and all the things forbidden to them here on earth. Now they will be happy, as we who remain can never be on earth."

One of the unexamined aspects of the September 11 attacks was the role that sexual deprivation played in turning young men into mass murderers. Fifteen of the nineteen hijackers on September 11 came from Saudi Arabia, "a theocratic kingdom that bans dating, cinemas, concert halls, discotheques, clubs, theaters, and political organizations," the *New York Times* reported. In Saudi Arabia, "religion and tradition prohibit unmarried men and women from mixing." Is it any wonder that a certain number of young men in places like Saudi Arabia—where all educational system is all Islam, all the time—will resent people who enjoy all the things that their religion and government forbid?

Like the puritan haunted by the fear that somewhere, someone is happy, the Islamo-fascist is haunted by the fear that somewhere, someone is enjoying the lap dances and the dates and the discos and everything else that his religion forbids him—at least until he gets to heaven. Once he gets to heaven, *then* he can have all the lap dances and dates and black-eyed virgins he can handle, on just one little condition: He has to die a martyr, which he can do by blowing himself up in an Israeli pizza parlor or flying a plane into the World Trade Center.

"The fundamentalist seeks to bring down a great deal more than buildings," Salman Rushdie wrote in *The Washington Post* on October 2, 2001. "Such people are against, to offer just a brief list, freedom of speech, a multi-party political system, universal adult suffrage, accountable government, Jews, homosexuals, women's rights, pluralism, secularism, short skirts, dancing, beardlessness, evolution theory, sex. . . ." The Islamic fundamentalists, Rushdie continued, don't think Westerners believe in anything. "To prove him wrong, we must first know he is wrong. We must agree on what matters: kissing in public places, bacon sandwiches, disagreements, cutting-edge fashion, literature, generosity, water, a more equitable distribution of the world's resources, movies, music, freedom of thought, beauty, love. These will be our weapons."

Reading Rushdie's comments after September 11 inspired me. Fuck Falwell, fuck Coulter, fuck bin Laden, fuck Walker, fuck fundamentalism, fuck Islamo-Fascism, and fuck plain ol' Fascism. Committing the sin of anger in New York City would be easy—much easier than it had been in Texas. Blasting away at paper targets at the

Bullet Trap in Plano didn't make me feel angry; if I committed a single sin at the Bullet Trap it was probably the sin of pride. I couldn't wait to get home and show my friends what a good shot I was, or to indulge my newfound skill at a slightly closer-to-home shooting range. (Have I mentioned what a good shot Paul, my instructor, thought I was?) In New York City, however, I had anger down.

"Why, I wondered, were not more of us angry [after the attacks on September 11]?" William Bennett asked in his quickie post-9/11 book, *Why We Fight: Moral Clarity and the War on Terrorism.* "Why did so many, especially the county's elite, seem to back away from any hint of righteous anger?"

Huh? Why weren't more of us angry? Everyone I knew was angry, and everywhere I went I met angry people. But according to Bennett, only a small number of right-thinking conservatives could see that the War on Terrorism was necessary and just. In the same essay in which he dubbed Bennett, Bork, and Buchanan "scolds," Andrew Sullivan expressed frustration with the right's inability to take yes for an answer. "As the country becomes more conservative," Sullivan wrote, "the right sees liberalism everywhere."

In *Why We Fight,* William J. Bennett can't bring himself to take yes for an answer. There's a reason peace rallies after September 11 were sparsely attended. The overwhelming majority of Americans agreed with Bill Bennett. We said yes. But Bennett and his fellow scolds could only see a resolve-sapping pacifism stoked by leftie cultural critics. Admittedly, some of what the left pumped out immediately after September 11 was idiotic, just as the comments of Jerry Falwell and Pat Robertson were idiotic. Americans were not, however, led down the primrose path by Susan Sontag, Katha Pollitt, and Edward Said. Thoughtful, angry lefties were marching in lockstep with Christopher Hitchens, not Noam Chomsky. We wanted to bomb bin Laden with bombs, and not, as Toni Morrison suggested, love.

"Little schoolchildren in our country are routinely taught to believe that America represents but one of many cultures [and] that there is no such thing as a better or worse society," Bennett fumes at the end of *Why We Fight*. Even Americans who believe Western society and culture is superior to that of, say, Saudi Arabia are afraid to speak up, "[because] saying so can get you into trouble."

Hell, Bill, I'll speak up: Western culture—liberal democracy, representative government, universal human rights—is superior to Saudi culture. Far superior. Personally, I would rather live in a country where I can buy a drink, kiss a guy, and rent a hooker without risking a public beheading—and like the overwhelming majority of Americans after September 11, I was angry at the people who wanted to take those things away from me, be they Bennett's enemy bin Laden or Bennett's buddy Jerry Falwell.

I had never been out on an adult-style date with a woman before. When I was growing up in Chicago, I dated some girls under duress, but those dates didn't take place in hipster bars and expensive restaurants. We were teenagers on the north side of Chicago in the mid-eighties, so our dates took place in bowling alleys and fast-food restaurants. I felt awkward on those teenage dates because I was dating them only so I could tell my friends and family that I had been on a date with a girl. With Emily I felt awkward because I wasn't worthy. Even if I had played her particular sport, she was still way out of my league.

It was a little after six o'clock when we arrived at the bar, in a short lull between after-work drinkers and the early evening partiers. Emily and I found a couple of seats together at the bar. There were a lot of men in the bar around my age, and these men looked at me—me in my jeans and T-shirt and tennis shoes—and quickly concluded that I wasn't worthy. What was an incredibly beautiful woman like Emily doing out on a date with a schmo like me? If I were a few decades older, and wearing a suit, like most of Emily's customers, they would have assumed she was attracted to older, more powerful men (or attracted to their money), and therefore not a woman they had any chance of getting for themselves.

But since she was with me, a poorly dressed guy around their age, the men in the bar assumed they all had a shot. Not only did they have a shot, but I had a woman I clearly didn't deserve, and they would be doing her a favor by taking her from me.

I could sense the envy emanating from the clumps of youngish men in their business suits, ties loosened or hanging out of their suit jacket pockets. It was fun to be envied, but there was an undercurrent of—well, of violence. Here and there in the bar the men were glaring at me, as if I had something that belonged to them, which in a way I did.

Emily and I were talking about New York—about the attacks, what else?—when one of the other men in the bar decided to do something about his envy. He strolled up to us and stood right behind our bar stools until we turned and looked at him.

"How are you guys doing tonight?" he asked. He was a good-looking guy, bigger than I was. He had a big smile but very small teeth, and his smile exposed two parallel lines of healthy, bright pink gums. He introduced himself and then asked me who I was.

"Are you this lovely lady's big brother?" Jim said. "Or are you her coworker?"

Jim laughed. Loud. The big brother/coworker question was supposed to be a joke, I guess. Emily laughed, but her laugh began after his did and ended before. She was being polite, deferential, upbeat.

"No, we're on a date," she said, gesturing towards me but—hey!—beaming at Jim!

Jim looked me up and down; then he looked back at Emily. "Where you from?" he said, turning to me.

"Seattle," I said.

"Shit, I thought all the dot-com boys had gone broke!" He laughed and put his hand on the bar between me and Emily, separating us. Then he turned his back to me. "Those guys didn't know how to run a business, and they never knew how to dress," he said, laughing his loud, mean laugh.

"He's probably spending the last of his stock options to take someone like you out on a date." Then he handed Emily his card. "Give me a call if things don't work out with the Microsofty here."

He stared at me when he called me a softy, smiling his big gummy smile. I think he wanted me to hit him. His gummy smile said, "I'm picking up on your date right in front of you, and what are you going to do about it?" He was clearly an alpha-male type, and I suppose he expected me to challenge him for alpha position, which I refused to do. I like to think of myself as an alpha male—all men do, don't they?—but I wasn't up for getting into a fistfight over a *woman*. Now, if he had attempted to steal my collection of show tune CDs, well, then I would've laid him flat. But Emily? He could take her off my hands for fifteen hundred bucks.

Jim lingered for a second, looking at me. I grinned at him, playing dumb. If he wanted to have a fistfight, he would have to throw the first punch. He gave me an angry, imploring look. It was as if he thought I was doing something wrong by not holding up my end of the deal. He seemed to think I was obligated to hit him so that he could hit me and win the girl.

"Let's go get something to eat," Emily said, taking my hand. Turning to Jim, she said, "It was great to meet you."

"Give me a call sometime," Jim said to Emily. "See you around, softy."

Emily had made reservations at a restaurant a block from the hotel.

"It's my favorite restaurant," she said. "I'm sure you'll love it."

Emily's favorite restaurant was also one of New York City's more expensive restaurants—and it was on me, of course; high-priced call girls don't go dutch. While we ate, I couldn't help but contemplate the sinfulness of paying someone five hundred dollars an hour to eat incredibly expensive food in her favorite restaurant. What sin is this? I wondered to myself while we ate small rounds of goat cheese that cost more than twenty-five dollars each. Was it greed on Emily's part for making reservations in such a pricey place? Was she getting a kickback from the restaurant? Or was it gluttony, even with tiny portions? Later in the evening, the same thoughts would flit through my head as we sat watching a hit show that's almost impossible to get tickets to—a show I would wind up paying Emily five hundred dollars an hour to watch. What sin is this? Greed on her part? Or stupidity on mine?

During the walk to the restaurant, I confessed everything—writer, doin' research, not interested in "hitting it off"—because my pride wouldn't allow me to let Emily think I was a coward. I didn't want her to think what I'd done in the bar, or hadn't done in the bar, made me somehow less of a man. I wasn't afraid of Jim, I lied. I was taking her to dinner and a show to pick her brain, not her booty, and anyway I wasn't the kind of guy who gets into drunken fistfights over women. Emily nodded. She'd picked up on that the moment we met in the lobby.

"Usually when I meet a man at his hotel the first thing out of his mouth isn't, 'Wow, I *totally* love your jacket.' "

While she would normally shoot down any guy who tried to pick her up when she was with a client ("Clients appreciate that"), Emily thought the guy was pretty cute, she liked aggressive men, and she didn't think it would bother me. After all, I liked her jacket.

The restaurant she took me to was one of those hushed places, where the tables are incredibly close together, making it nearly impossible to have a private conversation; it was the kind of restaurant where white, well-off New Yorkers gather to discuss the cartoons in that week's issue of *The New Yorker*. The food was tremendous, and we ordered quite a lot of it; yes, this was definitely gluttony. There were only four other couples in the restaurant the night we went, and we were off in a corner by ourselves, which made it possible for me and Emily to talk shop.

"Business has been way off," Emily confided. "Not for the

twenty-dollar blow-job crowd—their clients are local. But the vast majority of my clients are rich businessmen from out of town or overseas. They haven't been coming to New York City, obviously, so for me business is way, way down. It's been hard."

While Emily's business may have been down after September 11, PONY's Quan said that wasn't necessarily the case for other New York City prostitutes.

"I don't know very many prostitutes who rely very much on tourists for their income," said Quan. "Anyone who makes their living as a prostitute is looking to have regular clients, who tend to be local. Tourists are not regular clients. When people are being tourists, they're often traveling with someone, like their family. That doesn't make seeing a prostitute very easy."

Business travelers, however, do make good clients. "Business travel was way off after September 11," said Quan, "and prostitutes who do most of their trade with business travelers were losing money. Higher-end, three- and four-hundred-dollar-an-hour prostitutes had the most to lose. I also know some people who had clients that died on September 11."

Emily's business was gone, she said, because before September 11 she had carved out a niche serving Japanese and Taiwanese businessmen ("They adore—and will pay a lot for—tall blondes!"), and they weren't coming to town. She had an established group of regular clients, and she had stopped advertising her services. A few weeks after September 11, she was forced to put her Web site back up.

"I needed to get some new clients," she said, "some men who didn't have to fly to the city to see me."

Emily was everything she claimed to be in her Web site—beautiful, fun, charming, sexy. Emily wasn't a student, however, and this came as a shock to me. I was so invested in the paying-my-way-through-college-escort stereotype that I assumed Emily was doing postgraduate work somewhere or other.

"How long do you plan to keep doing this?" I asked. "If you're not going to school, what do you plan on doing when you get out of this line of work?"

Emily set her spoon down—we were working on desserts by this point—and shot me a disapproving look.

"Why would I get out of this line of work?" she said. "I'm making good money, and I live really well in the greatest city on earth. I work a few hours a night, three or four nights a week, and I have the rest of my time to myself."

"But you won't always make good money doing this," I replied. "Gravity comes for everyone."

She shrugged, then cracked her lavender crème brûlée with her spoon. In the first two years she was escorting, Emily sank every cent into a two-bedroom condo, which she now owned outright.

"Whatever happens, I'll always have a place to live."

What will she do for income when she gets older?

"I don't know. Maybe I'll do domination work," she said. "I'll set up a dungeon in my extra bedroom. There's good money in that, and you can do that until you're fifty."

"So you're happy doing what you're doing indefinitely?"

"I'm a ho. I like being a ho. Are you happy doing what you're doing indefinitely?"

"Yeah, but I don't have to see people naked or—"

"Or what?"

"I don't have to have sex with people I'm not attracted to."

"You're beginning to annoy me a little," Emily said, smiling at me, a singsong lilt in her voice. "I just want to get that on the table. I mean, do you know how many married women have sex with someone they're not attracted to every time they have sex with the husband? And what makes you think I automatically have sex with people?"

"Uh, the naked pictures? The hints on your Web site?"

"I don't have sex with anyone I don't want to have sex with. Men buy my time, that's all, and what—"

"—what happens between two consenting adults is perfectly legal."

"If I'm with a man I find attractive, something might happen. If I'm not attracted to him, nothing happens."

"Don't the guys expect it, though? Don't they get angry if you don't put out?"

"I guess you could say I'm attracted to a lot of different kinds of men. I would do you, for instance, even though you're not really my type."

"Well, if you had a dick," I said, "I'd definitely be into you."

"Thanks, I wouldn't be into you in a nonprofessional context," Emily continued, turning the spoon. She cocked her head to one side and squinted at me, as if she were trying to picture me naked. "No, I'm very much into muscular men, especially men who are at least a few inches taller than I am. That's what I love, and it's hard to find."

How big? How muscular?

"I like that classic V shape, a lot of muscle, no facial hair. Big, ripped guys, without an ounce of fat, but a little rough around the edges. The guy I moved here with looked like Henry Rollins. He thought he was Henry Rollins, too, but he only looked like him. That's my type. My current boyfriend is six-six and all muscle."

I asked Emily if her boyfriend minded the line of work she was in. She shrugged as she scooped up the last of her crème brûlée with her spoon.

"Why should he mind?" Emily said. "He's in the business himself."

It was almost midnight when the show ended. Emily walked me back to my hotel, and thanked me for dinner and the show. Then she informed me I owed her another fifteen hundred dollars, since we'd been together six hours. We had to leave the hotel to find a cash machine. I had hoped Emily might not charge me for the three hours we spent watching a hit show, but times were tight. ("I promise to put your money into my IRA," Emily joked, "so that you don't have to worry about me when I'm old.") By the time I got back up to my room, I had calculated just how much money I'd dropped into New York City's battered economy since arriving in the city eight hours earlier: $500 for the hotel room, $200 for theater tickets, $200 for dinner, $40 for drinks in the bar, $30 for a cab from the airport; and $3,000 for Emily—$3,970 total. I didn't pay any state or local sales taxes on most of the money, since the lion's share of it went to Emily, and Emily is officially part of the underground economy. But the money I gave her had to surface sooner or later. When Emily spent my $3,000 on food, clothes, and her condo's monthly dues, she would be paying taxes.

When I got up to my room after saying good-bye to Emily and three thousand of my publisher's dollars, I opened up my laptop computer and began to search for Emily's boyfriend.

During intermission at the theater, I pumped Emily for info about her boyfriend. I was fascinated by the concept of coming to New York and renting both halves of a straight couple. They had been seeing each other for a little more than a year, Emily told me. He was six feet six, white, with dark black hair and blue eyes, and he competed in "natural" body-building contests (no steroids).

"Are his clients women?" I asked.

Emily looked at me like I was from Mars.

"Brad does gay work," she said. "I wouldn't want him seeing women. Anyway, there's no money in women." Her boyfriend wasn't bi, she explained. He was a straight guy and a body builder who made money letting gay men worship his body—but that's all. Just worship, no sex.

"The gay guys he sees usually just beat off while they're with him," Emily said. "He poses, flexes. He's huge. Two hundred and forty pounds, all muscle," said Emily. "All he does is muscle worship. Gay guys pay him to let them feel his muscles, kiss his biceps, his calves. That's all he does with them. No sex whatsoever."

Emily and Brad met through a friend, a gay neighbor of Emily's who was a regular client of Brad's. As a loyal customer over a period of years, Richard had come to know Brad pretty well. Richard paid Brad two hundred dollars a week for the privilege of washing his gym clothes by hand; with Brad dropping by once or twice a week to drop off and pick up his gym clothes, he and Richard had become friendly. When Emily moved into the condo next door, she also got to know Richard. Soon they were friends, and in their conversations about men Richard discovered that he and Emily shared a passion for big, muscular guys. Richard didn't know that Emily was an escort when he threw a small party in his apartment with the sole purpose of introducing Emily and Brad. The couple didn't find out they were both escorts until a few months into the relationship. Another New York City miracle: A boy escort and a girl escort are set up on a blind date by a gay male client of the boy escort—it sounds like Nora Ephron's next movie. Brad eventually moved in with Emily, and as a token of appreciation, Brad no longer charged Richard for the honor of washing his gym clothes.

I wasn't really into muscle guys, but the idea of renting the boyfriend of the escort I'd been with all night, well, it was too delicious to pass up. If Brad was anything like Emily—who was beautiful and, once I stopped trying to be her career counselor, charming and delightful—I wanted to get to know him. And who knows? Maybe I was into muscle guys and I didn't know it. ("It's not until you run your hands over someone supersized that you can appreciate how wonderful all that flesh feels," the FA at the NAAFA convention told me.) Since I've always been into skinny, bookish guys, I'd never really had cause to run my hands over a guy with a lot of muscles. Maybe an hour with Brad would change my mind.

It took a couple of hours, but I finally found an ad for a guy who fit Brad's description on a male escort Web site: "Live your fantasy. 6'6", 240 lbs. ripped. I'm the straight guy at the gym you're always staring at. Massive, rock-hard, ripped abs, huge guns. Model looks, great face. $200 IN /$250 OUT. Muscle worship only. No sex." I called and left a message. Early the next morning I got a call from

Brad. He had an hour free late Saturday night. If I wanted the "in" price, I would have to go to his apartment, or he would come "out" to my hotel for $250.

Halfway through my weekend in New York City, I'd managed to commit five of the seven deadly sins. Anger, as I said, was easy; it was the reason I came to New York. Greed was taken care of by Emily's outrageously high fees. (Although I will admit that Emily was better looking than my lawyer, as advertised.) Gluttony was the outrageously expensive meal with Emily; envy in the form of the reaction of Jim, the man in the bar who wanted to get into a fistfight and run off with my very expensive date. Pride was my feeble attempt to explain to Emily why I didn't punch Jim in the bar, and lust, well, that would be taken care of by Brad, who would be coming to my hotel room late Saturday night.

I had just one sin left to tackle before Brad came by and took care of lust: sloth. I took a nap after Brad called, and that might have counted towards sloth, but napping did nothing to pump money into New York City's battered economy. I would have to be more proactively slothful. So I got up, got dressed, and headed down to the East Village to kill some time and score myself some of that leafy, green sloth the kids like so much.

I have a friend who lives on East Twelfth and Avenue A, and I often stay at his place when I come to New York. Walking around his neighborhood, men mutter "weed, weed," under their breath at passersby.

It was dark when I got to the East Village, and as I walked by Tompkins Square Park, a black guy in a satin Yankees jacket and an FDNY baseball hat walked past me muttering, "weed, weed, weed." I'd never said anything but "no, thanks," to weed mutterers before, so I wasn't sure how to initiate or close the sale. In fact, as I walked around the park, I found myself dwelling on the fact that I had never once purchased pot in my life. To satisfy my rather minimal need for pot, I had always relied on the kindness of a few potheaded friends, all of whom seemed more than happy to give me marijuana for free.

I think my potheaded friends are amused by how little it takes to get me high; again, I didn't start smoking pot until I was in my thirties, and I've never smoked enough to develop much tolerance for the stuff. I wondered for a moment if I might get arrested buying pot on the streets of New York. Then I figured that New York City's police department had better things to do right now than come between New York City's potheads and their pursuit of happiness.

"I'd like some weed," I said to the man in the baseball jacket. He looked at me, long and hard.

I began to panic. Did I say the right thing? What if he was a cop? What if I said the wrong thing and he decided to gun me down, drug-deal-gone-bad style?

"How much you want?" the man finally said.

I had planned to spend three hundred dollars on pot—I intended to get New York City's underground economy roaring!—but being a novice pot buyer, I didn't anticipate the reaction my request would get.

"Three hundred dollars' worth," I said.

"What you need so much for?" the mutterer said, looking pissed. "You a cop?"

"No," I said, "not a cop. You a cop?"

"No, I'm not a cop. What you need so much for? You settin' me up?"

Ah, I got it. If I was a cop, and I could get him to sell me a *lot* of pot, he might get sent away for a long stretch of time.

"I . . . uh . . . just need a lot of pot. I'm buying it for my friends. And me. They smoke a lot of pot, you see, so I need to get . . . a . . . lot."

"You a cop," the mutterer said, "you a damn cop."

The mutterer walked around the corner, off Avenue A, and onto East Fourteenth Street. I thought the deal was off and was about to split when the mutterer looked over at me and said, "You buying pot or not?" I walked around the corner. He asked me to show him the money. I pulled three hundred-dollar bills out of my pocket.

"You not a cop?" he asked again.

"Not a cop."

"How much you want?" he asked. I was confused by the question; hadn't I already indicated to the gentleman that I required three hundred dollars of his finest marijuana? In my confusion, I said the wrong thing:

"How much pot can I get for three hundred dollars?"

In retrospect, my mistake was so frigging obvious it makes my head hurt. I basically told the pot dealer that I had no idea how much pot three hundred dollars buys. Now he knew that I didn't know what I was doing. Since the sale of marijuana isn't regulated by the New York City Department of Consumer Fraud, Weights and Measures Division, I would have no one to complain to if he fleeced me.

"Okay," he said, "three hundred dollar' worth." He made a show of taking three bags of pot out of his pocket. He held out his left hand. I handed him three hundred dollars; he handed me the three bags of pot.

At my friend's apartment ten minutes later, I pulled out my three "hundred-dollar" bags of pot. I'd been had, Sean laughed. His friendly neighborhood pot dealer charged me three hundred dollars for three twenty-five-dollar bags of pot. I didn't feel like getting high (I didn't want to be fucked up when I met Brad at my hotel), and I told Sean that I would leave it all for him on one condition: He had to smoke a little of my very expensive pot, just to test it out. I wanted to know if I'd been completely had; I was overcharged, and I could live with that. But was it pot at least?

Sean smoked some in a little pipe, then sat back in his chair at his kitchen table and waited a minute or two. Then he smiled.

"Good news. This is *excellent* pot," Sean said. "You may have been overcharged, but you weren't ripped off."

Apparently some dealers by the park keep pot in one pocket to sell to locals and bags of chopped-up bay leaves in another to sell to tourists.

"They figure half the tourists don't know what pot looks like, and he's never going to see them again anyway," Sean said. "He probably sold you the real stuff because he thought he might see you again. So look at it this way: You got ripped off, but at least the guy who ripped you off didn't think you were a tourist. He thought he might see you again. He thought you were a New Yorker. Isn't that worth the extra two hundred twenty-five dollars?"

"**L**ook at these muscles, faggot," Brad said, one hand on the back of my head. "Faggot, look at these muscles. You could never have muscles like this. No faggot could. Yeah, you're a fucking faggot. I'm a man. A real man. You? You're a faggot. Faggot. Faggot."

Brad was slowly dragging my face across his massive chest as he called me a faggot, moving my face into one armpit, then onto his biceps, down his side, across his abs, and back to his other armpit. Then he ran my face through the whole upper-body circuit again. Brad was everything Emily told me he was—huge, gorgeous, a little rough—and while his demeaning you're-a-fucking-faggot rap probably qualified as a hate crime in New York City, the tone of his voice was oddly tender. He murmured the insults as if they were sweet nothings, which to some of his clients they no doubt were.

Brad didn't want to meet in the lobby; he preferred to come right to my room. I tried to watch some television while I waited for Brad to come to my room, but I couldn't concentrate on *Saturday Night Live*. (Tina Fey rules.) My heart jumped out of my chest when Brad knocked on the door. He told me to leave the money on the table by the bed, which I did, and he smiled and said hello as he came into the room. I expected him to pick up the money right away, but he didn't seem to notice it sitting on the nightstand. He was wearing black sweats, a black T-shirt, and a pair of running shoes, and his black hair was a little longer than it looked in his pictures. He walked to the middle of the room, looked out the window, then turned around and pulled his shirt over his head, tossing it on the end of the bed. He stood there for a second, letting me take him in, all rippling shoulder muscles, abs, and pecs. He slapped his abs with his hands and then held his hands out, palms up, as if to say, "Solid, huh?" I was transfixed—but not by lust, unfortunately. Brad was about as far from my type as men get; I like slightly sissy guys. Brad, towering over me, was none of those things. He was massive, a human SUV.

Brad reminded me that he was straight, and that he only did muscle worship. Then he asked me what I wanted to do—and he called me *dude*.

Oops. I didn't have a game plan. All I really wanted to do was meet Emily's great big boyfriend, pump a little money into New York City's underground economy, and piss off a few fundamentalists. I was satisfied just to see him with his shirt off. But he was mine for an hour, and I had to fill the time, so I explained that all my boyfriends had been shorter than I was and skinnier than I was, which was true. Then I lied and told Brad that I was curious what a big, muscular body felt like. I didn't want to get naked, I said, I just wanted to run my hands over him.

"Mostly," I said, "I just want to feel you up, I guess. I've never really worshiped muscles, so I'm not sure how that's done. Is it okay if I just feel them?"

"It's your hour, dude," said Brad. "I just came from the gym. I can take a quick shower if you like, and you can watch. Some guys like that; we can even shower together. Or if you like, we can do this with me all sweaty. Your call, dude."

I hesitated.

"It's good, clean sweat, dude. I don't smoke or drink, so my sweat is clean. Dudes tell me all the time that they dig it."

I opted to watch him take a shower, hoping it would kill fifteen or twenty minutes. He looked amazing naked, and I was amazed that this sort of beauty could be ordered up to my hotel room like a bucket of ice. He was one of those body builders with hugely broad shoulders but a very narrow waist. Like Emily, Brad was breathtaking. Richard deserves all the dirty laundry he can handle for bringing these two young people together.

Unfortunately, Brad was in and out of the shower in about five minutes. He invited me to dry him off. I demurred. I plopped down on the end of the bed, and when Brad came out of the bathroom he was wearing a clean pair of underwear. He walked to the edge of the bed, stood right in front of me, and began to flex and pose.

"Come on," he said. "Feel my body, dude. You know you want to."

Actually, I didn't want to—but I didn't want Brad to know that I didn't want to, so I began running my hands over him. He was male, and he was beautiful, but he was so far from my type that running my hands over his chest and shoulders and arms wasn't having much of an effect on me. Brad felt like an enormous armoire that someone had stretched turkey skin over, popped in the oven and roasted to a golden brown. I wasn't turned off, but I wasn't turned on. I was thinking to myself, Shit, do I really have to stand here like an idiot running my hands over this guy for the next fifty minutes?

I broke the law pumping money into New York City's underground economy. What I did with Emily probably wasn't illegal, but what I did with Brad—or what Brad was about to do to me, I should say—definitely was. There were 2,598 arrests made for prostitution in New York City in 1998, according to the New York State Uniform Crime Report. The average big-city police department spends 213 workhours a day enforcing laws against prostitution. In Los Angeles in 1993, one city official estimated that the ineffective enforcement of his city's prostitution laws was costing the city $100 million a year. In the city where I live, the police department seems much more interested in setting up prostitution stings than catching violent criminals. And why not? "You get up in a penthouse at Caesar's Palace," Las Vegas vice cop told the *Vancouver Sun,* "with six naked women frolicking in the room and then say 'Hey, baby, you're busted!' " Compared to regular police work, "busting prostitutes is fun."

The urge to alter consciousness is as old as humanity itself, as Salim Muwakkil points out, and so, too, is buying and selling sex. Prostitution has been and always will be with us, so the only rational argument about prostitution is not, "Shall we allow it or ban it?" but "How shall we make this thing that we can't stop less harmful and less dangerous for all involved?" Every problem moralists and virtuecrats cite as an argument for keeping prostitution illegal—violence, disease, child prostitution—is a problem that is either created or made worse by keeping prostitution illegal.

In Australia, where brothels are legal, a street hooker is eighty times more likely to have an STD than a woman who works in a brothel. In the Netherlands, where prostitution is legal, the rate of STDs among prostitutes is no higher than the rate of STDs in the general population. Edinburgh, Scotland, decriminalized prostitution, which is now permitted in public baths, which are licensed and regulated as places of "public entertainment." Streetwalking is permitted on particular streets in Edinburgh where hookers have plied their trade for centuries. After decriminalization, prostitution did not expand into other areas, as some predicted, and the health, social, and crime problems associated with prostitution actually decreased.

The owners of licensed bathhouses in Edinburgh are required to keep drugs out to hold on to their licenses, and they can't abuse or exploit the women who work in them very easily since those women can now take their complaints to the police without fear of being arrested themselves. In the areas where streetwalking is allowed, there's a policewoman on duty who works with the girls; as a result, prostitutes are subjected to much less violence in Edinburgh than they are in Glasgow, where it remains illegal.

Following Edinburgh's example, England is moving towards legalization, as is Germany. Even the Jesuit magazine *La Civiltà Cattolica* has come out in favor of decriminalizing and regulating brothels, which were closed in Italy in 1958.

"**D**ude, what gives?" Brad asked, breaking out of his pose.

What gives?

"You a cop, dude?"

This was the second time tonight that someone asked me if I was cop, and I laughed, further killing the mood Brad was trying to create. I had to explain to Brad that I laughed because I didn't think I looked much like a New York City cop.

"I'm sorry," I said, "I'm just not sure what I was supposed to be doing. I've never done this muscle-worship stuff before."

"Tell you what, dude," Brad said. "I'll take the lead. I'll do what most guys like, all right?"

All right.

"I'm going to be a little rough with you, okay?"

Okay.

That's when Brad grabbed the back of my neck and began steering my face around his upper body and calling me faggot. (It was better than being called dude.) Brad's body hair must have been thick and black, like the hair on his head, because there was stubble all over his body, and after my face took a few spins around his torso, I had a nasty whisker burn.

"You know what I want you to do, faggot?" Brad said, pulling my face out of his armpit.

"Uh . . . no, what do you want me to do?"

Brad wrapped his arm around my head, and holding on to my hair pulled my face up to his while at the same time flexing his biceps, which pressed into my jaw.

"I want you to get down on the floor and kiss my feet."

Okay . . .

"And I want you to call me a god, you faggot, while you kiss my fucking feet," Brad said, still holding my face up to his.

"Okay," I said, thinking, Okay . . . just . . . let . . . me . . . go . . . and . . . I'll . . . do . . . it. . . .

He pulled my face away from his and, keeping hold of the back of my neck, pushed me all the way down on the floor. I kissed his feet. I called him a god—ah, so this must be muscle *worship,* I thought to myself. Now I get it. Brad *was* aggressive, just like Emily liked her men. I wasn't embarrassed about worshiping Brad, or kissing his feet, although it's a little embarrassing to reread this story up to this point—and we're not even to the really weird stuff yet.

When I sat back on my legs and looked up at Brad, he had an erection, which was a lot more than I had. Brad looked down at me—way down—and smirked. Then he pulled his dick out of his underwear, whispered *faggot,* closed his eyes, and began to beat off.

This is some fucked-up shit, I thought to myself, and I was momentarily overwhelmed by feelings of guilt. It was less than a month since the attacks, and not fifty blocks away they were still pulling bodies out of the wreckage of the World Trade Center, and here I was goofing around in a hotel room with a big, straight, body-building, object-of-muscle-worship escort. It felt—oh, I dunno—somehow disrespectful. But all Brad was doing was what the president asked us all to do—go about our business. Maybe if this scene were turning me on, I thought, maybe if running my hands over the flesh of someone who looked like Brad were my favorite thing, I would've gotten turned on and, like all turned-on people, I might have forgotten about everything else in the world for the duration of our time together. If this scene with Brad represented "getting back to normal" to me, maybe it wouldn't feel so wrong.

But was it wrong? People all over the country were having "terror sex," as the papers dubbed it, hooking up with strangers in bars and going back to their apartments. Churches also filled up in the days immediately after the attacks, but so did bars and nightclubs. ("I believe that Americans are a virtuous people," wrote Ken Connor, president of the Family Research Council, in Reverend Moon's the *Washington Times*. "Our nation uniquely aspires to virtue. It is our national purpose and has been since its founding. This is why, since that terrible Tuesday morning, we Americans have returned to our foundational virtues [and] filled our churches.") Two months later, however, church attendance was back down to its pre–September 11 levels, but terror sex was still roaring. In February of 2002, *USA Today* reported under the headline, SKIN AND SIN ARE IN! that floor shows featuring naked women were returning to the stages in Las Vegas. Clearly the triumphalism of the virtuecrats and the scolds and conservative pundits after September 11 was premature. We were at war, it was a just war, and we were winning that war. But the nation wasn't being remade in the image of the Family Research Council.

I also wasn't the only tourist in New York City checking out the men on the weekend of October 5 through 7. While I cavorted in New York with Emily and Brad, 972 tourists from Oregon were in New York to show their support for the city. Nancy and Ken Bush (no relation to the Bushes of D.C., Maine, Florida, and Texas) came to New York on the "Flight for Freedom" tour organized by an Oregon travel agency, and they didn't sit around their hotel room feeling glum—that wasn't what Mayor Giuliani and Senator Schumer wanted them to do.

"We were frustrated by the attacks and wanted to do something to help," Nancy Bush told a reporter from the *New York Daily News*. What did they do? Nancy went shopping, went out to dinner, and caught a performance of *The Full Monty,* the Broadway musical about a troupe of male strippers. If Nancy Bush could come to New York to check out a half a dozen naked guys and feel patriotic about it, why shouldn't I feel patriotic about renting Brad?

"Kiss my feet, faggot," Brad said, bringing his right foot up to my neck, and using it to push my head down to his left foot. "Kiss my fucking feet, faggot. Faggot. Faggot."

I can take a hint. I went back to kissing Brad's feet. I was fully clothed, but Brad wasn't, having kicked off his underwear by this point. You notice strange things when you're waiting for someone else to finish up. While I was kissing Brad's feet, I noticed that there were little copper-colored dots in the royal-blue carpet. Then I noticed a quarter on the floor under the desk. Kissing Brad's right foot, I noticed he had stubble on his big toe. Apparently he shaved his toes, just like he shaved his chest, arms, and stomach. Then I kissed his left foot and—hey, what do you know!—his right big toe had about three dozen long, black hairs on it. One shaved toe, one nonshaved toe. Weird.

"Faggot," Brad said, breathing pretty heavily. "You're a faggot. What are you, faggot?"

"I'm a faggot?" I said, thinking, You're the one beating off, and I'm the faggot?

"That's right, you're a faggot. And what am I?"

"You're a god." You're beating off, and you're a god.

"That's right, I'm a—"

And Brad came.

There was an awkward pause. Brad stood there, breathing and shivering. I didn't know what I was supposed to do. Could I get up now? Or was I supposed to wait for permission to stop kissing his feet? Since Brad was so much bigger than I was, I decided to stay down on the floor until he gave me further orders.

"Hey, dude, thanks," Brad finally said, stepping back and pulling his foot out from under my face. "You can get up."

I walked to the bathroom and got Brad a towel so he could clean off his abs. Brad asked if I wanted to get off, and I took a pass. What I wanted to do, I said, was ask him a few quick questions.

"Fire away, dude."

First, what's with the unshaved right toe? Brad laughed and explained that he has a client who pays him for the honor of shaving his body. This particular client likes to leave the hair on one of Brad's toes so that he can fantasize about how different Brad's body would look if it wasn't kept shaved.

Listening to this, I had a you've-got-to-be-kidding look on my face.

"Dude, I know, it's freaky. But it pays the rent. That's not even the strangest guy I see," he said. "My next-door neighbor used to pay me to let him do my laundry. I see another guy who pays me to watch his TV and ignore him and drink his beer, only he wants me to walk up to him every once in a while and punch him in the stomach as hard as I can. This is a freaky business."

Okay, speaking of freaky: I'm the gay client, you're the straight escort. You had an orgasm, I didn't. Why were you turned on by what we were doing?

"It's a trip, dude." Brad laughed. "I didn't dig it at first, guys worshiping me. Ninety percent of the guys I see want me to call 'em fags and kiss my feet and call me a god. After a while, I don't know, it started to turn me on. I mean, there's another man kissing my feet. Some other guy is so intimidated by my body that he'll do whatever I tell him to. I guess humiliating other guys makes me horny."

Brad suddenly reminded me of Jim, the man in the bar the night before, the alpha male who tried to pick up Emily right in front of me. He was definitely straight, but he seemed to enjoy humiliating other men. Renting Emily allowed me to commit two of the seven deadly sins, gluttony and greed, and I had planned on renting Brad so that I could commit the sin of lust. It seemed ironic that it was Brad, a man who is about ten thousand times better looking than I am, who committed the sin of lust in my hotel room. Oh, I had sinned; by kissing Brad's feet and calling him a god, I had inspired a kind of semidetached lust in his heart, making myself the occasion of sin. He didn't lust after me; he was straight, after all. What turned him on, what he lusted after, wasn't who I was but what I was doing.

Brad was dressed now and heading out to see another client.

"He's a regular," Brad said.

Anything freaky?

"No," Brad said, "not really. Pretty much what we just did."

Brad walked to the door, snagging the money from the night-stand on his way. He tucked the money into a pocket on the side of his gym bag, and then turned to face me.

"Last chance for a feel, dude," he said, holding his arms out, smiling.

I wish I could write something like, "I took a pass," or, "Having learned so much about myself already, I didn't feel the need to further violate Brad," or "I looked at Brad and said, 'STOP CALL-ING ME "DUDE," YOU FUCKING MEATHEAD!' " Sad to say, I wanted my money's worth, and I figured I wasn't going to have the chance to run my hands over someone who looked like Brad ever again, so . . . I copped one last feel. It actually felt better to run my hands over his body with his clothes on; I couldn't feel the stub-ble on his chest and stomach, and he wasn't tensing his muscles, which made him feel a little more like a human being and less like an armoire.

I removed my hands from the nice man and thanked him for his time.

Brad opened he door and stepped into the hall. "See you around, faggot," he said, winking. Then he turned and walked down the hall towards the elevators. After I shut the door, I lay down on the bed and looked at the clock. Brad had been in my room for almost two hours. I was touched. While Emily had in-sisted I pay her to eat dinner and watch a play, Brad was too much a gentleman to insist that I pay him to have an orgasm.

Okay, *now* I was completely sinned out. I'd done my patriotic duty, and all I wanted now was a little legitimate room service. I found the menu in my room and ordered myself a bacon sandwich. As I lay in yet another hotel room looking out my window at yet another American Gomorrah, it occurred to me for the first time that there was a Bible in every hotel room I'd stayed in while I ran around sinning my brains out, thoughtfully provided by the Gideon Society.

Somehow despite the biblical reference in the title of this book and, of course, the book that inspired it[1] (I wanna give a shout out to my homey Bobby Bork), and despite all the reading I was doing while I worked on this book (I may be the only unreformed sinner in America who has plowed through the complete works of Messrs. Bork, Bennett, and Buchanan), I hadn't thought to sit down and reread the biblical story of Sodom and Gomorrah. I went to my nightstand, opened the drawer, and pulled out a familiar looking Gideon Bible, with its red cover and gold embossing.

The story of the destruction of Sodom and Gomorrah, "the cities of the plain," appears in Genesis chapters 18 and 19. Biblical scholars who aren't grinding the Bible-as-word-of-God ax theorize that the story of the destruction of two cities most likely derives from a pre-Israelite folk tale, perhaps recalling a volcanic catastrophe. Or, shit, maybe the same aliens who built the pyramids nuked the place. Who knows? In early Jewish and early Christian literature, Sodom and Gomorrah are held up as examples of sin and the destructive wrath of God. The story in Genesis takes place in the city of Sodom, but we never get to go inside Gomorrah, so we don't know if Gomorrah had a lot of trendy cafés, a lively performance art scene, and an alternative weekly newspaper—all features of our modern American Gomorrahs. The Bible doesn't have a lot to say about Sodom either, only that the city had "gates."

So what exactly were the people of Gomorrah up to? We first

1. Here's my brother Bill on the title: The source for Bork's title is probably as much Joan Didion's *Slouching Towards Bethlehem* as it is Didion's course, W. B. Yeats's poem "The Second Coming," which includes this line: "And what rough beast, its hour come round at last, Slouches towards Bethlehem to be born?" Didion's book of essays on the cultural revolutions of the sixties uses this phrase because of the sense people had that the world was changing, and Bork, by shifting the tile to another less happy city, implies that America is changing for the worse.

But all of this imagery is profoundly un-American if you look at its roots. Yeats believed things were going to hell in a handbasket because he thought history was cyclical, and at the end of our current 2,000-year-cycle we'd be plunged into a new dark age. His evidence for this coming dark age was the decline of the aristocratic order of the world, particularly his Anglo-Irish ascendancy, as Irish Catholics ousted the British. So when this phrase gets used by folks who claim to be all-American, they're really showing up their inborn elitism. Just as the Borks of the world seem not to have read the Sodom and Gomorrah story, they haven't read the poem they're alluding to either.

hear about the rumors of their sinfulness in Genesis 18.20, when God says to Abraham, "How great is the outcry against Sodom and Gomorrah and how very grave their sin!" The Hebrew word translated as "sin" is *z'aqa* which implies violence or injustice, not sexual depravity.

Still, when two angels visit Lot in Sodom—Lot being Sodom's only stand-up guy—a crowd gathers outside Lot's home: "The men of Sodom, both old and young, all the people from every quarter, surrounded the house." The men of Sodom wanted to "know" the angels, and Lot refused to hand God's messengers over to the men of Sodom. Instead Lot offered them his daughters: "I have two daughters who have not known a man; please, let me bring them out to you, and you may do to them as you wish; only do nothing to these men." (Lot may have been the only decent guy in Sodom, but I can't imagine he was ever named Father of the Year.) The fact that *all* the men of Sodom demanded that Lot release the two angels to them emphasizes the collective guilt of the entire city.

Here's an interesting fact: Nowhere in the story of the destruction of Sodom and Gomorrah are the men of Gomorrah mentioned. They don't crowd around Lot's house, demanding to "know" the visiting angels. Maybe there was a pride parade in Gomorrah that night—or a rap concert or a swingers' convention or a riverboat casino was opening—and the men of Gomorrah couldn't tear themselves away. On this point, the Bible is silent.

While the men of Gomorrah were up to God only knows what (and God, the Bible's author, isn't telling), it's clear that the men of Sodom wanted to subject the strangers at Lot's place to a mob rape. Many scholars believe that the account emphasizes the social aspect of the sin of Sodom, rather than the sexual aspect. The men of Sodom desired to humiliate and dehumanize the strangers, not enjoy sexual pleasure with them. The men of Sodom were breaking the sacred law of hospitality, since the angels are Lot's guests, and a good host isn't supposed to let his guests come to harm. (Lot's daughters, on the other hand . . .) Since the men of Sodom are such pricks, God decides to destroy both cities, "raining brimstone and fire on Sodom and Gomorrah, from the Lord out of his heavens."

By no stretch of the imagination is the United States of America "slouching towards Gomorrah." We may have a lot of those trendy cafés, performance art spaces, gay bars, and alternative weekly newspapers, and while we tolerate a huge number of things specifically forbidden in the Bible (shellfish, bacon, cheeseburgers, legshaving, divorce, adulterers, uncircumcised males, gays and lesbians, and so on), we *don't* tolerate the kind of mob violence that any unbiased reading of the Sodom and Gomorrah story reveals to be God's beef with the citizens of those doomed cities. The sinners of Sodom and Gomorrah, unlike modern American sinners, weren't content to sin with other sinners and leave virtuous Lot and his virtuous daughters and those virtuous angels the hell out of it. The men of Sodom sought to impose their sinful ways on Lot's guests, to violate and humiliate them, to "know" them in the biblical sense. (Picture an episode of HBO's *Oz* crossed with CBS's *Touched by an Angel*.) The people of Sodom and Gomorrah went from tolerably wicked in God's eyes to I'm-going-to-nuke-this-place wicked when they attempted to force their sins down the throats (or up the butts) of unwilling participants. (If the men of Sodom had contented themselves with raping Lot's virgin daughters, God might have spared the place.) While the men of Sodom and Gomorrah (and the children and women, too, I assume, since God destroyed them along with any unborn children the women were carrying at the time) were sinful, it wasn't until they tried to impose their sins on others that God pressed the button.

As I said at the beginning of this book, modern American sinners don't attempt to impose their sinful ways on their fellow Americans. We may do things that are injurious to ourselves—eat too much, gamble too much, fuck too much, shoot too much—but if it makes us happy, that's our right, and, remember, we were endowed with that right by our Creator, and our founding fathers saw fit to enshrine that right in our nation's founding document. Anyone who strives to deprive his or her fellow Americans of their right to pursue happiness is not only violating the original intent of founding fathers, *but also flying in the face of God.* (Take that, Alan Keyes!) As much as it annoys the virtuecrats and talk-show moralists, the American sinners have the same rights to life, liberty, and the pursuit of happiness as any other American. Bork, Bennett, and Buchanan are free to believe that our pursuit of happiness is sinful, just as we are free to believe that their virtues are vastly overrated.

Unlike Andrew Sullivan, I'm not convinced that the paleoconservative scolds are on their way out. Indeed, I think they're going to be with us for a long, long time. As I write these words, Patrick Buchanan's *Death of the West* remains on the *New York Times* bestseller lists, and books by his fellow scolds dot Amazon.com's Top 100 list. There are apparently a huge number of Americans, registered Republicans all, who never seem to tire of being told that they live in a morally bankrupt shithole; these people will keep American virtuecrats and scolds in book deals and speaking gigs for the rest of their natural lives. Isn't it odd how the same conservatives who complain about "blame America first" lefties never challenge the "nothing nice to say about America" paleoconservatives?

Books by virtuecrats and scolds go on for three or four hundred pages about what a shithole this country is—this Gomorrah, this moral sewer, this dismal state, these morally collapsed United States—but they all end with a paragraph or two of uplift. Bork, Bennett, and Buchanan all hold out hope at the end of their books. If she heeds the call of the virtuecrats and the scolds, America can right herself: ". . . The blessings of marriage and family life are indeed recoverable," Bennett writes at the end of *The Broken Hearth.* "If we do our part, there is reason to hope that those blessings may yet again be ours."

"We have so much to be thankful for," Buchanan writes at the end of *Death of the West.* "And while no one can deny the coarseness of her manners, the decadence of her culture, or the sickness in her soul, America is still a country worth fighting for and the last best hope of earth."

"We have allowed [our nation] to be severely damaged," Bork writes at the end of *Slouching Towards Gomorrah,* "but perhaps not beyond repair. As we approach the desolate and sordid precincts, the pessimism of the intellect tells us that Gomorrah is our probable destination. What is left to us is a determination not to accept that fate and the courage to resist it. . . ."

Like Bork, Bennett, and Buchanan, I'd like to end with a few hopeful words. Unlike Bork, Bennett, and Buchanan, I'm not tacking a few hopeful words onto the end of four hundred pages of "this place sucks," "moral sewer," "slouching towards Gomorrah," or "what a dump." I don't think my country is a shithole. Indeed, I agree with Buchanan that America is the "last best hope of earth," and, like Bennett, I believe the United States is worth fighting for— these United States—not some 1950s era dream of the United States. The country worth fighting for is the big, messy, complicated, diverse, fascinating place the United States is right now. What makes the United States the envy of the world (besides Hooters and Krispy Kremes, of course) is that this is a nation where full citizenship has nothing to do with race, religion, sex, political persuasion or, yes, personal virtue. Good or bad, religious or irreligious, male or female, left or right, of color or washed out—we're all Americans.

This is a country where the culture evolves and remains vibrant because people are free to challenge the existing order. The right to life, liberty, and the pursuit of happiness means that each of us is free to go our own way, even if the ways some of us may choose to go seem sinful or shocking to some of our fellow citizens. America is at its best when our freedom to go our own way is restricted only when, as Thomas Jefferson said, "[our] acts are injurious to others."

So like Bork, Bennett, and Buchanan, I have hope. I hope that people who disagree with the scolds and the virtuecrats will go right on ignoring them; I hope that our drug laws will one day be changed to reflect reality; I hope that more people who want to cheat on their spouses will do so with their spouses' permission; and I hope to one day spot Bill O'Reilly at a gay pride parade in heels and a bra. I hope that Americans who find happiness in sinful pursuits will always be able to exercise their God-given right to gamble, swing, smoke, eat, shoot, march, spend, and procure. And I hope that the Borks, Bennetts, and Buchanans will one day recognize that their right to pursue happiness as they define it is not threatened by the right of their fellow Americans to pursue happiness as we define it. It's a big country, after all, with plenty of room for saints and sinners alike.

ACKNOWLEDGMENTS

I had help.

For his many insights, his patience, and his good humor, I would like to thank my thoroughly brilliant editor Brian Tart. For blending encouragement and nagging so effortlessly, I have to thank my literary agent, Elizabeth Wales. My research assistant, Sean Taylor, contributed huge piles of facts and figures, in addition to providing me with above-and-beyond-the-call constructive criticisms. And thanks to Amy Hughes at Dutton for keeping so many balls in the air at once.

My brother, Bill Savage, to whom I've dedicated this book, is full of good advice and total bullshit in roughly equal measures—which pretty much makes him the ideal older brother. Bill read early and late drafts, encouraged me to keep writing, and got me completely shit-faced one night in Chicago when I was in despair of ever finishing this project. Thanks, Billy.

Much thanks to my good friends Tim Keck, Mike Ranta, David Schmader, Brad Steinbacher, John Goodman, and Jason Sellards for their support and encouragement. Thanks to the staff at the Tully's at the corner of Second and Marion in downtown Seattle, where I was allowed to sit all day for weeks while working on an early draft of this book; to Cafe Luna on Vashon Island; and to the staff of Cafe Septieme for keeping me fed while I worked twenty-hour days to meet my final deadlines. I wouldn't have been able to write this book at all if the card dealers, drug pushers, whores, adulterers, faggots, gun nuts, and gluttons I met along the way hadn't been so indulgent. Thanks, gang.

I wouldn't be able to finish this project—or any project—if it weren't for the love and support of my boyfriend, Terry, and my son, D.J.

Finally, I can't close without thanking William J. Bennett, Patrick Buchanan, and, of course, Robert Bork for inspiring me to write this book.

For a complete list of sources and notes, please visit the Web site,
www.skippingtowardsgomorrah.com